THE POLITICAL MIND

or

'HOW TO THINK DIFFERENTLY'

Kieran Laird

EDINBURGH UNIVERSITY PRESS

For my mother and father, Roseanna and Patrick Laird

Edinburgh University Press Ltd
22 George Square, Edinburgh

Typeset in Sabon
by Servis Filmsetting Ltd, Manchester, and
printed and bound in Great Britain by
Biddles Ltd, King's Lynn, Norfolk

A CIP record for this book is available from the British Library

ISBN 978 0 7486 2386 0 (hardback)

Contents

Introduction: The Political Mind

In 2000 an interesting argument developed between Apple Macintosh computers and the Church of Satan. Apple had been running an advertising campaign that used black-and-white photographs of famous historical people considered to have been influential in bringing about some change of perspective on behalf of their contemporaries superimposed with the slogan 'Think different'. This appealed to the Church of Satan, an organisation born in San Francisco in the late 1960s and citing individualist freethinkers such as Nietzsche, Twain and Franklin as influences, as well as including Freud, Jung and Foucault on its suggested reading list. The Satanists were also enamoured of the Apple logo of a rainbow-coloured apple with a bite taken out of it, which for them contained a reference to the forbidden fruit of the tree of knowledge. Accordingly, they produced a version of the Apple advertisement containing a photograph of their founder, Anton LaVey, with the 'Think different' slogan and Apple logo. They also included one of Apple's web badges, 'Made with Macintosh' on their website. Apple were not happy with what they saw as a copyright infringement, with the potential to blacken the goodwill accrued by the Apple brand through association with an organisation that many of their customers might object to. The Church of Satan came up with another picture in response, this time with the caption, 'We think TOO different', and the debate continued.

Although it lacks the attribute of grammatical correctness, the phrase 'think different' is an intriguing proposition made all the more so by Apple's reaction to their unexpected Satanic endorsement. How does one in fact think differently? It is not as easy as one might expect. Take the Church of Satan, for example. The central tenets of its philosophy expound a freethinking individualism which seeks to rid the mind of its cultural (and primarily religious) inhibitions, instituting instead a symbolic, dogmatic and ritualistic system focusing on Satan as a symbol of individual human instinct rather than the Christian source of evil. Given the engrained nature of Christian thought and the historical emphasis on the dualism of good and evil in Western culture, this sounds like an interesting project. There is, however, very little which is original in its underpinnings which draw heavily on Freud, Jung and Nietzsche as well as the individualistic psychology and techniques of the Human Potential movement current in America at the time of the Church's foundation. Indeed the only difference between the end result of the satanic philosophy and American libertarianism seems to be the ritualistic aspects associated with the former. The philosophy of the Apple Corporation may have had more in common with the Church of Satan than they cared to admit and the latter may be a lot less original than they suggest.

If an organisation built around an idea that would strike many in Western society as anathema cannot make us think differently, what can? That is the central question of the present work. It is for me an inherently political question as critique, resistance and change are all premised on the ability to formulate difference: an alternative, even if it is only the absence of certain elements of present circumstance. This also makes it an adversarial question, a satanic question in the etymological sense.

The present work turns around three interlinked aims. The first is to introduce neuropsychological material that may help to generate interesting political theory at the most base level of the creation of new thoughts, as well as serving to problematise some existing theory on a psychological basis. The second seeks to show how such psychological material may be used to critique contemporary Western society through an analysis of consumer capitalism. In this regard it is contended that contemporary consumer society creates anxiety in individuals through the role it plays in the creation of self-identity. It is argued that one of the mechanics of consumerism is an 'existential imperative', which has been built up over time through a reorientation of marketing strategy towards consumers as individuals. This existential imperative puts forth the message that people are individually responsible for the creation of the person they want to be with the market stepping in to offer goods and services which claim to facilitate this process. It is argued that there is a fundamental tension between this imperative to individual self-creation and the market mechanisms that are offered to help fulfil it. This tension leads to anxiety.

In order to connect individual anxiety to consumer capitalism we must present several claims. First amongst these is the claim that the individual self and collective society are co-original, that they are bound together in a 'chicken and egg' relationship, each serving to mould and create the other. This idea also feeds into the deeper line of argument about psycho-political change. Secondly, it must be established that contemporary society affects the individual self in the adverse way I suggest: that it causes anxiety. It is important to note at this stage that it is not consumer society per se which I argue causes anxiety, but rather the *tension within it* in terms of the model of self-creation it holds out and its mechanism of fulfilment. As will become apparent, I present the self as a fluid and mutable entity with no essential qualities. Rather, I will argue that the self is constructed using the social meanings of its surrounding environment. If consumerism allowed the self to be formed in the way the existential imperative urges I suggest there would be no anxiety; the latter arises from the fact that this formation is frustrated. This frustration is endemic to the present form of consumerism because products are marketed in terms of desires that must be kept insatiable in order to preserve the cycle of consumption.

The third premise is that self-creation in today's society is in some qualitative way different from the selfhood elaborated in response to previous societies. It can be claimed that there has always been anxiety, especially in the long periods of strife and insecurity that make up history. This is undoubtedly true. I believe also that one may indicate other points in history in which certain societal mechanisms have sought to mould the individual self for some purpose causing anxiety in the process. One example may be the manufacture of guilt by the medieval churches as a mechanism of spiritual, economic and political control. We now have a different set of social structures that mould our selfhood, however, and we have a different relationship to these mechanisms. In the wake of Enlightenment liberalism society focuses on the unconstrained individual and it is this idea to which the market has orientated itself with the existential imperative. It is therefore my task to introduce and investigate a set of psychological ideas and then show how they can be used to analyse the particular set of contemporary circumstances and the orientation of our self-identity within them.

The third theme, which hovers in the background during the discussions of the other two, is whether there is indeed a possibility of 'thinking differently'. I do not presume that thought can be wholly original, if that means unconditioned by any of the affective or ideological content of the thinker's surrounding culture. My reasons for this will become apparent as the book progresses through discussions on the formation of the conscious self. I am, therefore, concerned with the more humble question of how the ideas and affects of the social can be posed in juxtaposition, how one may open up cracks in certain sets of ideas using others as tools. 'Thinking differently' may therefore mean combinations and recombinations of pre-existing ideas or concepts in ways which serve to critique elements of the social and political world within which one is thinking.

Some readers will find the psychological material interesting but disagree with how I have deployed it and some may have sympathy with my analysis of society but are opposed to its neurological underpinnings. Finally, there will be those who disagree with my conclusions about the possibility for original thought mobilised in the political realm. My aim is merely to outline a set of interesting and potentially useful conceptual tools.

Given the confines of time and space there is also much relevant material that I have had to leave out. There are many internal debates within psychology over the nature of consciousness, nonconsciousness and the emotions. There is just as much disagreement over the same topics in political and social theory and philosophy. To do justice to every point of view would be an encyclopaedic task and one that I do not pretend to undertake here. I have also chosen not to discuss some topics that may have some relevance to the work, such as the copious material on brainwashing and the debate over sex and gender differences at the neurological and conscious levels. I can only recommend that the reader, if interested, seek out this material and connect it to that presented here.

Before I begin, however, it may be useful to take a brief overview of the ways in which other psychological theories have been used for political ends.

Behaviourism: The political automaton

On a very traditional level politics has been the study of how human beings order their social lives, how they come together and regulate themselves in societies, and how they conceive of the theoretical foundations for the institutions that they construct and allow to regulate their conduct. As such, the base unit of political analysis is the human being, how he or she acts, what motivates them, what he or she expects from society and what society, if it is to function, requires of them in return. Political science and theory will, therefore, act on the basis of an underlying notion of human psychology which serves to guide methodology and underpin theoretical constructions. Questions such as how the individual self is formed, how it functions and how it relates to the social whole are, therefore, of the highest importance to political thought and vast resources have been invested by the social sciences to investigate them. There have been many attempts to achieve this from several different angles, each with its own conclusions as to how politics should operate on the basis of its theory of individuals. Rawlsian liberalism, for example, takes a Kantian view of the human agent as essentially autonomous and hence advocates a political structure that maximises individual choice. Post-structuralists argue that there is no essential self apart from that which is conditioned and created and for their part try to move politics from its humanistic roots.

To this end, most social sciences proceed according to the Enlightenment assumption that we can unlock the universal laws that govern human behaviour. D. E. Broadbent, for example, claims that despite the fact that we have achieved so much we

> still steal, go mad, live unhappily together and threaten each other with weapons which might destroy the entire species . . . Perhaps the most hopeful road is to apply to behaviour itself the methods of attack which have proved so useful in dealing with the material world: to observe, experiment, and build predictive theories for further experimental test.[1]

As one of the main currents in psychology, classical behaviourism advocates the study of human action and cognition in terms of pure stimulus and response chains. It denies the utility of introspection and the study of mental states as well as any conception of the meaning an action has for the actor. People are seen by behaviourists as basically automatons – 'its' – complicated processing machines which respond at a neurological level to sense stimuli.

As John B. Watson, one of the founding founders of behaviourism, put it,

> psychology as the behaviourist views it is a purely objective natural science. Its theoretical goal is the prediction and control of behaviour. Introspection forms no essential part of its methods, nor is the scientific value for its data dependent upon the readiness with which they lend themselves to interpretation in terms of consciousness.[2]

For Watson, humans adapt and change themselves according to their environmental situation with their behaviour constituted by responses to certain situational stimuli. The latter is defined as 'any physiological change within the organism or any impinging object in the environment' with the former comprising the way the organism reacts as a consequence.[3]

Possibly the most influential of the post-Watsonian behaviourists is B. F. Skinner who shifted the focus within the paradigm from natural science methodology to scientific explanation with the development of specific terms and concepts that would accommodate this end. One such concept, which Skinner adopted in his analysis, was *mentalism*, which he used to refer to the type of circular or self-referential explanation that, he claimed, explains nothing. Examples would be replies to a question about an action that merely stated 'I just wanted to do it' or 'I did it on impulse'.[4] Skinner, however, sought to explain actions within a framework which was characterised by objectivity, determinism and a concern for what he saw as purely practical questions.

Such a conceptual schema does of course necessarily rule out a considerable amount of material that had hitherto been considered relevant in the study of human cognition and action. The whole field of the unconscious as a source of explanation, for example, was explicitly ruled out. Skinner did, however, share a lot of common concerns with Sigmund Freud. Both were interested in explaining human behaviour by focusing on individuals rather than groups, and believed that although humans are essentially not rational decision makers their behaviour is ordered by natural causes. Both were also keen to extend their findings to social problems.[5] Skinner, however, disagreed with Freud's construction of internal mental apparatus to account for behaviour. He argued that there is the inherent danger in using mentalistic explanations in that they themselves have to be explained, the question arising of how the wishes, ideas and values to which mentalism points originate.[6] He also took objection to Freud's three-level division of the mind into the conscious, preconscious and unconscious, claiming that behaviour is determined solely by environmental and genetic factors.[7]

The consequences of behaviourism for society as a whole were rigorously developed by Skinner and seem to have met with some degree of popular attention. His 1948 book *Walden Two* had sold 2 million copies by 1982, with sales on the increase.[8] In this, primarily fictional, work Skinner applies behavioural techniques to the running of a small community of about 1000 citizens. The general model provided by Skinner has served as the inspiration for several experimental communities such as Twin Oaks in Virginia and Los Horocones in Mexico. The latter of these provides to its citizens a detailed code of behaviour and emphasises the sharing of many items, such as clothes, as well as encouraging the precepts of equality and cooperation. The behaviourist idea of positive reinforcement is also used systematically in the classroom and in community management.[9] Whereas *Walden Two* outlined a fictional utopian community in which important human social activities are controlled beneficially by the manipulation of environmental conditions, *Beyond Freedom and Dignity* in 1971 focused more on countering the popular idea that human freedom is best served with the elimination of external control mechanisms. This, Skinner argued, is fundamentally mistaken and he puts forward the ways in which behavioural technologies can be developed to reap the benefits of constructive environmental control. For Skinner we are controlled all the time and the question is not how to 'free' ourselves through breaking the chains but how to replace oppressive chains with what can be better construed as props for our culture.

As well as these two books, Skinner also penned an important article for the May 1986 issue of *American Psychologist* applying the concepts of operant conditioning to everyday life. Entitled 'What is wrong with daily life in the Western World', it suggests that the feelings of depression, listlessness and boredom common to many people in our society are due to the fact that many contemporary behaviours have 'pleasing' as opposed to 'strengthening' effects. This leads to the erosion of the contingencies of reinforcement that shape and maintain a barrage of important behaviours. In plain terms, this means that, as we pursue the acquisition of numerous devices and practices which are alleged to make our lives easier, once the pleasing effects of these mental and physical devices wear off we are left without the many behaviours that would have been strengthened if we had been more active ourselves. As Nye puts it, 'our possibilities for enjoying life become more limited [as] our behaviours become more limited'.[10] Skinner points to several cultural practices which promote pleasing rather than strengthening effects, such as the fact that our behaviour is increasingly affected by the advice of 'experts', thereby robbing us of the direct consequences of self-made decisions which would serve to strengthen correct behaviour.

There would seem to be some obvious worrying political consequences stemming from the acceptance of the behaviourist paradigm. Given the suggestion that all of our behaviour is conditioned, a lot of power is placed in the hands of those who control social and educational institutions. The nature of the conditioning in which such institutions engage would also mean that its operation could pass relatively unnoticed and on a very basic level the possibility of rebellion would seem to be slim.

Not only has behaviourism directly pointed out solutions to modern ills itself, it has also served to influence the accounts and methodologies of other theorists. One example from American political science is the work of Robert Dahl on the operation of power in the USA. Dahl used the techniques of behaviourist social science in his analysis, defining power in such a way as to make it amenable to scientific methodologies of objectification and comparison. Although classical behaviourism was dealt a blow in the field of psychology by the influence of Freud, as well as the theories of Carl Rodgers, it would seem that a considerable amount of the theoretical underpinnings in the social sciences can be traced back to the behaviourist conception of the human agent. The naturalist, and specifically empirical, methodologies employed by a considerable number of political science researchers work on the basis that human action can be adequately interpreted by observation and experiment, via responses to questionnaires or overt non-verbal behaviour, both of which can be analysed by the researcher through the use of objective explanations of human action.

Perhaps one of the most prominent examples of where behaviourist thinking has entered political science is the collection of theories that form the rational choice approach. Rational choice works based on constructing a priori models about human agents and applying them either to the real world or to the running of counterfactual situations. According to the theory, human actions proceed relative to the attainment of actors' intrinsic desires, with the fact that desired objects are in limited supply leading to the development of various gambits and strategies. Rational choice is hence a very individualistic doctrine, having no interest in the behaviour of groups and societies except as collections of individuals and refusing to question the basis on which desires are formed. All desires, even social or communal ones, are regarded by the theory as instrumental.[11] As a brief illustration of the problems such theories can run into it may be useful to make two comments on this conception. On the one hand rational choice must take into account some psychological features of the human agent in order to explain why different people will form either maximax or maximin strategies in similar situations. These can be seen as choices that work on the basis of something deeper than the mechanistic fulfilment of desires, effected, as they are, by personality influences such as optimism and pessimism as well as things such as the desire for security or perceptual salience.[12] Rational choice also fails to adequately explain phenomena on the societal level, one example being the trust that is a necessary background to the formation of binding contracts and which would seem to rely on something deeper than a mutually beneficial game theory explanation.[13]

Behaviourism is currently enjoying a resurgence in popularity with the onset of the computational paradigm, a family of psychological theories which use modern computer processes as a metaphor for human cognition. Steven Pinker, for example, purports to collapse the problem of self into a conglomerate of neurocomputational processes – consciousness being activity in layer 4 of the cortex or the contents of the short-term memory, free will being the anterior cingulate sulcus or the executive subroutine, and morality being kin selection and reciprocal altruism.[14] The problem with these new theories may seem relatively obvious from the forgoing string of scientific jargon – we as human beings simply do not understand ourselves that way; it is counter intuitive at the most basic of levels. Neurocomputation does not correct the difficulties of the classical model and, despite taking the stimulus-response explanation to a new level of technicality through the attempt to tie it in with neurology, they still do not address the question of meaning in human life. Under their auspices, we may be amazingly complex machines, but we are machines none the less.

Freud: The politics of the unconscious self and society

The upsurge in behaviourism was partly a result of a swing away from the Freudian conceptions that had held sway in psychology for so long. Freud's ideas will be discussed in depth throughout this work, as they represent the most influential engagement with the unconscious to date, as well as being the ideas most-often deployed in political theory. It is not therefore proposed to engage his theory in any detail at this stage. Freud effectively challenged the security of the Cartesian cogito or Kant's transcendental conditions of human subjectivity with his tripartite division of the mind into ego, superego and id. For Freud the unconscious was a dynamic conception providing the motive power for psychological experience through instinctive strivings and impulses.[15]

Freud himself was not averse to drawing out the wider implications of his theory and in *Civilisation and its Discontents* he turned his ideas of individual neurosis outwards to examine society as a whole. Freud's main contention in this work is that civilisation comes about as the result of a trade off in which we repress some of our instincts in order to gain security from our primeval fears.

Aside from his own forays into the realm of politics, Freud's ideas have most often been deployed by theorists seeking a psychological foundation for Marxist politics, such as Marcuse, Reich and Lyotard. They have also been used to great effect by feminist theorists such as Kristeva, Butler and Irigray and served to influence, sometimes through opposition, the wider poststructuralist movement as in Deleuze, Guattari and Zizek as well as being filtered through Lacan into discourse analysis. Marcuse comments that there is a fatal paradox lying at the heart of Freud's work:

> The concept of man that emerges from Freudian theory is the most irrefutable indictment of Western civilisation – and at the same time the most unshakeable defence of this civilisation. According to Freud, the history of man is the history of repression . . . such constraint is the very precondition of progress.[16]

It was this conservative streak in Freudian theory that had to be overcome before critical use could be made of his concepts. One such attempt to do this came from Marcuse himself, working within the remit of the Frankfurt School to give Marxism a conception of human psychology to deepen its foundations. Marcuse sought to reintroduce the biological and instinctual factors that neo-Freudians had sought to play down, claiming that the jettisoning of concepts such as the unconscious and the death instinct had robbed the theory of its critical edge. The shift of emphasis from the biological organism to socially conditioned personality had only served to reduce the importance of the conflict between the individual and society. Marcuse thus shared with Freud the central idea that civilisation necessarily entails a tension between freedom and happiness, and between culture and instinct.[17] The difference between the two is that Marcuse sees this antagonism, not as a necessary corollary of the human condition, but of a specific historical form of society – industrial capitalism.

Marcuse also argued against the prevalent scientific rationality of Western civilisation, pointing out that its implied logic of subject against object meant that nature stood as something to be controlled and conquered. The reasoned faculties in the human psyche were therefore, elevated over the lower instinctual ones with many thinkers taking Plato's lead and claiming that reason demanded the subjugation of instinct.[18] I have deliberately steered clear of a discussion of the more intricate details of Freudian political theory, founded as it is on the much-contested base of Freudian psychology and tending to use psychoanalytic methods on the political level: for example, Marcuse's calling for the political use of sexual practices that society deems perverse in order to unchain the life instinct from societal constraint.[19] Again, perhaps the most relevant of the Freudian pantheon for our purposes is the work of Lacan.

The criticisms which have been levied against Lacan's political implications may be particularly instructive, pointing to the pitfalls which are to be encountered when the essentialist foundations of selfhood are removed. Frosh gives a succinct summary of the main stumbling blocks:

> If humanism is a fraud and there is no fundamental human entity that is to be valued in each person, one is left with no way of defending the basic rights of the individual, for the individual is apparently no more than her/his construction . . . It must be admitted that Lacan's position threatens to slip either into the essentialism it abhors . . . or into such a relentless structuralism that no content at all is allowed the human subject.[20]

Despite these reservations, most of which Frosh links with Lacan's insistence on the constructive primacy of language, he does point out that there are some interesting insights to be gleaned from Lacan's psychology. The most useful for political purposes is probably the idea that the self is an ideologically constructed entity, created through a process of engagement with the world that works not on the basis of a direct encounter but on mentally constructed fiction.

Another illustration of a political Freudian who came to dispute some of the tenets of the master's canon was Wilhelm Reich. He claimed that the unconscious forces in the mind were inherently good and it was societal distortion that made them bad. He advised that we should let these libidinal instincts express themselves and should not repress them.[21] Reich's ideas deteriorated in popularity, however, as his claims became more and more outlandish, culminating in his claim that he had built apparatus which could harness this libidinal energy, which he called orgone energy, and which could be directed at clouds to control climate[22] or could, through a space gun, also be used to repeal alien attacks.[23]

Humanism: Self-centred politics

There have been many attempts, both philosophical and psychological, to address the deficiencies in the behaviourist and similar conceptions. Husserl, for example, attempted to build on the phenomenological psychology of Bretano (or 'psychognostics' as the latter referred to it) by conceiving of the human subject as a knowing self. Naturalistic philosophy, for Husserl, failed in its tendency to view only the physical world as real with humans being conceived of as 'a unity of spatio-temporal being subject to exact causal laws of nature'.[24] Husserl's early writings reflect a rejection of this conception with his advocating of the 'phenomenological reduction' by which the empirical ego of the everyday world is 'put in brackets'. Spiegelberg explains this methodology by rendering it in its literal meaning of 'a leading back to the origins of which our all too hasty everyday thought has lost sight'.[25] Thus not only is consciousness disconnected from the world but also from the substantial ego, leaving, it is hoped, a pure consciousness freed from all earthly attachments. Herein lies the problem with the phenomenological reduction: it entails an individual transcendental subjectivity which transcends even the individual subject through rejecting all that makes him a human agent. Husserl sought to rectify this in his later work through the concept of *Lebenswelt*, a notion that Heidegger would later incorporate into his *Dasein* and, on a more social level, into the *Mitsein*. The *Lebenswelt* is the world of lived experience, which suggests an intersubjective dimension to the otherwise detached individual ego. Exactly how the two interrelate is left unclear in Husserl's work – and even in that of the later phenomenologists. However, the concept of the centrality of the life-world in the interpretation of human experience, together with the element of historical understanding gleaned from Dilthey's philosophy, was to act as a springboard for the development of philosophical hermeneutics,[26] one of its foremost proponents being Charles Taylor.

Taylor, in his volume of essays *Human Agency and Language*, mounts a concerted attack on the behaviourist approach in psychology and its knock-on effect in political science. Whereas classical behaviourism overtly rejected what it called 'mentalism' in the explanation of human action, Taylor founds his argument on a critique of the tendency toward 'physicalism' which behaviourism represents. In his critique he not only cites classical behaviourism with its account of 'correlating stimulus input and movement' but also its more sophisticated contemporary variants as found in attempts at computer modelling.[27]

Taylor points out the problems that all these theories have encountered when they come up against the purposive component in human action:

> This form of behaviourism could not cope with the purposeful, intelligent behaviour even of rats, let alone men [sic] . . . It could not match the regularities of behaviour characterised in terms of purpose and cognition with descriptions of environment and behaviour characterised as stimulus and response.[28]

In the face of this problem, behaviourism began to stretch its central concepts in order to try to facilitate phenomena that the core of the theory would explicitly reject. One example Taylor cites is the notion of 'response',

> which was meant to be identified *qua* 'colourless movement' – and there would be little point in launching on the behaviourist enterprise if it were not – [but] in fact was almost invariably classified in terms of the end goal of the action concerned.[29]

This kind of conceptual stretching seemed to lead to a situation in which a weak form of behaviourism emerged, one that seemed to state merely that experience serves to alter behaviour, a proposition that very few would want to dispute. Taylor's critique turns then on an identification of the distinction between weak behaviourism, which presents itself as a self-evident truism of everyday experience, and strong or classical behaviourism, which would seem to be untenable even from within its own camp.

One method that sought to overcome these problems was neurocomputational theories, good examples of which are the ideas of Susan Greenfield. Greenfield presents a more appealing account than does Pinker. She uses the idea that consciousness develops slowly and gradually and points to the fact that, whereas the brains of primates undergo most of their development in the womb, human development takes place for the most part after birth. This conceptualisation serves on the one hand to counter the unpalatable ideas of Skinner and Watson, who claimed that human cognition could reasonably be compared with that of animals. It also puts the behaviourist notion of conditioning on more-concrete ground. If human brains undergo most of their development postnatally, then it seems reasonable to suggest that they develop and mature under the influence of particular stimuli and environmental constraints.[30] As we increasingly interact with our environment, more of the appropriate neurons are connected to facilitate the most effective signalling, and therefore enable the best responses in given situations. Activity and growth, therefore, go hand in hand with even small changes in lifestyle or environment being reflected in changes in neural circuitry.[31] Despite being a more sophisticated variant on the initial idea of stimulus and response, Taylor believes that such an approach inevitably runs into the same root problem as the classical model:

> whether human functions that on a phenomenological level seem to involve a flexible know-how and perception of things which is not reducible to brute data and an exactly specified procedure can be matched by a machine which does operate on particular input by just such an exact procedure.[32]

The concept of brute data is an important one because it serves to link Taylor's critique of behaviourist psychology and his objections to the more 'scientistic' methodologies in political science. Taylor's argument is that a social science that wishes to fulfil the criteria of empiricism must reconstruct social reality as a collection of brute data. This brute data claims to represent both people's behaviour and the subjective reality of an individual's beliefs as attested by their responses to questioning or their overt non-verbal behaviour.[33] In order for behaviourism to make the type of causal claims it does, based on a purely mechanistic or 'physicalistic' model of human action, it also has to break down the complex web of human interaction into discrete 'bits' of data which it can then process. The move towards computational modelling has only exacerbated this problem with the flattening of interpretation increasing at every step towards more rigid 'brute datafication'. There is an obvious appeal to this initiative in terms of both psychological and political investigation. It is incredibly easy to process, find correlations between and construct models with discrete bits of concrete information. It is a process that facilitates the ordering and conceptualising of an inherently disordered mental and social reality. The problem is, however, that it excludes those elements of cognition, action and social orientation that are developed and carried on through the self-interpretations of the agents involved.

Taylor's foremost critical point, which he places in opposition to the psychological and social scientific idea of brute data, is that humans are self-interpreting animals. This ties him into the hermeneutic stream of political theory in which emphasis is placed on the meanings associated with human action as deployed in social settings. Such perspectives follow Hegel in contextualising human consciousness within social and historical frameworks.

In the subject-centred mode of political theory, there are those perspectives that follow a more Kantian idea of the subject, taking their cue from his attempt in the *Critique of Pure Reason* to differentiate the causally conditioned phenomenal or empirical self from the noumenal transcendental self. The latter of these is then taken to be the moral and rational agent. It would be too simplistic and constitute an interpretive brutality to suggest that Kant merely painted a rational individual subject, whose mind was linked to but not bounded by social context. His lectures on pragmatic anthropology, underlining the study of the connection between body and mind, belie such a view. It is true however that there is sometimes a tendency in the tradition of political theory which has followed Kant to lay less emphasis on the connections between mind and world, or even mind and body, leading to an overestimation of its rational abilities.

It has been the subject of much debate to compare and contrast the strands of political philosophy that have emphasised either the contextualised or 'unencumbered' and rational individual. For the purposes of the present study, what the perspectives share is a concentration on the conscious element in mental thought, with their differences lying only in the constitution of consciousness and the parameters of its abilities. This emphasis on consciousness serves to bracket off much of our mental life and fails to present an adequate picture of critical possibility. It does not question the possibility of how we may think differently.

Postmodernism: Taking the self out of politics

Postmodern perspectives do not share such optimism about our abilities, however. They share their pessimism with the Frankfurt School, which combined Hegelian and Freudian concepts to critique the hold which instrumental rationality has on contemporary society. Whereas the Frankfurt School, and those who continue its concerns, sought to shift the emphasis from one form of rationality to one thought to be less oppressive, postmodern thought often gave up on rationality altogether and sought to erase the conscious human self from the baseline of political and social theory. Rather than posit an essentially transcendental subject as the epistemological foundation, Foucault sought to start with a specific socio-historical context and then investigate how a sense of self was created within it. This mode of inquiry had already been advocated by structuralism and had led to interesting political interventions such as Althusser's structuralist reading of Marx with a psychoanalytic influence. For structuralism there was no essential self, merely the illusion of one created by language usage and the functioning of external structures. Foucault and those following him did not look for transcendent structures in each society, however, preferring to examine the particulars of each social and temporal context with its ruptures and changes. Foucault examined the way in which subjects were created sexually in different societies, Lacan pointed to the idea that we have to lean on the 'otherness' of language to create ourselves in terms that are never quite our 'own' and Kristeva talks of the sense of 'foreignness' inside us which leads us to discriminate against the external stranger. The commonality in these positions is the abandonment of an internal self and the positing of a shell built around an internal void and entirely constructed from external meanings derived from language and behavioural patterning. Our sense of self is thus entirely constituted, in this set of theories, by the discourses surrounding us.

The psychology envisaged by normative political philosophy generally posited a centred rational self capable of coming to reasoned political judgements which then formed the basis of political intervention. It is this vision that underlies Rawls' veil of ignorance, Habermas' communicative rationality and Taylor's narrativity. Freudian theory had problematised this essentially Cartesian view, however, and the Kantian or Hegelian assumptions coupled to it. The Enlightenment project of rational social and political progress guided by reason began to move a little further out of reach. Both Descartes and Kant assumed that the human mind had innate structural features that would allow it to transcend the psychological conditioning impact of the world around it. Hegel, although he and those who followed him gave greater attention to the contextualised nature of thought, still firmly held to a teleology that promised eventual emancipation.

Freud showed how rationality was not the main motor of mental life and how much of what surfaces in consciousness is the product of inherently irrational forces. To this was added the idea, in postmodern and poststructuralist philosophy, that the conscious self was no more than the manifestation of the world surrounding it. We shall encounter the work of Jacques Lacan and the idea that language is the greatest shaping influence in constituting the self later in this work. There will also be discussion of Foucault's reliance on the creative nature of power and Deleuze's emphasis on desire. Another structuring influence, and one that for the purposes of this introduction is a prime example of the use of psychological underpinnings in political theory, is Althusser's concept of ideology.

In *For Marx*, Althusser argued that society operates on three interconnected levels: economic, political and ideological. The economic level is the final determinant of social relations but the three are so intertwined that one cannot discuss one in isolation from the others. In terms of the subject, Althusser argued that it is ideology that constitutes the main motor for the creation of subjectivity. The function of ideology is to manufacture a relationship between the individual and the concrete realities of existence. Through the mythology of connections it establishes, it essentially manufactures the subjectivity it sets out to coerce. This conception was then carried to another level by Foucault who, in his early works, argued that the subject is created by the structures of the different forms of knowledge that surround it. These forms of knowledge are themselves created, not by any conscious human agency, but by emergent discursive processes. In his later work, the very notion of the self, and not just the particular form it may assume, is seen as the product of specific socio-historic discourses and practices.

For Lacan, Althusser and Foucault, the lesson of structuralism was that what mattered was not the individual subjective consciousness, especially in its rational element, but rather the external structures beyond it that constitute the subject from outside. There is no subject before social structure for such theorists, no innate core of selfhood that can be used as a foundation for thought and action.

From a political point of view, this has ramifications for both the practice of intervention and its constituent basis. Although someone like Taylor can point to an authenticity to be recovered or an evolution to be continued in terms of the subject, postmodern views have no real basis for telling us why one set of discourses provide a 'better' subject than another, other than that any system will always exclude someone and create resistance within it. As in other political theory, the view of the subject will determine the political possibilities afforded, even wherein it is claimed that the subject has been dethroned as the focus of analysis. If there is nothing internal to, or transcendental in, the subject that may act as the foundation for political intervention, then our options are limited by the very discourses we seek to resist.

The politics of synapses?

I have great sympathy with the postmodern position, as will be seen in the coming pages. The idea that political possibilities are bounded by external discourses serves to heighten the importance of the satanic question: how do we think differently? In order to examine this idea, and because of my belief that political theory must be founded on a conception of the subject (even if that conception is of a self that lacks an essential *quidditas*), I propose to examine neuropsychological material relating to the nature of consciousness and unconsciousness. This will serve both as a justification for my sympathy with the postmodern view of the nature of the self and reposition thinking differently as a socio-biological question.

The mode of argument used in this book can be seen in terms of a series of conceptual machines through which the central argument advances. The main concern with a method of building theory that divorces concepts from their original contexts and re-territorialises them in relation to others from different backgrounds is that one will end up with an incoherent and contradictory jumble of ideas that lose the central contention one was trying to present. I hope that the following discussions avoid such a fate.

This method raises an interesting philosophical question as to the nature of concepts and the relation they bear to the bodies of theory that contain them. One may argue that a concept is defined in terms of that which surrounds it in the contemplative universe it inhabits. Divorcing a concept from its background would, in this case, be akin to taking a word from an unknown language and trying to integrate it into one's own speech. One would lose the hermeneutic associations that that word had for its original speakers. Our language reflects, to a large extent, our world and the history of experiences that its speakers have passed through. Etymologically, a word is a deep and complex thing. In the intellectual world a concept is likewise, it operates in terms of the ideological grammar of that which surrounds it.

I hold that a concept can be more than this, however. An idea held up to the light of consideration can be as aesthetically pleasing as an object of art and can be appreciated in its own terms. It may have an elegance all if its own. More than this, it may have utility. Not only are concepts works of mental art, they are also tools. I mean this in the oldest possible sense. Before we create a specific tool for a specific purpose, we always use whatever we can to complete the task. Our forebears did not possess machine tools but, rather than leave a task undone, they utilised pieces of rock or wood: whatever they could improvise. Such is intellectual endeavour. In the face of new experiences to be analysed and new questions asked, the theorist must survey the range of conceptual tools that grow around him or her and harvest those needed for the particular task at hand. A concept holds its place in a body of theory because it fulfils a certain task. If it can complete another task in another body of ideas then it can be divorced from its original home and utilised elsewhere.

This idea of concepts in terms of utility is also one that helps to keep coherence, since one is only introducing specific ideas in order to fulfil a specific function in terms of the overall argument. It is this method that I have followed in this book, passing the argument through the conceptual machines necessary to both build it up in terms of supporting argument and refine it in theoretical terms.

Chapter 1 serves to introduce the neuropsychological work on consciousness and nonconsciousness that I discuss throughout. This material is prefaced with a look at how conceptions of consciousness have evolved over the years. Chapter 2 goes on to discuss various themes in the philosophy of mind in order to provide a philosophical context within which to set the neuropsychological work. One of the objections levelled against such research and its utility in social thought is its reductionist tendency. Chapter 2 argues that in functionalism we are able to combine the materialism with context sensitivity as well as being able to differentiate between different levels of consciousness. Herein, we also begin to engage the central concern of the book with discussions on the interactions between both body and mind on the one hand and consciousness and nonconsciousness on the other, to start to unpack how change can be brought about.

Chapter 3 goes on to complicate the idea of thought further, as well as introducing the social element of thinking through discussion of affect and emotional regimes. Then follows an examination of the emotional regime instigated by consumer capitalism though the lens of Zygmunt Bauman's concept of *unsicherheit*. Chapter 4 examines the role of narrative in conscious self creation and concludes with an investigation of the impact of Deleuze's concepts of difference and repetition on the creation of original thought.

Chapters 5 and 6 then take the ideas of self, consciousness and nonconsciousness thus far presented and investigate their political potential, focusing on consciousness in Chapter 5 and nonconsciousness in Chapter 6.

The help and support that I have been lucky enough to receive during the writing of this book has come from a variety of sources. The ideas herein started life in my PhD thesis and I owe thanks to those within the School of Politics (as it then was), Queen's University

Belfast, who have been kind enough to give me both their time and comments when the work was in that form. Primary thanks must go to Iain Mackenzie who has been an unfailing source of faith, advice and support throughout the entire life of the project, as was Moya Lloyd. I have also had the benefit of comments from John Barry, Shane O'Neill, Vincent Geoghegan, Debbie Lisle, Denis Smith and Jane McConkey on various aspects of this work, including pointers towards ideas and authors that both helped shape the development of its ideas.

On a personal level, I must also thank my family, my mother and father Patrick and Roseanna Laird, my sister Marcella and my niece Naomi, for their constant support and encouragement over the years. Marcella has also been kind enough to give me the benefit of her professional experience in the field of mental health, as was Gary Erwin, also of Muckamore Abbey Hospital, Antrim. Many thanks also to Ciaran Dougherty, Aidan McDonnell, Ciaran O'Neill, Chris O'Reilly, Vincent Perry, and Liam Polley, who over many years have become my extended family. Aidan McDonnell was also kind enough to proofread and provide his comments on the work. To these people I have been lucky to add those friends I have made since switching from academia to a legal career and I thank those people for their support during the latter stages of the work.

Thanks also to Nicola Ramsey and those others at Edinburgh University Press who have been supportive, helpful and understanding during the writing and publication process.

Final thanks must go to my partner Miranda without whose love, support and presence I would get very little done in any area of life.

Notes

1. Broadbent, *Behaviour*, p. 9.
2. Watson, as quoted in Morris, *Western Conceptions*, p. 115.
3. Morris, *Western Conceptions*, p. 116.
4. Baum, *Understanding Behaviourism*, p. 29.
5. Nye, *The Legacy of B. F. Skinner*, p. 75.
6. Ibid. pp. 76–7.
7. Ibid. p. 80.
8. Ibid. p. 74.
9. Ibid. p. 98.
10. Ibid. p. 109.
11. Laver, *Private Desires, Political Action*, p. 27.
12. Elster, 'The nature and scope of rational choice explanation', p. 320.

13. Hollis, *Philosophy of Social Science*, p. 135.
14. Pinker, *How the Mind Works*, p. 561.
15. Morris, *Western Conceptions*, p. 93.
16. Marcuse, *Eros and Civilisation*, p. 11.
17. Morris, *Western Conceptions*, p. 338.
18. Ibid. p. 343.
19. Outlined in Geoghegan, *Reason and Eros*, pp. 52–6.
20. Frosh, *Politics of Psychoanalysis*, p. 137.
21. Cattier, *Life and Work of Wilhelm Reich*, pp. 138–49.
22. Boadella, *Wilhelm Reich*, p. 289.
23. Ibid. pp. 302–5.
24. Morris, *Western Conceptions*, p. 370.
25. Spiegelberg, *Phenomenological Movement*, p. 132.
26. Morris, *Western Conceptions*, p. 374.
27. Taylor, *Human Agency and Language*, p. 125.
28. Ibid.
29. Ibid. p. 126.
30. Greenfield, *The Human Brain*, pp. 139–41.
31. Ibid. p. 147.
32. Taylor, *Human Agency*, p. 128.
33. Taylor, 'Interpretation and the Sciences of Man' in *Philosophy and the Human Sciences*.

1

The Neuroscience of Consciousness

It has become a standard refrain of contemporary social theory that, as we begin the twenty-first century, our culture seems as incoherent and fractured as our mental life. Ideas exist in juxtaposition, contradicting each other at certain levels and complementing at others. The exploration of the interrelationship between these planes and layers of culture, as well as those of consciousness and selfhood, are what fuels art and literature and what occupies the psychiatrist's couch. At the heart of our culture is still the irresistible promise of Enlightenment rationality: that the world is there to be explained and bettered. The raw optimism of this original programme has been tempered over the years by certain provisos, exceptions and downright rejections, from romanticism and spirituality, to chaos, quantum and the uncertainty principle.

The strata of our psychological beliefs have built up, giving rise to a situation wherein our legal systems place emphasis on the individual's responsibility for actions as if they were all consciously taken, whilst more and more people turn to New Age practices to tap into unknowable forces they intuitively sense beyond our rational grasp. These currents entwine around each other, creating complex relationships. The turn to mysticism, for example, is unlike the submissive medieval attitude to religion. The idea that our place in the world is preordained and we live at the revocable benevolence of an almighty God has mutated through our enlightenment-tinged psyche to become another tool in the individual's kit for controlling their personal world.

One of the aims of this book is to explore the complex relations between the entwined strands and associations of our culture and the entangled, contradictory planes of our minds. This first chapter tries to peel back some of these mental layers before penetrating them in later chapters with the influence of our social environment. I have chosen to start at the bottom, working from what is regarded as the dark depths of the unknowable unconscious, up to the contemporary dissection of the nonconscious, before breaking the surface to the more familiar ideas of narrative selfhood.

Historical trends in the theory of the unconscious

The unconscious is an idea made famous and popularly accessible in our culture by the work of Sigmund Freud and his followers. So successful has been the Freudian monopolisation of the term that when we think of the unknowable portion of our mental lives it is usually in terms of drives and dark impulses bubbling to the surface through dreams, jokes and slips of the tongue, as well as neuroses and complexes.

Freud was, however, preceded and succeeded by a long line of alternative visions that have not proved as fascinating to the popular mind. In order to elucidate some of these other ideas, I shall pick out three historical strands in work on the unconscious – the supernatural or noumenal unconscious, the natural unconscious and the mechanical unconscious – in order to prepare the ground for a discussion of contemporary work on consciousness and unconsciousness.[1]

The supernatural unconscious

In the *Iliad*, no one seems to blame Achilles for his behaviour, even though he may now strike us as a thoroughly unlikeable character. His aggression and cruelty, as well as the speed with which he perceives an insult, are attributed to the action of his passions: beyond his conscious control and mostly inspired by the gods for their own ends. He is not, therefore, held to account because his rational mind can neither know nor control these impulses. The gods act almost as an external unconscious in this and the later Greek myths. Their behaviour exhibits many of the features we associate with the unconscious. They are irrational and demand instant satisfaction of their desires, often going to extreme lengths to attain it. In these stories, the inherently rational behaviour of humans is influenced by these capricious and erratic beings and those caught in the web of their machinations cannot be blamed.[2]

With the advent of Christianity, the polarisation of this dynamic was reversed. The irrational impulse now lay in humans themselves and it was through the intercession of a supremely benevolent deity that these impulses could be overcome, by way of divine grace for example. The soul, as that fragment of the divine residing in humans, now became the rational component of mental life, the equivalent of what we now term consciousness. Augustine, for example, claims that the awareness that we are alive is the awareness that we have a soul, therefore equating it with self-consciousness.[3] Aquinas later defines the soul as 'the principle of intellectual activity . . . also termed the mind or intellect'.[4]

There are hidden influences outside this, however, not open to the introspective analysis pioneered by Augustine, and exhibiting a lasting influence into the nineteenth century. That which lay outside of rational consciousness, whether attributed to the actions of the Greek gods or the inaction of the Christian God, was deemed ontologically separate from consciousness, supernatural and outside reasonable analysis. As Augustine states 'I myself cannot grasp the totality of what I am'.[5]

The natural unconscious

The unconscious may not have been amenable to direct analysis using introspection but its influence and presence could be inferred. This presence came to be seen as a natural and not supernatural phenomenon. One example is Plato's tripartite division of the soul into reason, spirit and appetite.[6] The division is hierarchical with spirit, even though irrational, being seen as the ally of reason, with appetite playing the disrupting influence. Here reason can be equated with consciousness, with spirit and appetite as unconscious desires and drives to be controlled. In the *Phaedrus*, for example, we get the image of reason as a charioteer keeping the unruly horses of spirit and desire in check. Plato does not simply privilege reason over the other two elements of the soul, however. The guiding organisational theme in *The Republic* is that of balance rather than subjugation.

Justice in the individual results from a balance of conflicting mental and physical attributes, just as justice in the state consists of a balance between all the different components of the *polis*, each knowing their place and acting within their own sphere of influence. This can be seen clearly in Plato's discussion of the virtue of self-discipline.[7] Therein it is claimed that a person is 'master of himself [sic]' when the better element in one's personality controls the worse element.

Further on in Book 4, the harmonic connection between individual and state is directly highlighted. 'The state was just when the three elements within it each minded their own business . . . [and] each of us will be just and perform his proper function only if each part of him is performing its proper function.'[8] The individual and state are interconnected in this statement, not only because they mirror each other but also because, for the individual to perform his or her proper part in society, the internal elements of the mind must be in harmony.

Balance within leads to balance without and both are seen as forms of health, physical and political.[9]

In this conception, the irrational parts of the psyche are seen to have an important place in mental functioning. An excess of reason is just as unwanted, though not as dangerous, as an excess of spirit or appetite and the philosopher, who privileges reason above all else, is portrayed in the *Phaedrus* as being in the grip of a type of madness. Through spirit we desire honour and, in times of battle, this element is to be given a freer reign in order to imbue us with courage. Appetite is necessary for our everyday survival causing us to desire food and procreation. The irrational parts of our mental life are therefore portrayed as natural and essential components, with rational consciousness given the task of keeping their wilder tendencies in check.

This view of the unconscious as a type of natural instinct can also be seen in Schopenhauer's 'will to life'. In the conception of the supernatural unconscious, that which lies outside conscious availability was equated with a Kantian noumen. Schopenhauer proposed that this noumenal entity was 'Will'. Through introspection, the turning of consciousness inward, Schopenhauer argued that a bodily action arising from what we think of as volition is in fact the same thing as volition itself. The body and its actions are objectified Will: the structuring of Will in terms of the Kantian categories of space, time and causation in the phenomenal world.

We do not each possess an individual will, however. Multiplicity belongs to the phenomenal world whereas behind it lies a single unitary Will, 'a blind, irresistible impulse' or 'an endless striving'.[10] Schopenhauer defends the use of a word that usually implies directionality of thought to describe a directionless force by claiming that we can understand the concept more easily by relating it to our own experience of volition. Given that the Will is an endless striving actualised through many different phenomena, and this includes animals, plants and inanimate objects as well as humans, it can never find tranquillity or contentment, often coming into conflict with itself, leading, for example, to war.

The root of all evil for human subjects is, according to Schopenhauer, slavery to the Will. Human beings are essentially irrational, guided by desire and emotion as the Will seeks satisfaction, with the intellect merely a tool developed and maximised to serve this end. Human intellect is able, however, to go beyond the pursuit of what is necessary for mere survival and use its surplus energy to attempt to break free from the hold of the Will. In the short term, this may be achieved by way of aesthetic contemplation, with art being viewed only for its aesthetic significance and not as an object of desire. Through this, we may achieve a level of disinterested tranquillity. The long term, and more satisfactory option, is to follow a Buddhist type of path, to realise the fleeting nature of happiness and turn surplus rationality to a disgust with, and renunciation of, the Will.

We therefore get a fascinating relationship between the consciousness and unconscious in Schopenhauer, which is worth examining a little further as it precursors both Freud and Nietzsche and will become important again in later chapters.

In the supplement to Book 2 of *The World as Will and Idea* entitled 'On the primacy of the Will in self-consciousness', consciousness is seen as an epiphenomenon of the Will:

> for consciousness is conditioned by the intellect, and the intellect is a mere accident of our being, for it is a function of the brain which, together with the associated nerves and spinal cord, is merely a fruit, a product, of the rest of the organism, and even its parasite in so far as it does not directly engage with its inner mechanism but merely serves the purpose of self-preservation by regulating the relations of the organism with the external world.[11]

This is a direct precursor of the ideas that we shall encounter in the next section of this chapter. Consciousness is equated with knowledge and it is argued that the Will is in the position of that which is known. The known is seen as primary to the knower. Echoing Augustine, 'certainly the intellect is on a familiar footing with the Will, but it will not be privy to all its business'.[12]

The idea of free will, as presently conceived, is alien to Schopenhauer. We have little conscious control over our actions. 'The intellect is originally a stranger to the Will's decisions' supplying the motives on which the Will acts but becoming privy to the consequences almost like a third party and always trying to discover the Will's intentions.[13] This then bears on our conscious ability to influence the Will. This influence can be wrought, however, through such techniques as consciously bringing to mind images or memories which affect the Will. An unpleasant thought, for example, can cause 'anxiety to constrict the heart, and the blood [to] flow sluggishly Even though the intellect can lead the Will in this way, likened by Schopenhauer to a nursemaid exciting gladness or sadness in a child through stories, the Will reasserts its primacy 'by prohibiting the intellect from entertaining certain ideas, by suppressing certain train of thought' which it knows will cause it pain, a mechanism Freud would later characterise as repression.[14] Whereas Plato depicted self-control as holding the three elements of the soul in balance, with the emphasis on the rational element if any, Schopenhauer holds that the Will's control of the intellect is 'being master of oneself'.[15]

In Book 4 of *The World as Will and Idea*, however, the denial of the Will to life is seen as a way in which the intellect can act, no longer as the supplier of motives for the Will to act upon, but as a 'quieter of the Will'.[16] On the one hand, knowledge may lead the Will to act in new directions, 'but it can never make the Will want something actually different from what it has hitherto wanted; this remains unchangeable, for the Will is, after all, only this willing itself, which would otherwise have to be suspended.'[17] The Will cannot be suspended, but it can be denied. After a long period of gradual penetration into the nature of reality, leading to a realisation of the negative nature of happiness as the momentary cessation of desire and a cultivation of compassion for others, a person may take the next step to total renunciation or aestheticism.

> Anyone who has reached this point still always feels, as a living body, as concrete manifestation of Will, the natural disposition towards every type of volition; but he deliberately suppresses it by forcing himself to refrain from doing all he would like to do, and on the contrary, to do all he would not like to do, even if this has no purpose beyond that of serving to mortify the Will.[18]

This must be a continuing struggle, however, as there is always the danger of the Will reasserting itself.

At the end of the work, Schopenhauer asks whether this triumph of the intellect over the Will, of consciousness over the unconsciousness, is not a contradiction of his earlier characterisation of the Will as prime originator. In answer it is claimed that the Will is still the base of reality but that the phenomena which emanate from it can stand in opposition to it. The example is given of the fact that the genitals will still exist, as visual manifestation of the sexual impulse, even though that impulse has been quelled and is not acted upon. The contradiction between the primacy of the Will and its denial by the intellect, through a changed mode of knowledge, is a reflection of the deeper contradiction of the conditioning of the unconditioned Will when it enters the phenomenal world.[19]

Schopenhauer's work was carried on by his foremost disciple, Eduard von Hartmann. Von Hartmann sought to reconcile Schopenhauer and

Hegel by positing a teleological element to the Will. Still in the pessimistic vein, he argued that as the intellect grows so too grows unhappiness and that the material advancement of civilisation is only an unconscious mechanism for the self-perpetration of the race. Full development will be culminated when the intellect has been refined to the point where it recognises the futility of volition and desire and the human race commits mass suicide.[20] (An interesting tangential line of thought can be drawn from Schopenhauer, through Von Hartmann to Camus' idea of suicide as the limit of critique.)

Nietzsche, on the other hand, preferred a more dynamic life-affirming interpretation. In Nietzsche, like Schopenhauer, we find the argument that the role of consciousness is overrated in the wake of Kant and intellectualist philosophy, rather, 'consciousness is a surface'.[21] He regards there being little difference between waking and dreaming: 'all our so called consciousness is a more or less fantastic commentary on an unknown, perhaps unknowable, but felt text . . . Must one really say . . . experiences are fictions?'[22] Nietzsche folds consciousness into the body and sees the mind as no more than the functioning of the body: 'body I am entirely and nothing else; and soul is only a word for something about the body'.[23] The idea of consciousness only arises out of the social necessity for communication.[24]

Nietzsche embraces becoming and it is this aspect of his thought that Connolly subsumes within his own concept of 'technique'. There is, however, a greater appreciation in the former of the limited role of consciousness within this process. There is an embracing of fatalism on Nietzsche's part, a rejection of free will as commonly understood as complete conscious control. We are not passive in the face of uncontrollable external forces but we must learn to accept our place amongst them. Action on our part can influence the world but we in turn are influenced by an internal, as well as external, world that we cannot seek to fully control. Freedom for Nietzsche comes from a genuine acceptance of this; 'my formula for greatness in a human being is *amor fati* [love of fate] . . . Not merely [to] bear what is necessary, still less conceal it . . . but *love* it'.[25]

Not only should we accept that consciousness is limited, Nietzsche claims that we must actually realise the dangers it poses as part of our mental life. 'Consciousness is only the last and the latest stage in organic development and as such is less developed and less strong'. Nietzsche holds that the relatively immature consciousness should be 'thoroughly tyrannized' by the unconscious, if this were not so we would 'perish sooner than necessary' the victim of every fleeting thought or idea. In this conception, consciousness is an intermittent variable whereas the unconscious is a foundational constant.[26]

The threads of Plato, Schopenhauer and Nietzsche can be seen to come together in Freud. It is with Freud that the naturalisation of the unconscious becomes complete at a psychological as well as cultural level. There is also a noumenal element to the unconscious, however, in that its depths can never be fully plumbed and will remain mostly unknowable. Freudian metapsychology underwent many changes and was constantly refined throughout his life in light of the therapeutic work undertaken by him and others. For our purposes, it is useful to follow the standard division into three successive periods: the affect-trauma model, the topographical model and the structural model.

The early affect-trauma model was based on Freud's observations, with Franz Breuer, of hysterical patients.[27] Whereas Breuer believed that the dissociation of the conscious and unconscious minds occurred in psychotic patients when pent up pressure from emotional forces broke through to the surface as psychotic symptoms, Freud argued that the separation occurs in mentally healthy individuals also.

The idea of the unconscious was generally current in Vienna at the time and Freud and his circle of acquaintances were familiar with the work of Schopenhauer and von Hartmann. Freud sought to move the idea from the philosophical realm and to connect it with his recent clinical experience. The function of the psychic apparatus is conceived at this stage as being to adapt the organism to the pressures of the external world (traumas). Ideas incompatible with conscious beliefs are repressed by an ego that develops as the child grows older, forced into the unconscious, which is then disassociated from consciousness. In this early version of the ego, we see it having to deal with the outside world, foreshadowing the final structural model in which it will be torn between external and internal pressures. At this point, however, it is more in control, performing the repressive function itself and consigning mental contents to unconsciousness as a form of self-protection.

This phase of Freudian metapsychology was relatively short, extending only from the 'Neuro-psychosis of defence' [1894] and *Studies on Hysteria* [1895] to its replacement mainly by Chapter 7 of *The Interpretation of Dreams* [1900].[28] The succeeding topographical model is so called because the mental elements are now organised vertically in terms of depth instead of the relatively horizontal differentiation between conscious and unconscious in the affect-trauma model. Alongside the conscious and unconscious, another entity, the preconscious, is posited and the structure of these three components is analysed more thoroughly than before. In the interests of clarity, given the overlap between content, I will capitalise Conscious, Unconscious and Preconscious when referring to them as nouns to differentiate from adjectival descriptions of the contents of these systems.

Again, the Unconscious is made up of unsatisfied impulses and strivings, usually sexual or aggressive, which seek fulfilment. They are considered dangerous to the organism and are therefore kept in check, away from conscious functioning and able to reach the surface only in a disguised form, such as sublimation wherein wishes are culturally transformed into more socially acceptable goals. The Unconscious, however, contains the reservoir of psychic energy that powers mental life and is therefore in the driving seat, even if its impulses are only acted on in a distorted form. Enjoyment of public speaking or acting, for example, is seen as the product of crude sexual exhibitionist wishes that must find discharge and do so in a less dangerous form.

The primary motor of mental activity is the seeking of mental equilibrium through the discharge of tension caused by the wishes of the Unconscious. The Unconscious knows no rules, acting only in terms of the 'pleasure principle' by which it strives endlessly for satisfaction.[29] Its contents do not operate in accordance with the Kantian precepts of time, space and causation and exist in contradictory and random association.

The main function of the Preconscious is to act as a filter protecting the Conscious from the dangerous promptings of the Unconscious, by transforming its wishes into more acceptable forms that range from purely mental activity, such as dreams, daydreams and hallucinations, to derivatives of wishes acted out in a different form in the real world. It too is unconscious, representing one of the major changes from the affect-trauma model. No longer is the repressive and filtering mechanism conscious, thereby paring back the remit and abilities of the conscious mind. In effect, there are now two levels of censorship: the boundary from the Unconscious to the Preconscious and that from the Preconscious to the Conscious.

In addition to those elements of the Unconscious which have succeeded in getting through, either in a suitably modified form or by forcing their way through unaltered, the Preconscious also contains mental representations brought about through contact with the outside world and preconscious cognitive and imaginative functioning. Much of the automatic processing which we shall see in the next section is attributed in the Freudian models to the Preconscious, such as subliminal perception, the automaticity of repeated tasks and the sudden epiphanies of problem solving. The Preconscious 'thinks' whereas the Unconsciousness does not, it merely wills, as in Schopenhauer.

The influence of the external world leads the Preconscious, and the Conscious, to operate according to the 'reality principle'. In contrast to the very simplistic operation of the Unconscious – what Freud termed the 'primary process' – the Preconscious and Conscious have a more complex functioning, the 'secondary process', conditioned by logic, reason and external codes of moral, conduct and behavioural expectation.

The smallest part of mental functioning is that which takes place in the Conscious and which, unlike the other two, has the quality of that adjective attached to it. There is not a lot of emphasis on the Conscious in Freud's second phase, reflecting its limited role and the primacy of the Unconscious. The Conscious contains those thoughts that have made it through the second level of censorship from the Preconscious, as well as those elements of the external world that are receiving direct attention at any particular time. The transitory quality of consciousness is illustrated by Freud's analogy of the mystic writing pad, a Victorian toy consisting of a wax block covered with clear celluloid that could be written on with a stylus. When the celluloid was separated from the wax block, the writing disappeared from the surface, leaving it clear, but the imprint, or trace, was still left on the underlying wax. Thoughts fleet across the surface of consciousness, being wiped off with the direction of attention elsewhere, but still leaving an imprint on the Preconscious.[30]

Clinical experience and internal theoretical inconsistencies over the gestation of the second phase pointed to problems with the topographical model. One example was the idea that preconscious thoughts could become conscious if attention was turned towards them, which contradicted their primarily unconscious nature. Another was the re-evaluation of drives.

For most of the second phase, the primary drive was thought to be sexual, but clinical experience of subjects' repetition of destructive patterns led Freud to formulate the idea of the 'death instinct' along with the 'life instinct'. The death instinct, or Thanatos, has its roots in the notion that the instincts that guide human action represent the organism trying to regain a past state of psychical equilibrium, which, for Freud, had its ultimate expression in death. The life instinct, or Eros, on the other hand, is comprised of those instinctual forces that seek to maintain the organism's own existence in the face of external dangers so that it may live out its life course and die a 'natural' death from internal causes.[31] The death instinct could not be adequately incorporated in the topographical model, however, given its premise that the primary driving energy would always be libidinal or sexual.

The second phase of Freudian metapsychology saw behaviour and thought as primarily motivated on the internal level by unconscious wishes passing through the censorship processes of the Preconscious. The third structural phase, however, paid a lot more attention to the influence of the external world on behaviour. The dichotomy of the Conscious and the Unconscious was also relegated to the background as two of the new mental structures, the ego and superego, contained both conscious and unconscious elements, and more emphasis was placed on the processes of transformation that unconscious wishes went through before reaching the surface.

The id is synonymous with the Unconscious of the topographical model. Its contents are unfulfilled instinctual and socially conditioned childhood wishes inaccessible to consciousness, although now the aggressive drive takes equal place with the sexual drive as motivating factor. Again, the id is the entity with the dynamic power that activates the other structures. There is more emphasis now on developmental factors with the positing of psychosexual stages, which must be resolved as the child develops. Failure to resolve a stage will lead to a fixation in the id affecting future development and behaviour. Failure to resolve the anal stage, for example, may lead to an obsession with tidiness and cleanliness in later life. Failure to resolve the oral stage will lead to excessive eating or alcohol and drug abuse.

The superego is also conceived developmentally, arising out of the internalisation of authority and codes of conduct derived from parents, and later teachers and peers, which serve to regulate the actions of the ego. The notion has its precursor in the 'ego ideal' of the second phase,[32] the internalisation of parental rules and expectations, but is now widened out and incorporates the functions of a conscience giving rise to unconscious feelings of guilt which guide many of the ego's actions.

Finally, in the structural phase, there is the ego trapped between the competing demands of the id, the superego and the outside world, serving three masters as Freud puts it.[33] The ego is not to be simply equated with the Conscious of the topographical model, as the id is with the Unconscious, because it may contain unconscious elements within it. (Indeed confusion is caused by Freud also claiming that its contents are akin to that of the topographical Preconscious.)[34] Consciousness is seen as a quality only possessed by some of the ego's contents and the old topographical Conscious is merely a sense organ of the ego, with the id and superego only having access to consciousness through the ego.

The function of the ego is to control both contact with the outside world, through activities such as perception and action, and the competing demands of the outside world, id and superego. These conflicts are resolved by transforming unacceptable wishes using defence mechanisms. In the *New Introductory Lectures on Psychoanalysis*, the ego is described as merely a portion of the id that has been modified by contact with the outside world and, in an analogy similar to that used by Plato, it is described as being like a rider on a horse. The horse, the id, supplies the energy whilst the rider directs its movements and goals.[35] The relationship is not always harmonious, however, especially given the repressive checks and demands of the superego, and the conflict between the psychic structures is manifested by anxiety.

The boundaries between the three structures are not rigid and may change. Indeed the aim of psychoanalysis is claimed to be the strengthening of ego to make it more independent of the demands of the superego and to claim mental territory from the id. As Freud puts it, 'where id was, there ego shall be'.[36]

As well as assigning the ego a role similar to Plato's reason, Freud also perceived the parallels between his theory and Schopenhauer's. When outlining the death instinct to his audience of readers he anticipates the comment, 'that isn't natural science, its Schopenhauer's philosophy!'[37] The difference is pointed out that Schopenhauer recognised only the aggressive of the Freudian drives, in his theory of human conflict as the competing desires of the Will, whereas Freud gives equal weight to the life instinct. It could, however, be argued that Schopenhauer could just as well incorporate both of these drives into the functioning of the Will, as seen above in the discussion of the preservative as well as destructive tendencies. In this regard, Freud confuses the theory of von Hartmann, with his suicidal culmination of the world cycle, with that of Schopenhauer. On the other hand, the Freudian life instinct parallels the affirmative aspects of Nietzsche's will to power and the idea of drives is common to both.[38]

The mechanical unconscious

Whereas the emphasis so far has been on the unconscious element of mental life as irrational, in terms of opposition to the rational soul or being driven by irrational instinct, there is a current of theory that has not viewed it as such. In the *Monadology*, Leibniz introduced the ideas of apperception (self-conscious awareness) and unconscious perceptions and habit, of which he claimed three quarters of our mental life is composed.[39] In the nineteenth century, theorists such as William Hamilton, Thomas Laycock and William Carpenter characterised unconscious functioning as including lower-order mental processes occurring outside of awareness, such as the functioning of the human perceptual system, the ability to divide attention between tasks or become aware of outside stimuli during concentration, as well as the automaticity of thought and lack of awareness of one's feelings.

Carpenter, for example, formulated the concept of 'unconscious cerebration' to describe the automaticity of many actions that occur without conscious volition through 'cerebral reflexes'. If a hypnotist could distract or relax the conscious mind, Carpenter suggested, one could be put in direct contact with these reflexes.

Similarly, Thomas Henry Huxley argued that all animals function mostly on the basis of unconscious automatic processes. Consciousness, according to this theory, is an epiphenomenon with the unconscious as the initiator of action:

> The feeling we call volition is not the cause of the voluntary act, but simply the symbol in consciousness of the stage of the brain which is the immediate cause of the act. Like the steam whistle which signals but doesn't cause the starting of the locomotive.[40]

Likewise, Hermann von Helmholtz (and his assistant Wilhelm Wundt) pointed to the vast array of rules that humans must learn to navigate in the world, using the example of perceptual rules, such as those governing the perception of movement, to suggest decisions made with the help of unconscious inference.[41]

With these theories, we have a different view of the unconscious. No longer is it seen as the repository of energy, alien intents or repressed instincts to be held in check, but rather as a mechanism like clockwork. It does, however, comprise the greater part of our mental lives and instigate a large portion of action. Whereas the Freudian conception has proved vastly influential in psychology, culture, art, literature and politics, this more prosaic version can be seen as laying the foundations for contemporary theory based on neuropsychological study.

It is this latter, neuropsychological work that it is the intention of this book to seek to discuss in a social and political context, and the rest of this chapter is devoted to outlaying the relevant theories in this field.

The nonconscious: How individual are you?

In order to distinguish between earlier conceptions of the unconscious part of mental life, I shall follow contemporary neuropsychological practice and restrict myself to using the term 'nonconscious' both as an adjective and noun. This has the benefit of framing that which happens outside of conscious awareness in terms of impersonal automatic processes without imputing to it any maleficent motives which may flow from Freudian associations.

Libet and the mysterious half-second

Benjamin Libet defines consciousness as being analogous to awareness.[42] Given that up to 98 per cent of our brain activity happens beyond conscious awareness, this leaves an awful lot outside.[43] Although millions of bits of information flood into our senses with each passing moment, our consciousness only processes an average of sixteen bits per second. The human consciousness discards millions of bits of sensory data per second, preferring to present an ordered and organised picture of some of our environment, rather than a chaotic snapshot of everything. The radical upshot of this fact is that 'to be aware of an experience means that it has passed'.[44]

Research into subliminal perception carried out in the 1970s and 1980s sought to show how a subject can perceive and process a stimulus at a level below that of consciousness by, for example, the presentation of a stimulus too quickly to become conscious of it. It became clear that most of the information that passes through a person's senses is not picked up by consciousness, even when this information has a demonstrable effect on behaviour.[45] The ratio of what we sense to what we perceive can be put at one million to one.[46]

One example of this in the clinical setting is the research into priming conducted in the late 1980s by psychologist John F. Kihlstrom. Priming is a good starting point since it involves cognitive processes requiring recognition of words and other meaningful objects, as opposed to mere perception. Subjects are shown two presentations by means of a tachistoscope, an apparatus for briefly presenting visual stimuli, the first being presented so rapidly that the subject cannot consciously perceive it. The second stimulus is then presented, consisting of a word or an image that the subject has to consciously process by commenting on whether or not it is a real word or possible object. It was found that, when there was a link between the two stimuli, subjects were quicker and more successful in identifying what the second picture showed. In other words, 'one can learn something from a stimulus that is so brief that one does not perceive it'.[47]

Kihlstrom commented on the possible repercussions of such findings:

> Such information processing activity would be nonconscious in the double sense: neither the stimuli themselves, nor the cognitive processes that operate on them, are accessible to phenomenal awareness. Such doubly nonconscious processes nevertheless exert an important impact on social interaction. Through the operation of routinized procedures for social judgment, for example, we may form impressions of people without any cognitive awareness of the perceptual-cognitive basis for them.[48]

Our senses take in millions of bits of sensory data per second and yet only between sixteen and forty are processed by our conscious minds. The idea that nonconscious stimuli can influence our conscious thought is not particularly radical, more counterintuitive is evidence that suggests that our consciousness lags behind sensory input. Building on the ratio of sensory input to conscious awareness, Libet asserts that it takes half a second of sensory stimulation registering in the cortex before our conscious mind becomes aware of the stimulus.[49] This means that the world we are aware of is that of half a second ago.

Libet's experiments examined the relationship between the objective neurological signs of stimulation by an event and the subjective conscious experience of it, by comparing direct stimulation of the sensory cortex with stimulation of the skin. It was found, at the end of the nineteenth century, that stimulation of the areas of the cortex relating to the body's sense of touch leads to the feeling that the corresponding part of the body is being stimulated. Stimulate the part of the cortex relating to feet, for example, and one experiences the feeling of one's feet being tickled. The cortex is usually never exposed to direct stimulation, being protected in the ordinary course of events by the skull, and has no sense of touch relating to itself. When stimulated, therefore, it projects the feeling out into the area of the body relevant to that part of the brain stimulated. It was found that it took half a second of stimulation of the cortex for nineteenth-century subjects to become consciously aware of it, via the feeling that some other part of their body was being aroused.[50] In everyday life, however, we experience a sense of touch as if simultaneous with the stimulation. To sum up, if the area of one's cortex relating to feet is stimulated one feels a sensation in one's feet half a second later, whereas, if one has one's feet tickled it is experienced immediately.

Libet took this knowledge and tried to answer the question of how, given that it seems to take half a second of neural activity to become conscious of an action, we experience the world in 'real time'. The results of his experiment showed that it took half a second of activity in the sensory cortex before consciousness occurred but that the subjective experience was posited as simultaneous.

Libet set up an experiment in which the sensory cortex was stimulated to induce a tingling in one hand, whilst simultaneously the skin of the other hand was stimulated directly. The timing of stimulation of cortex and skin could be varied. The subject was then asked which they experienced first or if both were experienced at the same time. The results were as follows:

> Even when skin stimulation of the left hand did not start until 0.4 second after the sensory cortex was stimulated in a place corresponding to the right hand, the patient said 'Left first'. A peculiar result: it takes 0.5 second for us to become conscious of stimulation of the sensory cortex. Something similar would be expected of skin stimulation, because some neuronal activity is required before the stimulus can be felt. In just 0.1 second, a stimulation of the skin can sneak in front of a stimulation of the sensory cortex . . . Stimulating the skin leads to activity in the cortex, which, after half a second leads to consciousness. But consciousness is experienced as if it set in very shortly after the stimulus, because the subjective experience is referred back in time.[51]

In other words, the brain creates the illusion that consciousness is attained virtually simultaneously with the onset of a stimulus, whereas, in fact, Libet's research finds that a stimulus may be presented and nonconsciously acted upon before the conscious mind even knows of its onset. Conscious awareness of stimulation occurs after 500ms but the experience of awareness is referred backwards to the time of the primary evoked potentials, electrical changes in the cortex signalling nonconscious registering of stimulation, which appear 10–30ms after stimulation.[52] This antedating of conscious awareness is how we then believe we experience stimulation instantaneously.

Given that it is established in psychological research that subjects may view images in a considerably different manner to the way in which they are presented, what Freud would view as repression, this half-second delay gives a time-frame to allow other inputs to modulate the content and character of an experience before it reaches consciousness. Libet points out that this creates the possibility that what we experience as reality can be greatly influenced by individual character and past experience.[53] This preconscious modulation is characterised by Michael Gazzaniga as 'the interpreter', a left-brain device which ties together the various automatic processes of our mental lives and weaves them into a sense of self by reference to memory of past experience. As would be expected, this conscious interpreter is prone to make errors of perception, memory and judgment given the limited information fed to it from the nonconscious.[54]

Based on research conducted into the readiness potential, the electrical activity across the surface of the brain that precedes a physical action, Libet also asserts that there is a gap of half a second between our initiation of an action and our becoming conscious of it. In fact, he claims that we are conscious of acting only after having done so.[55]

The reason for this mental illusion is purely practical: we need to know when we are affected by a stimulus, not when we have become aware of it, but there are implications of the half-second delay and the small bandwidth of conscious processing for our sense of self and free will. There have been few replications of Libet's experiments, due in no small part to the difficulty of finding suitable subjects during open-head surgery. There are supporting studies cited throughout the literature, however.[56]

Wegner points out that we are unsure as to what nonconscious mental processes the readiness potential actually represents. He does claim that these processes, by their regular occurrence before movement, obviously have some relevance to ensuing events. Since the readiness potential could signal nonconscious processes leading to both the will to action and the action itself, the suggestion is that 'conscious wanting, like voluntary action, is a mental event that is caused by proper events'. Again, he highlights the idea that the experience of will is not the first stage in the processes but an event further down the mental chain. In fact, it might not even be a link in the 'causal chain leading to action' rather 'it might just be a loose end – one of those things, like the action, that is caused by prior brain and mental events'.[57]

Empirical findings such as those into the bandwidth of consciousness (the ratio of what our senses take in to what reaches consciousness), subliminal perception and Libet's experiments would seem to suggest that our conscious mind does not preside over our lives as much as we would like to believe. 'People are not conscious of very much of what they sense; people are not conscious of very much of what they think; people are not conscious of very much of what they do.'[58]

Gazzaniga and LeDoux: Why did you do that?

Not only do we act outside of conscious control but it would seem that consciousness is so unhappy about this state of affairs that it actively creates a series of complex fictions in order to account for the substantial gaps in its knowledge. This is illustrated by a study that was carried out by Gazzaniga and LeDoux with a young boy, referred to as P. S., who had undergone an operation to surgically split the two sides of his brain as a treatment for severe epilepsy.[59]

The right-hand field of vision in both eyes is processed by the left-hand side of the brain whereas the left field is processed by the right half. The left and right hemispheres of the brain have different abilities, with the left-hand side housing the verbal aspects of the linguistic faculties. P. S. was shown two pictures, one visible via his left-hand field of vision (a snow-covered scene) and the other visible via his right-hand field (a chicken's claw). He was then asked to choose which from a range of picture cards corresponded to what he saw. P. S.'s right hand pointed to a chicken while his left pointed to a shovel. In other words each side of his brain moved the corresponding hand to an object related to what it saw, independent of the other side. When asked why he had pointed to what he did P. S., without any hesitation, answered '"I saw a claw and I picked the chicken, and you have to clean out the chicken shed with a shovel." '[60] The left hemisphere, not having a ready explanation for what the left hand had pointed at, as it had not seen the picture of snow, fabricated its own explanation for what had happened. The conscious mind is that which weaves together the millions of bits of sensory data available to us and combines them with lifelong memory and current motivation in order to give us a gestalt picture of the world, which helps us make sense of it at any particular point in time:

> We all feel that the conscious verbal self is not always privy to the origin of our actions, and when it observes the person behaving for unknown reasons, it attributes cause to the action as if it knows but in fact it does not. It is as if the verbal self looks out and sees what the person is doing, and from that knowledge interprets a reality.[61]

The self is, therefore, robbed of its essential core as a means by which the human agent primarily engages the world on a reasoned basis amenable to explanation. It is, rather, presented as a collection of distorted images thrown together to obscure the fact that we have no intrinsic selfhood and is brought into reality only through encountering the social rules which we must adhere to in order to express this incoherent bundle to others. Indeed, from their observations of split-brain patients, Gazzaniga and LeDoux suggest that the mind is not a psychological entity but a sociological one, a collection of mental subsystems (emotional, perceptual, motivational, etc.) whose various behaviours come to be either interpreted or controlled by the verbal self. 'The uniqueness of man [sic], in this regard, is his ability to verbalize and, in so doing, create a personal sense of conscious reality out of the multiple mental systems present.'[62]

Following directly on from the P. S. study, we can see the primary role of narrative in self-construction. When presented with a situation requiring an explanation that his conscious mind did not understand, P. S.'s mind wove a coherent narrative based on what it had observed. At a deeper level, when confronted with nonconscious initiation of action as described in Libet's research, the subject will seek to interpret the situation in such a way as to render it explicable in both personal and social terms. It is this mental function of narrative interpretation that Gazzaniga attributes to the left-brain 'interpreter', the device that creates the conscious illusion of being in charge of actions by interpreting present actions in light of past events.[63] The location of the device in the left brain illustrates its necessary connection to linguistic faculties, as illustrated in the P. S. study wherein it was the left brain which supplied the rationalisation of action. Indeed Gazzaniga attributes the theory to this study.[64]

An interesting question is whether we would develop a sense of narrative self if isolated from society. It would seem that our conscious self is inherently tied in with our ability to communicate with others. This is illustrated in both the P. S. study, in terms of linguistic ability, and in the work of Daniel Dennett, who sees the conscious self as a centre of narrative gravity, the product, not the source, of spinning self-narratives.[65] It is difficult to imagine a narrative that does not articulate itself through language or some similar system of representation. Given that it would be impossible to argue that people without linguistic abilities are devoid of a sense of self, it is better to think of narrative in terms of representation rather than language.[66] What is important is that the system of representation is a *social* construct, a means of explaining and justifying our actions to others.

Like Nietzsche, Norretranders assigns the conscious 'I' the function of facilitating social interaction.[67] This idea is characterised by both Norretranders and Dennett as a 'user illusion'.[68] The user illusion is a term taken from computer science that refers to the user interface displayed on the monitor of a terminal and with which the operator interacts without any required knowledge of the mechanics of the hard- and software which underlie the computer's operations. The term seems to have gained hold in the wake of functionalism's turn to computer science and artificial intelligence research as a way of probing the basics of conscious operation.

We begin to see how the vision of nonconscious functioning presented by such research can be tied into political theorising. We have to grapple with the idea that consciousness may not be the prime originator of much of our action or even the largest part of our mental functioning. That the conscious part of our mental life is largely socially constructed is also highly relevant, though it is a current that has been present in political thought for some time. It can now take a different direction, however, in working out its interaction with the nonconscious. It is on these two levels that we shall proceed with the next chapter investigating the philosophical mechanics of importing such neuropsychological material.

Notes

1. These headings are loosely based on those used in Reed, 'The separation of psychology from philosophy', pp. 329–35.
2. For a fascinating extension of this argument, see Jaynes, *The Origin of Consciousness*.
3. For an excellent text on Augustine in this regard, see Hölscher, *The Reality of the Mind*.
4. Aquinas in Sahakian, *History of Psychology*, p. 23. See also Kenny, *Aquinas on Mind*.

5. Augustine, *Confessions*.
6. Plato, *The Republic*, Bk 4 §2 and translator's note pp. 207–8.
7. Ibid. Bk 4 431–2b.
8. Ibid. Bk 4 441d–e.
9. Ibid. Bk 4 444d–e.
10. Schopenhauer, *The World as Will and Idea*, Bk 4 §54, Bk 2 §29.
11. Schopenhauer, *The World as Will and Idea*, Supplement to Bk 2, p. 87.
12. Ibid. p. 94.
13. Ibid. p. 92.
14. Ibid. p. 91.
15. Ibid. p. 92.
16. Schopenhauer, *The World as Will and Idea*, Bk 4 §54.
17. Ibid. §55.
18. Ibid. §68.
19. Ibid. §70.
20. Von Hartmann, *The Philosophy of the Unconscious*. Schopenhauer had himself dismissed suicide as a resignation of defeat to the Will.
21. Nietzsche, 'Ecce Homo', p. 710.
22. Nietzsche in Kaufmann, *Nietzsche, Heidegger and Buber*, p. 55.
23. Nietzsche, 'Thus spoke Zarathustra', Bk V §354.
24. Nietzsche, *The Gay Science*, p. 111.
25. Nietzsche, 'Ecce Homo', p. 714
26. Nietzsche in Assoun, *Freud and Nietzsche*, p. 110.
27. Freud and Breuer, *Studies on Hysteria*.
28. Freud, *The Interpretation of Dreams*.
29. For the pleasure and reality principles see Freud, 'Formulations on th two principles of mental functioning', in *On Metapsychology*, and fo the Unconscious in general see 'A note on the Unconscious in psycho analysis' and 'The Unconscious', in the same volume.
30. Freud, 'A note upon the mystic writing pad', in *On Metapsychology*.
31. Freud, 'Beyond the Pleasure Principle', in *On Metapsychology*.
32. Freud, 'On narcissism: An introduction', in *On Metapsychology*.
33. Freud, *New Introductory Lectures*, p. 110.
34. Freud, 'An outline of psychoanalysis', in *Psychoanalysis: Its History an Development*.
35. Freud, *New Introductory Lectures*, pp. 109–10.
36. Ibid. p. 112.
37. Ibid. p. 140.
38. A detailed comparative exposition of Freud and Nietzsche is impossib here. For an excellent study see Assoun's, *Freud and Nietzsche*.
39. Leibniz, *Monadology*.
40. Huxley, 'On the hypothesis that animals are automatia', in Talli *Hidden Minds*, p. 32.

41. Hermann von Helmholtz, 'Empirical theory of perception and the theory of unconscious inference' [1860], in Sahakian, *History of Psychology*.
42. Libet, *Mind Time*, p. 13.
43. Gazzaniga, *The Mind's Past*, p. 21.
44. Norretranders, *The User Illusion*, p. 128; Libet, *Mind Time*, p. 70.
45. Norretranders, *The User Illusion*, pp. 159–61.
46. Ibid. p. 161; Wilson, *Strangers to Ourselves*, p. 24.
47. Norretranders, *The User Illusion*, p. 170.
48. Ibid. p. 171.
49. Libet, *Mind Time*, pp. 34–46.
50. Norretranders, *The User Illusion*, pp. 230–1.
51. Ibid. pp. 234–5.
52. Libet, *Mind Time*, p. 75. He goes on to describe how he experimentally tested this hypothesis but the technical details are unnecessary here.
53. Ibid. pp. 71–2.
54. Gazzaniga, *The Mind's Past*, pp. 1–2.
55. Libet, *Mind Time*, pp. 126–34.
56. E.g. Libet, *Mind Time*, p. 135; Norretranders, *The User Illusion*, pp. 226–8; Wegner, *The Illusion of Conscious Will*, pp. 54–5; Gazzaniga, *The Mind's Past*, pp. 74–6.
57. Wegner, *The Illusion of Conscious Will*, p. 55. For an interesting discussion of the criticisms of Libet see Dennett, *Consciousness Explained*, pp. 156–66.
58. Norretranders, *The User Illusion*, p. 259.
59. Gazzaniga and LeDoux, *The Integrated Mind*, pp. 148–51.
60. Ibid. p. 148.
61. Ibid. pp. 149–50.
62. Ibid. p. 51.
63. Ibid. p. XIII.
64. Ibid. pp. 24–5.
65. Dennett, *Consciousness Explained*, pp. 429–30.
66. Helen Keller is a good example of a self exposited in non-linguistic terms.
67. Norretranders, *The User Illusion*, pp. 269–71.
68. Ibid. pp. 289–93; Dennett, *Consciousness Explained*, pp. 216, 219–20.

2

The Politics of Neuroscience

The neurological material in the foregoing chapter operates within an ontology and epistemology that many in the social sciences have long fought against. At its hard scientific edge, this belief holds that human behaviour is fully explicable through close study of the operations of the brain. All social science and theory would therefore, in time, be superseded by an all-embracing explanatory vocabulary of neuro-physiological brainstates. Before we can proceed to unpack such material for use in a political context, this fundamental concern must first be addressed.

It is argued that the best way to engage with this debate is to move a step up (or down) from neuropsychology, to the philosophies of the mind that are built on it. This chapter will begin with a short exposition of the materialist philosophy of mind and objections to it from social theorists. It will then go on to discuss the most recent and fullest attempt to connect political theory to neuroscience, working from a dualist perspective, William Connolly's *Neuropolitics*. Finally, it will be suggested that a fruitful engagement between the two spheres can be centred around two connected planes: the mind (through the functionalist philosophy of mind) and the role of the body in cognition. This approach avoids objections to strict reductive materialism, allowing neuropsychological material to be used in a thoroughly political manner.

The materialist problem

Materialist philosophy of mind generally resolves itself into two streams: reductive and eliminative. Both begin from the presupposition that the 'common sense' psychological ideas we deploy in everyday life are, in some way, wrongheaded. These common-sense ideas (generally, and somewhat disparagingly, termed 'folk psychology') include such propositions as a person who goes without liquid will tend to feel thirst; or, at a higher level, a person who has a lot to do before an important deadline will tend to feel stressed, and a person who ends a long term relationship with a partner will tend to feel some degree of loss. Materialism holds that folk psychology is radically incomplete in its explanations; it cannot, for example, explain sleep or intelligence. Materialists claim it has not advanced in centuries, surviving only through a lack of alternatives. Where reductive and eliminative materialism differ is over the role neuropsychology has to play in regard to such folk psychology.

Reductive materialism, sometimes called identity theory, believes that folk psychological propositions are reducible to propositions about brainstates. When a person feels thirst, that feeling is identical with, and hence reducible to, a certain neurophysiological state in the brain. A common analogy is drawn with the way in which heat in liquids and molecular motion are both reducible to thermodynamic theory. The familiar categories of folk psychology (thoughts, desires, pains) will survive by being reduced to statements about the central nervous system.

Eliminative materialism is more sceptical about the survival of folk psychology in any form. Theorists such as Patricia and Paul Churchland hold that the common-sense understandings of our own and others' mental lives are patently false and will simply be disproved and replaced by, not reduced to, an adequate neuropsychological theory. Based on this theory, the analogy is with the way 'that oxidation theory (and modern chemistry generally) simply displaced the older phlogiston theory of matter transformation'.[1]

Bennett and Hacker, in their book critiquing many of the conceptual problems with the methodology and claims of contemporary neuroscience, rigorously deny the criticisms aimed at folk psychology by materialism. Firstly, they argue that the former is neither a theory in any rigorous, technical sense, nor a set of law-like causal statements. It is rather a set of characterisations based upon practical reasoning. It is unreasonable, therefore, to take it to task for not explaining sleep or IQ in the same way 'it would be to blame our common or garden vocabulary of sticks and stones, chairs and tables (and attendant humdrum generalizations), for failing to come up with theories of matter and laws of mechanics'.[2]

They go on to argue against the ontology of the reductionist project. On a global level, it is patently untrue to claim that everything in the world of human affairs is composed of matter. Political parties, economic development, society and culture are examples given. Whilst it is tautologically true to say that we are physically composed of no more than our nervous systems, it is false to claim that our behaviour can be seen as no more than the behaviour of cells – in the same way that a painting is more than just brush strokes or a novel is more than an assemblage of words:

> The behaviour of sentient creatures in general is explained partly in terms of their goals, and of human beings in particular also in terms of reasons and motives, not in terms of the material of which they consist. Even more obviously, the explanation of events and processes such as Hannibal's victory at Cannae, or the decline of the Roman Empire, the Industrial Revolution, or the rise of Romanticism has nothing to do with the matter of which the explananda are made since they are not made of anything.[3]

This criticism ties into those made by political theorists worried about the implications of the reductionist stance stemming from neurological material. One prime example is the work of Charles Taylor. Taylor's starting point is that humans are self-interpreting animals:

> This means among other things that there is no adequate description of how it is with a human being in respect of his existence as a person which does not incorporate his self-understanding, that is, the descriptions which he or she is inclined to give of his emotions, aspirations, desires, aversions, admiration, etc.[4]

Our actions are, at least partly, constituted by our own understandings of them. Our everyday language describes actions in just such a way, as being relative to a purpose that has some meaning for us.[5] Since the language that we use to describe our actions is the only means we have to understand them, especially in a social context when we are trying to understand the actions of another or make someone else understand ours, it seems that any psychological explanation must take account of these understandings and their vocabulary. We are intentional and motive-driven beings and when we must give an account of ourselves and our behaviour, as we must inevitably do in society, this must be expressed in terms of a vocabulary that has a shared meaning in our society. We cannot speak our own private language of volition. Concepts such as 'shame' both move us to act and then help us explain our actions, both to ourselves and others, *post facto*, and they are irreducible and untranslatable concepts; they cannot be explained except in self-referential terms.

A concept such as shame would seem to be impossible to isolate in terms of a neurological brain state. It would be possible, for example, for the same identifiable feeling to be experienced by various neurophysical instances. This is a point we will come on to discuss in more detail in the last section of this chapter. It is hard to conceive of a situation, such as reductionism envisages, in which we cease using a word like shame and talk rather of a certain brain state. The latter, though it may adequately express the neurophysical event, in no way conveys the conscious experience of what it is like to feel shame. To appreciate the notion, and what it *means* to the subject and what effect it will have in him or her, it has to be tied into an understanding of social context.

Given the problems presented by a purely reductionist approach to neuropsychology we must countenance other interpretations of such research. One example of a different engagement from a political perspective is the dualism adopted by William Connolly.

William Connolly and neuropolitical dualism

In the preface to his book *Neuropolitics: Thinking, Culture, Speed*, Connolly explains that his aim is to explore the intersections between thinking, technique, ethical judgement, cultural pluralism, speed and cosmopolitanism. This collection of themes is honed at the beginning of the first chapter to an exploration of the role of technique in thinking, ethics and politics, through an accentuation on compositional and creative thinking and the relationship between thinking and culture. The argument proceeds through chapters exploring the complex and layered nature of thinking, perception, conceptions of science, language and affect, time, religious experience and pluralism.

Connolly uses neuroscientific work from thinkers such as Damasio, Ramachandran and Varela, and seeks to establish a link to conceptions of thought in the work of philosophers such as Spinoza, Bergson, Nietzsche and Deleuze to build up a picture of the multi-layered nature of thought. This picture is then connected to a conception of culture, which calls for a recognition of complexity to study it and an attitude of deep pluralism to regulate it.

Whereas one may be sympathetic to Connolly's aims, issue may be taken with the moves that he makes with his material. In order to establish the foundational notion of technique in thought, an examination of the psychological ontology of perspectival parallelism underlying it is needed. Though Connolly does little work himself in bolstering this position, one may draw a comparison between his stance and that of the property dualism of David Chalmers, whose arguments can be mobilised to support him. Materialism is never far away from Connolly's perspective, however, and his aims might better be accomplished with recognition of this. Although perspectival parallelism may initially allow Connolly to sidestep debates on consciousness and nonconsciousness in his work, an examination of technique in thought necessitates an engagement with these themes to determine its possibility.

In the first move to outline his position, establishing the complexity of thought, Connolly gives us a rich and diverse range of sources and engagements. He anticipates and dismisses some of the criticisms that might be posed to the use of neuroscience to inform cultural theory claiming that, through resisting the reduction of cultural phenomena to neurological processes, cultural theory ignores the possibilities of such cross-fertilisation. In what can be seen as one of the most controversial moves in the book, Connolly answers the objection that neurochemical explanations cannot account for phenomenological experience by adopting a modified version of Spinoza's parallelism, referred to later as 'perspectival parallelism'.

In *The Ethics*, Spinoza establishes what is sometimes referred to as a double-aspect position in which mind and body, though of one substance, are separate in terms of attributes and coordinated, with each mirroring, but not causing, changes in the other.[6] Connolly follows Stuart Hampshire's rendering of this position as two separate human perspectives which one can switch between: phenomenological/internal experience and external observation of the body and brain during experience. Hampshire claims that humans can view the behaviour of individuals teleologically, in terms of desires, aims and appetites, or mechanically as the effect of external causes. On this account, neurological changes can affect thought but thought cannot be wholly explained neurologically.[7] Perspectival parallelism is linked to what Connolly describes as 'immanent naturalism'. In opposition to eliminative naturalism, which collapses experience of consciousness into mechanical nonconscious processes, and mechanical naturalism, which denies anything outside perception claiming that the human brain can be completely represented and explained, immanent naturalism posits a role for external influences on thought, such as culture, which are not amenable to full explanation.

The interesting question here in terms of politics is that of mental causality, how our thought patterns are influenced and changed by either internal or external sources. Spinoza is more complex regarding this question than he may first appear. On the one hand, mind and body are separate and distinct and there can be no question of either influencing the other. 'The body cannot determine the mind to think, nor the mind the body to motion . . .',[8] though for each bodily state there is a corresponding mental state and this is how the two spheres appear to match up in experience. Each can, however, only operate causally within its own sphere of influence and it is only thought, therefore, which can affect thought. *The Ethics* is, in a large part, concerned with psychological improvement and Spinoza is therefore anxious to show how the mind can be used as a tool for ethical advancement by acting on itself. The basis for this possibility lies in his axiom that whatever exists there always exists something else stronger that can destroy it.[9] A negative emotion can therefore be overcome by a stronger positive emotion.

We can fill out Spinoza's parallelism in terms of the perceived correspondence between body and mind with some of Leibniz's later insights. Whereas Spinoza is a substance monist, in terms of conceiving all reality as one substance perceived as either thought or extension (mind or body in our case), Leibnizian reality is made up of an infinity of monads all of which are the same *kind* of substance. Spinoza can be seen to have left open the possibility of indirect interaction between mind and body by asserting that for each bodily action there is a corresponding mental state; the mind can perceive the body drinking and hence feel thirst, for example. This is an interesting way of interpreting the P. S. experiment, although only in relation to the actions of the left brain. Leibniz takes this further with his theory of expressionism in relation to the two spheres – a particular mind so 'expresses' its own body that if one could somehow read that mind, he/she would have a perfectly clear idea of the body. Even though the two do not causally interact, they run parallel due to a divinely attuned, pre-established harmony. This principle does not work the other way around, however, in that examining the mechanical hardware of the body cannot give us an idea of the mind.[10]

As was mentioned in the last chapter, Leibniz, in *The Monadology*, introduces the ideas of apperception (self-conscious awareness) and unconscious perceptions and habit, of which he claims three quarters of our mental life is composed.[11] He is thus able to advance Spinoza's conception through filling out the mind's idea of the body with perceptions which can lie outside of conscious awareness.

If we tie this back into the possibility that the body can indirectly influence the mind through the latter's perception of the former, we may have a basis for asserting from this perspective that there can be nonconscious influences on our thoughts. Although this is an idea that will become important in the following sections, it is not a route that Connolly takes. In following Hampshire's rendering of Spinoza in terms of *perspectival* parallelism and combining it with affect, Connolly sidesteps the conscious/nonconscious split when he begins to analyse the role of technique in thought.

As stated above, Connolly draws the distinction between eliminative naturalism, the reduction of conscious experience to nonconscious processes; mechanical naturalism, which denies the 'supersensible field' and holds that non-human nature as well as human brain structure is amenable to full and complete explanation; and his own position of immanent naturalism. This latter posits a transcendental field that 'mixes nature and culture':

> To immanent naturalism, consciousness emerges as a layer of thinking, feeling, and judgement bound to complex crunching operations that enable and exceed it. The immanent field is efficacious and inscrutable (to an uncertain degree), but not immaterial . . . Moreover, the immanent field, while currently unsusceptible to full explanation and unsusceptible in principle to precise representation, may retain some amenability to both cultural inscription and experimental tactics of intervention.[12]

So, whilst maintaining that 'all human activities function without the aid of divine or supernatural force',[13] Connolly seeks to retain an ineffable element in human cognition through the link between culture and thought.

When it comes to thought, he follows the *Oxford English Dictionary* definition of 'to cause (something) to appear to oneself', 'to form connected ideas of any kind' and 'to form a definite conception by a conscious mental act, to picture in one's mind'.[14] This definition has the advantage, he claims, of embracing both conscious and nonconscious processes within the realm of thought. A technique in relation to thought is anything that intervenes to change 'the direction of thinking or the mood in which it is set'.[15] In the multilayered picture of thought which begins to emerge, Connolly quotes Hampshire's claim that an observer must shift attention back and forth between humans as perceivers of their world and as perceived objects within it, emphasising that the observed individual does not have the ability to shift between these first- and third-person perspectives in personal experience. Like Taylor, therefore, perspectival parallelism asserts the impossibility of fully translating subjective conscious experience into psychochemical processes, because the former draws on a larger cultural context of reference than the latter. As with Spinoza's parallelism, changes in the psychochemical process are mirrored by changes at the level of thought, and vice versa.[16]

This standpoint is echoed, to a certain extent, by that of property dualism. As opposed to Cartesian substance dualism, property dualism asserts that body and mind are not separate substances but rather that the properties associated with each are not conflatable. There is a difference, for example, between the neurobiological property of pain and the conscious property of feeling it. This idea is clearly expressed by David Chalmers: 'conscious experience involves properties of an individual that are not entailed by the physical properties of that individual, although they may depend lawfully on those properties.'[17]

It can be seen that there are prima facie similarities between property dualism and perspectival parallelism. There may be room to argue, for example, that the latter is a type of the weaker form of property dualism to which Chalmers refers. This means a position compatible with some form of materialism, since it states that the term dualism applies to any element that is not directly reducible to the physical level. Chalmers gives the example of physical fitness as a property that still has a direct causal link with microphysical properties. Property dualism for him, however, entails a regard for 'fundamentally ontologically new' properties which do not have such a link. Given that Connolly states above that the immanent field that gives rise to thought is not immaterial, there is room for arguing that his position is akin to the weaker form of property dualism as defined by Chalmers. The door is left open by Chalmers, however, who states that 'it remains plausible . . . that consciousness arises from a physical basis even though it is not entailed by that basis'.[18] If we connect such a statement back to the more Spinozian base of perspectival parallelism that has thought and psychochemical processes mirroring and causing changes in each other, then we may for the purposes of the present investigation conclude that Chalmers' property dualism and Connolly's perspectival parallelism have enough in common to merit arguments in one being used to bolster the other.[19]

This is an important consideration, since Connolly devotes little time to arguing for his ontology aside from presenting it as a means to placate cultural theorists, who reject using neuropsychology for fear of its reductive character. Chalmers' rejection of materialism may therefore be deployed in Connolly's support. Chalmers employs an impressive battery of arguments against reductive materialism on the basis that, for the latter to work, it must prove that consciousness is logically supervenient on the physical plane. In other words, certain physical properties of a system must conceptually or logically entail certain phenomenal properties. But, according to Chalmers, one can conceivably envisage a world in which the physical facts are the same as ours but in which consciousness does not arise. Secondly, we have no link between the facts of consciousness and the physical facts and, lastly, there is no present analysis of consciousness that can 'ground an entailment from the physical to the phenomenal':[20]

> The failure of consciousness to logically supervene on the physical tells us that no reductive explanation of consciousness can succeed. Given any account of the physical processes purported to underlie consciousness, there will always be a further question: Why are these processes accompanied by conscious experience?[21]

Two examples of arguments in the first two categories are Kripke's zombie argument and Jackson's knowledge argument.

Kripke attacks the identity thesis in materialism which holds that mental states and physical states are identical: for example, that pain is identical with c-fibres firing. This must be a necessary identity, Kripke argues, and not just a contingent one: when we designate pain in the identity thesis we must *necessarily* be talking about c-fibres firing. But the identity does not seem to be necessary, he claims, and it is possible to imagine a zombie world in which c-fibres may fire without any pain (psychological 'zombies' are exact physical copies of humans without any accompanying consciousness). For Kripke, it is impossible to describe the firing of the zombies' c-fibres as 'pain' since an integral element in pain is the *feeling* of what it is like, which the zombies lack. The purely physical description of pain as being exclusively identical with the brain state of c-fibres firing is therefore false.[22] This argument echoes that of Charles Taylor above. One can also think of hospital patients receiving morphine; their c-fibres are firing because their biological state is one inducing the nervous system to respond with pain but they do not feel pain because of the neurochemical blocking action of the drug. Hence, the physical, but not the conscious, component is missing and one would not say such a patient was 'in pain'.

In Jackson's argument, Mary is a neuroscientist who specialises in the study of the way in which the brain processes colour. She knows all the neurophysiological facts on the subject. She has, however, been born and lived all her life in a black and white room. When she sees a red object for the first time she will, it is argued, learn new facts, specifically what it is *like* to see the colour red. Jackson therefore argues that the physical facts are not an exhaustive account of reality and dismisses materialism on this basis.[23]

Hampshire's rendering of perspectival parallelism does not seem to rule out the materialist stance, however. He does say that 'it will be useless . . . to consider . . . a thoughtful person as if he or she were a piece of machinery', although this is primarily 'in our present state of knowledge', thereby leaving open the possibility of a materialist explanation in the future.[24] In terms of what Connolly wants to achieve with perspectival parallelism, a materialist approach may be viable however.

The main illustration of this is Daniel Dennett's heterophenomenology. Like Connolly, Dennett claims that we can never have a pure Cartesian phenomenology, in terms of accurately analysing our own thoughts and then using the first person plural to generalise those analyses to everyone else. Neither can we fully understand people, as the behaviourists sought to do, from a purely third person perspective by observing their actions. The method he extols is to transcribe the verbal interactions, reports and results of psychological experiments into a text and then to treat this text as a record of intentional speech acts. Other physical acts, such as button pushing, are also transcribed into the text and treated as intentional acts representing a conscious assertion on the part of the subject.[25]

In interpretation, the text produced constitutes the subject's heterophenomenological world, which for the purposes of investigating consciousness may or may not tally with the 'real' world. 'The . . . method neither challenges nor accepts as entirely true the assertions of subjects, but rather maintains a constructive and sympathetic neutrality, in the hopes of compiling a definitive account of the world according to the subjects.'[26] Heterophenomenology can be seen as taking two of Hampshire's perspectives, the first and third, and commingling them. The theorist can then turn to trying to explain why the subject experiences the inner world in a particular way. 'Then the question of whether items . . . portrayed [in the subject's heterophenomenological world] exist as real objects, events and states in the brain . . . is an empirical matter to investigate.'[27] Some of the ways in which materialists such as Dennett and others do this are explored below. For the moment, the important point is that the concerns for which Connolly mobilises perspectival parallelism and denigrates materialism may be overcome easily, and in a remarkably similar fashion, within materialism itself.

One of the points which recommends the use of Spinoza to Connolly is that the former allows reference to techniques of modifying thought patterns 'without adopting a reductionist image of thought in doing so'.[28] As an example of how this can be carried out, Connolly refers first to neuropsychological evidence provided by V. S. Ramachandran, who used a device called a mirror box as a technique of reducing pain in phantom-limb patients. Whereas, before, these patients felt pain in the area where the lost arm, for example, used to be, Ramachandran found that sessions using a device, which allowed patients to see a limb where theirs would be if it remained, reduced such pain. Connolly quotes Ramachandran as claiming that the plasticity of the brain allows such visual input to 'eliminate the spasm of a non-existent arm and then erase the associated memory of pain.'[29]

Connolly later links this idea to that of self-artistry in Nietzsche, tactics of self in Foucault, technique in Hampshire and micropolitics in Deleuze[30] and claims that:

> the thoughtful application by oneself of techniques to one's entrenched patterns of affective thought can both track the institutional technologies through which the visceral register has been organised and activate presumptive responsiveness to new social movements of pluralisation. You allow effects promoted at one level to filter into others, doing so to enable new thoughts to come into being or to refine the sensibility in which your judgements have heretofore been set. For thinking, memory, sensibility, and judgement are interwoven.[31]

It is not the intention here to directly engage with the political element of Connolly's argument;[32] he does, however, give some everyday examples of techniques which can be used to alter thought. These include listening to music whilst reading to relax the mind and make it more receptive, going for a run after trying to address a particular problem, giving in to previously ignored feelings of regret and misrepresenting a troubling perspective to minimise its disturbing effect.[33]

Much like Spinoza, there are two parallel but connected elements to this use of technique to influence thought. One may unpack the idea as either the conscious mind seeking to influence the physicality of the body through laying down new neural networks, or it may be conceived as the conscious mind seeking to influence the nonconscious mind. It will be remembered that Connolly refers to an immanent naturalist position conceiving consciousness 'as a layer of thinking, feeling, and judgement bound to complex crunching operations that enable and exceed it.'[34] It would seem, therefore, that he views technique as operating in the first manner as a mental process resulting in neurophysiological change.

Connolly does not talk of the Freudian unconscious or of a more neuropsychological nonconscious. In *Neuropolitics* the role of this level of our mental life is discussed in terms of affect. Connolly takes his departure from Nietzsche's discussions of affect, one example being the process by which the bulk of sensory material is filtered out leaving only a tiny proportion to reach the level of consciousness. This is in turn marked by what has taken place before it. Affect is also the means by which emotion plays a role in sorting through preconscious perception, bringing old memories to the surface to connect with new stimuli and thus emotionally charging and recharging each. Connolly finds in Nietzsche the way in which the nonconscious, imbued with affect, can be disciplined by the conscious mind. Nietzsche claims that the conscious mind has a defining, ordering and structuring role through logic and language. It enables us to devise techniques with which to work on nonconscious levels of thought and assess the impact these techniques have. He also folds the mental and physical aspects together:

> [A] mere disciplining of [conscious] thoughts and feelings is virtually nothing . . .; one first has to convince the body. It is decisive . . . that one should inaugurate culture in the right place – not in the 'soul' . . .; the right place is the body, demeanour, diet, physiology, the rest follows.[35]

Given that these are the kinds of changes that Connolly is trying to provoke, how does this sit with his underlying ontology of perspectival parallelism? Being a variety of monism it does not fall prey to the usual pitfalls of substance dualism, prime among them the question of how body and mind interact causally. If Connolly were a substance dualist then his use of the mind to reconfigure the brain would be severely problematised. Given that the parallelism is *perspectival* and not in terms of parallel substances the question is again begged of whether Connolly's position is not simply a materialist one, or, if it is not, then if it could be better rendered as such. If the mind is simply conceived as being a function of neurological processes then the question of causality would be a lot easier (although, as we shall see in the next section, the principle direction of causality would be problematised). If we search in Connolly for a robust dismissal of materialism in favour of perspectival parallelism as a basis for his philosophy, we find little beyond the separation of immanent naturalism from eliminative or reductive naturalism.

We can again turn to Chalmers in this regard and his attack on materialism cited above. It will be remembered that Chalmers claims that it is possible to imagine a world in which the same physical facts do not entail the phenomenological facts of our world. He claims that we do not have the right sort of link between neurophysiology and consciousness, and that the concept of consciousness itself cannot be analysed in such a way as to provide one. He is, however, a property and not a substance dualist and he does try to establish what a connection between the physicality and the mentality of thought might be. This is done through an exposition of certain principles as a foundation for working towards a fundamental theory of consciousness.

The principle of structural coherence links awareness and consciousness by asserting that the structure of awareness mirrors the structure of consciousness, and vice versa. For Chalmers, awareness is the psychological correlate to consciousness – where there is one there is the other – and thus this principle can provide a link between the phenomenal and the psychological.[36] The principle of organisational invariance states that consciousness arises from the functional organisation of the brain; any given system with the same fine-grained neurophysiological organisation will have qualitatively identical experiences.[37]

Chalmers characterises this as a non-reductive functionalism as opposed to harder-edged reductivist functionalism; he does however concede that both accounts are 'playing in the same ballpark'. He likens his approach to Dennett's definition of cerebral celebrity, for example. Dennett argues that consciousness is composed of those mental contents that can monopolise mental resources in such a way as to have an effect on memory, behaviour and so on. Whereas Dennett elevates this principle to a 'conceptual truth', Chalmers argues that his perspective requires merely the potential for global control, not its exercise in all cases, as the basis for consciousness. This would allow experience on the fringes of the visual field to be conscious, whereas for Dennett they would not.[38] The main point for Chalmers is that consciousness is 'determined by functional organisation, but need not be reducible' to it.[39]

Even if we bolster Connolly's psychological ontology of perspectival parallelism with dismissals of materialism drawn from Chalmers we are still left with the question of how techniques operate on thought. Even with a monist position, how does the nonmaterial influence the material? This is not a question that a position such as Connolly's can adequately answer. We are still waiting on the fundamental laws of interaction that Chalmers anticipates. If we leave this aside for the minute and accept the argument that the mind i something above the neurophysiology of the brain, and not reducible to it, the need remains to dissect the components of the mind itself. An analysis of technique can be seen to turn on two fulcrums: the mind-body interaction question and the conscious-nonconscious interaction question.

As stated above, Connolly does not engage directly with debates over consciousness and nonconsciousness. These are, however, unavoidable if we want to understand how the application of technique can operate, since in parallelist or property-dualist positions the emphasis is usually on consciousness. Certainly, with Connolly, techniques must be consciously applied to affect change on the nonconscious register, which in turn gives rise to change in conscious thought. Although there is an appreciation of the connectedness of the two levels, with conscious thought arising from the nonconscious, there may be a danger of privileging the causal role of consciousness over nonconsciousness. It is to this danger that the next section turns.

Connolly refers to the half-second delay suggesting, like Libet, that it gives time for the cultural inscription of thought. He sums up by saying that the:

> unconscious dimension of thought is at once *immanent* in subsisting below the direct reach of consciousness, *effective* in influencing conduct on its own and also effecting conscious judgment, *material* in being embodied in neurological processes, and *cultural* in being given part of its shape by previous inscriptions of experience and new experimental interventions.[40]

He does not, however, draw the strong conclusions of this research regarding conscious potential to affect thought when discussing technique, nor does he accept the materialist position from which such research operates.

If the conscious mind has a limited causal role in mental life and certain physical actions, then Connolly's use of technique in thought would be likewise limited. The applications of such techniques would be one part of the mind seeking to make sense of itself.

The idea becomes even more interesting in relation to Connolly with Dennett's assertion that the nature of our user illusion can in turn affect the hardware (or 'wetware' as the literature likes to refer to it) of our brains.[41] Unlike computers, the use, or disuse, of certain patterns of thought leads to changes in the actual physiology of the brain, as the neural networks supporting those patterns fall into abeyance and have their resources reallocated elsewhere. This is the argument

Ramachandran makes and it is also that of cognitive behaviour therapy. These are both inherently materialist perspectives, however, and again pose the question of whether what Connolly seeks to achieve could not be better done through materialism rather than perspectival parallelism.

Cognitive behaviour therapy works on the basis that many people experience problems due to a discrepancy between their internal and external lives, with their external environment creating needs that they are not mentally able to fulfil. Therapy then seeks to help clients adjust their internal world to fit their current external situation. For our purposes the relevant aspect of cognitive behaviour therapy (CBT) is that it seeks to adjust mental life through 'the use of strategies that aim to identify and *rectify* dysfunctional cognitions'.[42] CBT differs from standard behaviourism in the primary function it accords to cognition. It holds that cognition (ideas, beliefs, expectations) and affect have a foundational role in behaviour and that to change behaviour one must change the cognitions that underlie it.

Aside from the belief that one can use the conscious mind as a powerful tool to change underlying patterns of mental operation, the cognitive behavioural model may mirror perspectival parallelism in citing two perspectives, the internal and external. In this model, dysfunction occurs when the two perspectives do not run in sufficient tandem.

Although he may cite such a therapeutic stance in support of his claims for technique in thought, the use of such methods highlights the way in which such material can be brought to bear in a critique of Connolly. The use of techniques in thought presupposes a highly developed, critically reflective faculty on the part of the subject implementing them. CBT works by honing the patient's reflective capacity, using such techniques as keeping a journal, to the point where therapy is patient- and not therapist-driven. The research discussed in the preceding chapter minimises the role of such a reflective consciousness, positing it as an after-effect or epiphenomenon of mental functioning at lower levels. When we combine the conscious-nonconscious axis to the mind-body axis of the previous sections, the problems of Connolly's approach are seen. The problems can be remedied, it is argued, by embracing a materialism that addresses both these issues, seeking a position that may not place such an emphasis on consciousness. We must also balance this with the problems of pure materialism driven to reductive or eliminative extremes, as seen in the previous section.

How do we politicise neuroscience?

The functionalist philosophy of mind threads a path through these difficulties and may afford a portal through which dialogue can be held with political theory. It is firmly rooted in materialism, overcoming the dualist problem, works on the basis of a nonconscious-conscious continuum where there is no hard and fast boundary between the two, and allows culture an important role in mental processes.

At base, functionalism holds that the mind is a function of the brain. It draws the distinction between the function of an object and the set of material arrangements that allow that function to be discharged. The function of telling the time, for example, can be carried out in a variety of ways such as using standing stones, sundials, water clocks, mechanical clocks or atomic clocks. So too the function which we term 'mind' can be realised by any number of material arrangements, one of which happens to be the human brain.

Functionalists believe that reality is layered in certain nonreducible but importantly interdependent ways. For the purposes of illustration, let us revisit Taylor's concept of shame. Taylor holds that shame is an inherently social concept, irreducible to the pure mechanics of brainstates. Functionalists agree. The properties exhibited by a heart are not just the properties of the various atomic particles that go to make it up. Likewise, the properties of the mental state of shame are not merely those of the various neurochemicals which actualise it at a material level. Shame is a higher-level entity than brain chemistry, with its investigation rightly lying with the higher-level social sciences, as opposed to the lower-level natural sciences, with physics as the bottom base, which investigate neurochemistry. Even though the higher levels are dependent on the lower, they are sensitive to certain aspects of reality to which the lower are blind, being concerned with the mechanics of minutia. Physics can tell us which particles are behaving in what ways to create a sunset; neuroscience can tell us what inputs, chemicals and brainstates are involved in the perception of the sunset; but both are unable to grasp the complex web of associations and feelings induced by its contemplation. This latter aspect, the qualitative experience of a certain situation, is termed the 'qualia' in philosophy of mind literature and it is qualia that Kripe and Jackson discuss in the last section.

Just as functionalism posits a hierarchy of sciences to deal with levels of reality in the world, Daniel Dennett tries to explain consciousness with a hierarchical theory of levels of processing, awareness and allocation of mental resources. Dennett argues that what we term as consciousness first emerged as habits of mental stimulation, such as making vocalisations when there was no one else to hear and, hearing it oneself, answering one's own question, or drawing two parallel lines in the dirt and being reminded to bring one's vine rope to cross the river later.[43] These mental 'tricks' improved exponentially with the growth of language.

Language in turn led to the internalisation of 'memes'. Memes are a concept used by Richard Dawkins to express units of culture (ideas), which take up residence in the brain creating minds. Dennett characterises this process as parasitic. Memes behave and evolve like genes, the successful being those which for any reason succeed in replicating and surviving. Such ideas include the wheel, the alphabet, symphonies or Joyce's *Ulysses*:

> The haven all memes depend on reaching is the human mind, but a human mind is itself an artifact created when memes restructure a human brain in order to make it a better habitat for memes . . . the most striking differences in human prowess depend on microstructural differences induced by various memes that have entered them and taken up residence.[44]

Dennett goes on to compare memes to being akin to software installed on the hardware of the brain's architecture, a *virtual machine* in the same way as a chess-playing program on a computer turns the latter into a chess-playing machine for a while. The installation of the virtual machine of language in the brain will lead it to process in different ways; it will, for example, turn it into a serial processing device when we think through a task in the 'first this . . . then this' mode. The software analogy is useful, Dennett argues, because human consciousness is too recent to have been cemented at the material level of the brain and is the product of cultural evolution, which gets programmed into brains at an early age. Consciousness is therefore a cultural innovation of representation, usually and most powerfully through language, superimposed on actions carried out by subroutines that jostle for position, the most successful of which manages, by a process of elimination, to utilise the largest share of mental resources. These subroutines are nonconscious and chaotic in their jostling, operating in a parallel manner opposed to the serial nature of conscious thought. There is no single stream of consciousness, 'ghost in the machine' or 'central meaner', just a virtual machine (Dennett terms it the 'Joycean machine') that by its lower-level nonconscious actions discards the 'suggestions' of some subroutines and promotes others until the point where one becomes realised in action or speech and is then interpreted by the higher conscious levels of the machine.

In order to fill out the mental picture given by functionalism it is useful to consider the idea of embodiment. Theorists such as Hubert Dreyfus, Francisco Varela and Andy Clark take their cue from phenomenology, arguing that one cannot understand cognition and consciousness without situating the mind in the lived experience of both body and world. Dreyfus, for example, argues against the possibility of artificial intelligence on the basis that, when trying to get a machine to think, programmers seek to equip it with a representation of the world from which to proceed. Following Heidegger, he argues that humans do not carry round such a representation in their heads but that we represent the world in each situation as we experience it, one action leading to another with no real prearranged scheme.[45]

This fits in quite well with the picture of competing subroutines given by Dennett and is picked up in the work of Andy Clark. Clark also holds that the world is its own representation, but goes further, following Heidegger and Merleau Ponty, in unpacking the various ways in which cognitive functioning can be projected out into it, using it as a scaffold for the ordering of mental action or a workspace in which it can be carried out. Much of human intelligence is based on environmentally specific tricks and strategies, using our environment to mould and orchestrate behaviour. He characterises the mind as a 'leaky organ', mingling messily with both the body and our outside environment, citing developmental studies to illustrate how infants will use the world around them by mechanically interacting with it in a haphazard trial-and-error manner. As one grows, the mode of interaction becomes more complex but the use of, and dependence on, the external environment remains. One simple example, cited by both Clark and Dennett, is the use of a pencil and paper whilst doing arithmetic.

Like Dennett, Clark sees the use of language as the most important external patterning of thought. Unlike the former, however, he does not see its effects as being a subtle restructuring of brain physiology but rather as an external resource complementing the indigenous representation and computation of the brain. Language confers the ability to reconfigure computational space through inner and outer speech, directing attention and ordering action, and writing, which is used as an external memory device. These functions free up internal mental resources allowing more complex cognitive action.

Humans are, therefore, 'distributed cognitive engines' with thought depending on sustained interaction with the external environment, via the body, to 'transform inputs, simplify searches, aid recognition, prompt associative recall, [and] offload memory'.[46] The role of the body is fundamental in such a presentation. Varela uses the term 'enaction' to underline the idea that:

> cognition depends on the kinds of experience that come from having a body with various sensorimotor capabilities, and second, that these individual sensorimotor capacities are themselves embedded in a more encompassing biological, psychological, and cultural context . . . sensory and motor processes, perception and action, are fundamentally inseparable in lived cognition.[47]

Clark makes a similar point with his 'action loops', citing infant studies to show how young children acquire action-specific knowledge about things such as slopes, as well as perceptual studies involving adults. He uses such evidence to argue that we should move from a 'visuocentric' framework, in which cognition, and perception in particular, is primarily driven by vision, to a 'motocentric' framework driven by specific action routines involving the interaction of various local factors, such as bodily growth, environment, brain maturation and learning.[48]

These approaches emphasise a fluid interpenetrating set of relays between the mind, body and world that can be connected quite explicitly to the concerns of political theory. The idea of discourse in Foucault and Butler, for example, can be seen as a political explication of how different types of neuron-software affect the body. For Foucault the body is political because it is directly operated upon by the subtle effects of power contained in the many social institutions and cultural webs that make up our everyday life. Our bodies have to be in certain places (school, church, workplace) and perform certain functions in society: 'The body is . . . directly involved in a political field; power relations have an immediate hold upon it; they invest it, mark it, train it, torture it, force it to carry out tasks, to perform ceremonies, to emit signs.'[49]

Power infests the body; it penetrates and reforms it in certain ways. Power, for Foucault, is an essentially productive force: the prison regime is a set of ideas and practices; it is a machine which takes criminals and produces useful members of society; people who's bodies will be at work or at home when they are meant to be, it renders 'individuals docile and useful, by means of precise work upon their bodies'.[50] Another good example of a discourse which operates on bodies is the military. 'By the late eighteenth century, the soldier is something that can be made; out of a formless clay, an inapt body, the machine required can be constructed.'[51]

For Foucault, the body is something which is extremely malleable; it is clay which can be formed, trained, manipulated into various shapes and patterns of behaviour. The idea of a 'natural' body is at any point in time merely the product of various social discourses.

The military is a good example of a purely artificial system that manipulates bodies, but the argument also holds for processes seen as 'natural'. In *History of Sexuality vol. 1: The Will to Knowledge*, Foucault takes a 'natural' process/act/impulse to examine the effects of power on bodies. 'The purpose of . . . [this] study is . . . to show how deployments of power are directly connected to the body – to bodies, functions, physiological processes, sensations and pleasures.'[52] Foucault seeks to show how sexuality is operated upon by various discourses including, for example, religious doctrine on sex, the scientific study of women, the study and regulation of children's sexuality and the advent of population control with the attendant study and manipulation of a nation's sexual practices. Our notions of sexuality, and consequently our practice of it, are therefore subject to change in different times and places. Sexuality is not 'natural'; it is constructed according to time and place.

If bodies are malleable and discourses changeable then political and social groups can effect change. In *Gender Trouble*, Butler argues that there is no such thing as a naturally sexed body. She rejects the usual distinction, which claims that the difference between the sexes is natural whereas that between genders or sexualities is cultural. For her the idea of sex is not tied to the body but is, like gender, a production of Foucauldian discourses.[53] Butler argues that gender is a form of bodily signification. In other words, the gender we adopt has an impact on the 'sexing' of our body. In this way gender is *performative*, a notion rooted in linguistic theory which claims that a speech-act creates that which it names.[54] One often-used example of this in language is the marriage ceremony wherein the pronouncement of the vows by bride and groom means they are married. In the same way that acting out a marriage constitutes (or creates) a married couple, the acting out of a gender will constitute the identity it is purported to be. This acting out takes place on the surface of the body – 'gender is the repeated stylization of the body, a set of repeated acts within a highly rigid regulatory frame that congeal over time to produce the appearance of substance, of a natural sort of being.'[55] Gender is a set of 'acts, gestures, enactments . . . [and] corporeal signs'.[56] Once this is realised one can deconstruct the acts which constitute a particular gender and produce a sexed body, and see them within the framework of the social discourses which produce them.

One can go further than this however. One can use this knowledge to try to disrupt particular patterns of gender and sex by turning the acts that constitute these patterns against themselves. One way of doing this, which Butler suggests, is drag. For Butler, the performance of drag serves to highlight the difficulty of the notion of an original sex. It 'plays upon the distinction between the anatomy of the performer and the gender that is being performed' and uses the interplay of 'anatomical sex, gender identity, and gender performance'.[57] Drag does not parody the original gender but parodies the very idea of an original.

Butler's ideas are of course controversial. She, like Foucault, in claiming that the body 'has no ontological status apart from the various acts which constitute its reality', is criticised for denying the actual physical substance of the body. Critics suggest that there are physical limits to what the actual body can do and that it is not a blank sheet on which anything may be inscribed by discourse. In a later work, Butler attempted to address these concerns by introducing the idea of 'materialization'. However, this seems less a defence or a reworking of her beliefs than a restatement in that again she claims that there is no natural body only a process of 'materialization that stabilizes over time to produce the effect of boundary, fixity, and surface we call matter'.[58]

Work on embodied cognition is one part of a wider movement within cognitive science that is seeking to connect with influences outside the pure, hard, natural sciences.[59] A good overview of these trends is given in a collection of essays exploring the idea of social neuroscience edited by Cacioppo and Berntson. In their own essay in the collection, they argue for an interdisciplinary, multilevel analysis to understand complex systems of cognition. Such an effort would seek to extend analysis from the macro (social) level to the micro (neural).[60] This is, in some ways, akin to the project undertaken in Foucauldian analysis which seeks to connect macro power knowledge formations with micro effects on the self and body. Foucault's study of the various discourses surrounding sexuality sought to uncover some of the effects of power on our sense of self as did his analysis of the use of behavioural constraints and training in order to create soldiers and prisoners. The use of functionalist and embodiment theories of mental life can add new dimensions to such work. These ideas give us the ability to pursue the effects of power to ever-deeper levels, and to ask valuable questions, such as whether we can talk of power at a neural level.

The most important question for the present work is, however, the potential problems and opportunities that the use of such theoretical tools may present for resistance and critique. Before these issues are dealt with in Chapters 5 and 6, the next two chapters will seek to use these tools to explore the effect of contemporary socio-political discourses on our mental life and the generation of our sense of consciousness. The following chapter will assess the role of affect in culture and cognition before investigating the emotions that our own culture may generate and the effects they may have. Chapter 4 will examine the idea of narrative in the generation of the conscious self in our society, arguing that this may not be an ontological given based on the picture of cognitive functioning we have painted. It is argued that narrative is tied to a vision of linear temporality that does not exist in our mental lives, as illustrated by Libet and Gazzaniga and Le Doux in Chapter 1.

Notes

1. Churchland, *Scientific Realism*, p. 5. Other major works on eliminative materialism include Churchland, *Neurophilosophy* and *Brain-Wise* and Crick, *The Astonishing Hypothesis*.
2. Bennett and Hacker, *Philosophical Foundations of Neuroscience*, p. 373.
3. Ibid. p. 358.
4. Taylor, 'Interpretation and the Sciences of Man' in *Philosophy and the Human Sciences*, p. 189.
5. Ibid. p. 195.
6. Spinoza, *The Ethics*.
7. Hampshire, 'Introduction' in Spinoza, *The Ethics*, pp. x–xi.
8. Spinoza, *The Ethics*, Part 3, Prop. II.
9. Spinoza, *The Ethics*, Part 4, Axiom.
10. Leibniz, *Monadology*, §17.
11. Ibid. §14, §21–28. The idea is then given a fuller treatment in Leibniz, *New Essays on Human Understanding*.
12. Connolly, *Neuropolitics*, p. 86.
13. Ibid. p. 85.
14. Ibid. p. 87.

15. Ibid. p. 88.
16. Ibid. p. 89.
17. Chalmers, *The Conscious Mind*, p. 125.
18. Ibid.
19. There is also room to consider the possible relation between Connolly's immanent naturalism and Chalmers' naturalistic dualism. The latter states that, although we may view consciousness as a natural phenomenon, we must extend our view of what natural denotes beyond merely conflating the term with materialism (Chalmers, *The Conscious Mind*, p. 128). Chalmers also states that it is possible that his dualism could turn out to be a variety of monism in much the same way as matter and energy turned out to be two aspects of the one thing, although he is adamant that it cannot be a material monism (ibid. p. 129).
20. Chalmers, *The Conscious Mind*, p. 93.
21. Ibid. p. 106.
22. Kripke, *Naming and Necessity*, discussed in Chalmers, *The Conscious Mind*, pp. 146–9.
23. Jackson, 'Epiphenomenal Qualia', discussed in Chalmers, *The Conscious Mind*, p. 140.
24. Hampshire, 'Introduction', p. xi.
25. Dennett, *Consciousness Explained*, pp. 76–7.
26. Ibid. p. 83.
27. Ibid. p. 98.
28. Connolly, *Neuropolitics*, p. 8.
29. Ramachandran, *Phantoms in the Brain*, p. 56, quoted in Connolly, *Neuropolitics*, p. 12.
30. Connolly, *Neuropolitics*, p. 107.
31. Ibid. p. 108.
32. Anyone seeking such a discussion should see Vázquez-Arroyo 'Agonized liberalism'.
33. Connolly, *Neuropolitics*, pp. 101–3.
34. Ibid. p. 86.
35. Nietzsche, *Twilight of the Idols*, no. 47, quoted in Connolly, *Neuropolitics*, p. 77.
36. Chalmers, *The Conscious Mind*, pp. 219–25.
37. Ibid. pp. 219–25.
38. Ibid. p. 229.
39. Ibid. p. 275.
40. Connolly, *Neuropolitics*, pp. 83–5.
41. Dennett, *Consciousness Explained*, p. 207.
42. Marshall and Turnbull, *Cognitive Behaviour Therapy*, p. 30, emphasis added.
43. Dennett, *Consciousness Explained*, pp. 196–7. Dennett presents these examples as deliberately oversimplified thought experiments.

44. Ibid. p. 207.
45. Dreyfus, *What Computers Still Can't Do*, pp. xxxi–ii.
46. Clark, *Being There*, pp. 68–9.
47. Varela et al., *The Embodied Mind*, p. 173.
48. Clark, *Being There*, pp. 39–40.
49. Foucault, *Discipline and Punish*, p. 25.
50. Ibid. p. 231.
51. Ibid. p. 135.
52. Foucault, *History of Sexuality vol. 1*, pp. 151–2.
53. Butler, *Gender Trouble*, pp. 6–8.
54. Ibid. p. 25.
55. Ibid. p. 33.
56. Ibid. p. 136.
57. Ibid. p. 137.
58. Butler, *Bodies that Matter*, p. 9.
59. Embodied cognition is itself part of a growing sub-movement seeking to establish a dialogue between the work of Husserl and cognitive science. A good summary of such work, as well as an excellent introductory essay on the foundations of such a dialogue, can be found in Petit et al., *Naturalising Phenomenology*. Interesting as this broader project is, I have chosen not to discuss it in any detail because it is in danger of sometimes neglecting the role of the nonconscious in mental life, which is one of my primary concerns. The embodied cognition theories do not lapse into this neglect, however, and can be seen to follow on from the functionalist conception of mental life as a series of levels without rigid distinctions. They also make use of the valuable idea of emergent properties wherein the action of many different low-level mechanisms can give rise to complex phenomena the generation of which would be quite impossible for any to achieve in isolation.
60. Cacioppo and Berntson, *Essays in Social Neuroscience*, pp. 108–9. The authors then give examples of such multilevel analysis: one a top-down study of the affect of social factors on autonomic cardiovascular health and a bottom-up study of autonomic effects on higher-level cognition and behaviour. Many of the other essays in the collection also serve as valuable examples of such work, for example Michael J. Meaney's discussion of his own work on maternal effects on responses to threat in rats, pp. 4–13, or Stephen J. Suomy's work on the connection between genetic and experiential factors in aggression in rhesus monkeys, pp. 15–29.

3

The Political Use of Emotion

So far we have seen research from neuropsychology that illustrates the role which nonconscious processing plays in our mental lives. This is connected to the world around us through the role of the body in processing and cognition. One further aspect of this picture is emotion and affect. This chapter will seek to investigate the emotive aspect in thought and the debates as to its biological or social nature. Without going too far down the well-worn road of the nature/nurture debate, it is fairly uncontroversial to claim a socially constructed aspect to emotional experience and expression, even if one believes it to be at the purely linguistic level. It will be argued that the discourses of different societies help shape different emotions and, after a general examination of the nature of emotion, particular socio-historic examples will be given.

Emotion has generally been an underinvestigated political tool given the rationalistic bent of political theorising. The situation is getting better however following on from the feminist critique of the simplistic reason/emotion dualism. In the context of the present work, emotion is a useful tool on several levels. It takes its place beside other forms of nonconscious processing to further problematise the ideal of reasoned engagement with the world, but it is also a particularly important illustration of the effect of discourse in shaping thought processing at all levels. I am wary, however, of arguing that a society can be indirectly 'oppressed' through its prevalent emotional discourse. As we shall see, such a claim would involve arguing that there is some form of 'natural' emotional expression that becomes thwarted in some way. Undoubtedly, many societies have sought to directly repress subjects through actions and ideas specifically designed to work on the emotions. Indeed these form some of the most effective forms of repression, serving to instil demoralisation and hopelessness in the populace or to whip up fear and hatred of an internal or external group for political purposes. We shall however investigate the emotional discourses prevalent in our society before coming back, in the last two chapters, to see if we can harness emotional resistance.

The psycho-social nature of emotion

One of the first interventions into the psychological study of emotion was William James' 1884 article 'What is an emotion?' This later appeared, with minor amendments, as the chapter on emotion in *The Principles of Psychology*.[1] James' basic argument is that the experience of an emotion follows the physiological response to an event. Indeed an emotion is nothing more than the feeling of bodily changes engendered by an event. In his famous example, we see a bear, this causes us to run and, upon perceiving that we are fleeing, we feel fear. This can be seen as closely allied to Liebniz's conception in the last chapter that the mind will perceive the body drinking and hence feel thirst.

One of the problems with James' theory is that, since he claims that emotions are merely the perception of physiological states, this negates those that are preceded by no such physical expression. At the end of both the original 1884 article and the 1890 chapter, he goes so far as to claim that moral, aesthetic and intellectual feelings are not emotions at all but purely cognitive acts. He also fails to differentiate between those physical occurrences that are emotions and those, like perceptions of temperature or pain, which are not.[2] What James did, however, and the reason he is still cited in contemporary literature, was to couple emotion to bodily expression.

This did not prove a popular move in many circles as it serves to downplay the role of cognition in emotion. A contrary position is the attribution theory of Schacter and Singer. They argue that, given a physiological arousal, the brain interprets the internal and external causes and attributes an emotional label to it. Instead of seeing the bear, fleeing and feeling fear because we perceive ourselves running, we see the bear, experience physiological symptoms such as increased heart rate, freezing, sweating and so on and, given what we think the threat is from a bear, interpret the emotion as fear. This interpretive cognitive element gets round the problem in James' theory wherein one would be unable to distinguish between emotions that proceeded from the same physiological symptoms. Given a pounding heart and sweaty palms, for example, how do we know whether we are afraid of, or in love with, the bear? Schachter and Singer are able to claim that we are able to correctly attribute fear rather than love based on experience, knowledge and context.

In an experiment designed to test this idea, subjects were injected with adrenaline to artificially induce physiological arousal through stimulation of the autonomic nervous system. Attempts were then made to prejudice the attribution of emotion through the presentation of pleasant or unpleasant stimuli. As predicted, those presented with pleasant stimuli came out feeling happy, those presented with unhappy came out feeling sad and those presented with neutral material felt nothing in particular.[3] The problem is, however, that this is fine for explaining emotions post facto but fails to tell us how the machinery is initiated in the first place. What makes us run or start sweating at the sight of the bear? Magda Arnold fills in the gap with her appraisal theory. We see the bear, make a nonconscious appraisal of the situation that leads, not automatically to an action, but to an 'action tendency', and our feeling of fear results from the tendency to run.[4]

The difference between James and subsequent theorists is useful in that it highlights the possible role of biological or social inputs in emotion. If one follows James' line, then social environment has little role in emotional experience and expression, whereas in the Schachter-Singer theory attribution is a socially guided enterprise. Arnold's appraisal theory can also be seen to be driven by social factors, although at a nonconscious rather than conscious level, since in order to make an appraisal one must have some frame of reference or knowledge base from which to make it. Her theory does allow more room for instinctual tendencies than Schachter and Singer's in that our jumping and feeling fear as a result of a loud bang behind us comes, not so much from our store of collective knowledge, as from an ingrained survival mechanism. It could be argued that such instinctual reactions fit better with James' theory in that we tend to jump first and then feel the surge of fear.

One can get a better idea of how complex these issues have become with the help of contemporary neuropsychology. In biological terms, certain regions of the brain send commands to other regions and throughout the body, via chemicals in the bloodstream and electrochemical signals along neural pathways, which act on other neurons, muscular fibres or organs and ultimately lead to the release of further chemicals into the bloodstream. This culminates in a change in the global state of the organism. Change occurs both in the body expressed as muscular and organ behaviour, and the brain, through the release of substances such as monoamines and peptides in the brainstem and basal forebrain, which alter the mode processing of other brain regions (in terms of speed or focus, for example), triggering specific behaviours.[5]

Such operations happen at a level below that of conscious awareness and a conscious emotion is only triggered when the consequences of the changes engendered are sensed by consciousness. The first-order neural changes are mapped in second-order changes that engage the self-image and bring the emotion to consciousness. Antonio Damasio describes the above process, whereby changes in the body prefigure changes in both the body state and cognitive state, as a 'body loop'. It uses both humoural (chemicals in the bloodstream) and neural signals. Emotions can also be triggered by purely neural means through the action of the brain regions, such as the prefrontal cortices, which make it seem as if the body state has changed and induce neural changes accordingly. This Damasio calls an 'as if body loop'[6] and it is this which differentiates his model from what would seem like a contemporary Jamesian account.

LeDoux agrees that emotional states happen primarily below the level of awareness and only come to consciousness when the latter becomes privy to what is happening at lower levels. He points out, however, that there is a very unequal relationship between the two levels. It is relatively easy for an emotional state to displace more mundane contents in conscious awareness, whereas it is a lot harder for non-emotional events to displace emotions in consciousness. Trying to wish one's way out of depression, for example, rarely works. Though we may set up situations that provoke emotional reactions (movies, rollercoasters, drugs), we have very little conscious control over our emotions. In biological terms, the connections running from the emotional systems to the cognitive systems are much stronger than those operating in the other direction.[7]

This, like the instinctual reaction to take one's hand out of the fire without too much analysis, is an evolutionary mechanism that makes utilitarian sense. Another example is the emotion of fear. In terms of the evolutionary biology of the brain, the thalamus is a far cruder device than the cortex. Both the sensory thalamus and the higher-level sensory cortex are able to send signals to the amygdala, the subcortical region that then triggers a response. Whereas the cortex has the advantage of high-level processing, the thalamus has the advantage of speed.[8] When walking through the woods we see a large shadow. The thalamus sends a signal to both the amygdala and the cortex and by the time the latter has realised that it's not that damn Jamesian bear that seems to be dogging our every step, the former has flooded the system with adrenaline to either fight or run.

It should not be thought that whilst the thalamus is transmitting panic signals the cortex is coolly weighing up the pros and cons of the situation, however. The experience of emotion profoundly affects cognitive processing as mentioned above. In this regard, Damasio formulates his somatic-marker hypothesis around evidence from patients with damage to prefrontal regions of their brains. These patients were able to function in a perfectly rational manner but revealed a reduced ability to function advantageously in situations of risk and conflict, as well as 'a selective reduction of the ability to resonate emotionally' in such situations.[9] He claims that the selective reduction of emotion, rather than freeing reason from the confines of the irrational, can actually impair reasoning ability in certain circumstances, such as those involving personal or social situations, reason or conflict.

When weighing up a set of hard personal choices in the mind we sometimes get an unpleasant gut reaction to one of them. This Damasio calls a somatic marker: it marks an image or idea as having a certain danger or unpleasantness attached to the consequences of pursuing it and, even though consciousness still has the final say, it aids the cognitive process of rational reflection. The perception of danger, or of a positive outcome, is a result of learned experience or cultural influence and can operate at the conscious level during a rational decision-making process, or nonconsciously as an intuition or general mood if the nonconscious is working on a problem.[10]

One good example of a somatic marker, as well as the induction of emotion without consciousness, is the case of 'David'. David has one of the most severe learning and memory impairments ever recorded due to extensive damage to both of his temporal lobes, including the hippocampus (the important region in the creation of new factual memories) and the amygdala. David cannot learn any new fact and cannot therefore learn to recognise any new person, place or thing no matter how many times he meets them. In one experiment, Damasio set up a situation wherein David engaged in controlled activities with three different people over the course of a week. The first behaved pleasantly towards him and rewarded him whether he requested something or not, the second was emotionally neutral and engaged him in neutral tasks and the third was unfriendly and engaged him in extremely boring tasks. David was then asked to look at sets of four different photographs, one of which would be one of the three people he had encountered. When asked to pick out of the four photographs who he would go to if he needed help, or who he thought was his friend among them, he chose the friendly person 80 per cent of the time his picture was present and the unfriendly person almost never. The neutral person was chosen about 25 per cent of the time in line with chance in a set of four photographs. When confronted with photographs of the three people he had encountered he was unable to tell the experimenters anything about them but still consistently chose the pleasant person when asked who among them he thought was a friend. Damasio concludes that there was no conscious input into these decisions. Rather they were inspired by the emotions induced during the experiment and a nonconscious reinduction of these emotions during testing.[11]

Though there does seem to be room for societal influence in such neurological work, in the pairing of somatic markers with certain events and situations for example, the emphasis is very much on the biological underpinnings of emotion. This concentration on how the body and brain are hardwired leads LeDoux to state that all emotions are biological functions of the nervous system and Damasio to cite certain 'basic' emotions shared by all humans. Damasio refers to six basic emotions of happiness, sadness, fear, anger, surprise and disgust, as well as 'secondary' or 'social' emotions such as embarrassment, guilt, envy and pride, and 'background' emotions such as well-being, malaise, calm or tension. All these emotional levels share a biological foundation, being patterned collections of chemical or neural responses playing a regulatory role in the life of the organism, in terms either of responding to external phenomena or regulating the internal state to make it ready for a specific reaction. These processes are hardwired: biologically determined by evolution and 'depending on innately set neural devices', although the expressions and meanings of emotions can be changed by culture.[12]

This idea is most famously associated in contemporary times with Darwin. Darwin studied emotional expression in humans and animals, arguing that emotions were primitive states of physiological arousal linked to instincts and serving to promote survival by reacting to threats and signalling future intentions.[13] The notion that there are certain basic universal emotions is an old one, however. *Li Chi*, a first-century BC Chinese encyclopaedia, lists 'joy, anger, sadness, fear, love, disliking and liking'; the Stoics listed 'pleasure or delight, distress, appetite and fear'; Descartes, bucking the trend by citing more positive than negative, claimed 'wonder, love, hatred, desire, joy and sadness'; Spinoza opts for pleasure, pain and desire; and Hobbes mentions 'appetite, desire, love, aversion, hate, joy, and grief'.[14] There is also very little consensus on the secondary emotions, with Descartes expanding his list to forty-one, Hobbes to forty-six, Spinoza to forty-eight and James McCosh listing over one hundred in 1880.[15]

Contemporary research into basic emotions takes its lead from Paul Ekman's cross-cultural experiments in the early 1970s, in which subjects were shown photographs of posed emotional facial expressions and asked to identify which emotion the person in the photograph was experiencing. Ekman claimed that his results confirmed pan-cultural emotional expression for the same six basic emotions cited by Damasio above.[16] As well as judgement tests of facial expressions, Ekman also carried out component analysis of facial expressions induced in subjects. In one experiment, subjects from Japan and America were shown a stress-inducing film and their spontaneous facial expressions and bodily changes analysed, revealing close similarities between the two cultures.[17]

Goldie points out some problems with a simplistic reliance on these results, however. Such studies only focus on 'emotional responses in terms of bodily changes and facial expression' and the ability to match certain facial expressions to certain emotions. Nevertheless they neglect other aspects of emotion, such as intentionality. We must also ask what these expressions are expressions of. Subjects in judgment tests were asked to match photos to emotions from a set list but when, in another study, they were freely allowed to choose a single word for the expression forty different words were used for what had originally been termed 'anger' and eighty-one for 'contempt'. Subjects also preferred to provide an explanatory story for the expression rather than a single word.[18] It would seem that the universality found in Eckman's original experiment could be put down to the limited set of choices provided by experimenters of one particular culture.

One of the important considerations arising from this is the problem of language. Emotion terms in one language are often hard, if not impossible, to translate. The Anglophone concept of emotion is not the same as other languages' nearest equivalent: indeed some cultures have no term for emotion at all, subsuming the idea into terms for feeling and sensation. There are also differences across cultures as to what the basic emotions actually are. Finally, the English terms for specific emotions frequently do not translate into other languages, and conversely many emotion terms in other languages lack a simple term in English.[19]

In his historical study of Anglophone emotion terms, Dixon attacks the idea, adopted by Damasio, that Western thinkers until the late twentieth century, under the influence of rationalism and

Christian theology, have dismissed and ignored emotion as irrational, bodily based and involuntary. He claims that previous periods had no concept of emotion as we understand it because they deployed a different vocabulary, with terms such as 'passion', 'sensation' and 'affection', which gradually lost their individual subtleties and became subsumed within the umbrella notion of 'emotion'. The latter modern concept only gained common currency, he claims, with its usage in the 1820 lectures of physician-philosopher Thomas Brown, which finally secularised its study, although it had previously been used in a similar way by Hume.[20]

Dixon makes the point that our contemporary notion of emotion is itself over-inclusive. He claims that it is impossible to achieve consensus on what an emotion actually is given the diversity of mental and physical states that the term must cover. It is also robbed of its explanatory value since some emotional responses are treated as being akin to sneezes whereas others are treated like crimes, making inquiries into motivation and responsibility problematic.[21]

Cultural anthropological studies serving to highlight divergences across cultures in regard to emotion can be linked to work in social history investigating the changes within a particular culture over time to severely problematise the position that there are universal basic emotions. At the other end of the spectrum lies social constructivism that claims, in its strongest formulation, that there is no such biological basis to emotion, that it is an entirely learned sociocultural product. Emotion can thus only be understood with reference to the linguistic and cultural system within which it is embedded. It is an inherently intersubjective process, dynamic and changeable in line with historical, social and political context. As such, the feeling of an emotion places one firmly within the framework of meaning surrounding it within a particular culture:

> By reifying 'anger', we can be tempted into the mistake of thinking that anger is something inside a person exercising its invisible and inaudible influence on what we do. But to be angry is to have taken on an angry role on a particular occasion as the expression of a moral position. This role may involve the feeling of appropriate feelings as well as indulging in suitable public conduct. The bodily feeling is often the somatic expression to oneself of the taking of a moral standpoint.[22]

As Lupton points out, bringing us back to Butler and the idea of performativity at the end of the last chapter, one does not 'have' so much as 'do' an emotion.[23]

This position is echoed by Kitayama and Markus in their introduction to an edited collection on the influence of culture in emotion. They make the point that neuroanatomical analysis cannot distinguish shame from guilt or explain the cultural differences in different cultures' reactions to the same problems. To help with such explanation they propose a functionalist conception of socially shared emotional scripts 'composed of physiological, subjective and behavioural processes' developing as 'individuals actively, personally and collectively adapt to their immediate sociocultural, semiotic environment'.[24] Referring to literature on local biologies, they argue that the physiological aspects of an emotion are profoundly affected by social processes, being 'organised and modulated' by the action of emotion scripts:

> In short, . . . culture can penetrate deeply into virtually every component process of emotion, not only the cognitive or linguistic elements that are directly provided by the culturally shared pool of knowledge, but also physiological and neurochemical elements, which need to be adjusted or tuned for the individual to accomplish a reasonable degree of adaptation and adjustment to the pertinent cultural environment. Furthermore, if emotions are literally formed through individuals' active pursuit of adaptation to their cultural environment, the emotions will in turn function to maintain and regulate, or, in some cases, to challenge the very cultural environment to which they have been tuned.[25]

Emotions result, in this theory, from adaptation to the environment or, as expressed by another author in the same volume, the way people interpret and appraise their environment.[26] This brings us back to Schacter and Singer and the appraisal theory cited above. Indeed such work seems to provide the psychological touchstone around which much constructivist cultural anthropology on emotions is based.[27] One problem with such a foundation is that it entails having a definition of culture with which to work. Early studies drew on Geertz's notion that culture provides a model of social life, which is then used as a template for action.[28] As Reddy points out, this means that if culture conditions our every thought and dream we have no possible outside position on which to criticise or own. Catherine Lutz, in her influential study into emotions in Micronesia, turned to Foucault's concept of discourse to provide a critical tool. 'Like Foucault, I am interested in how emotions – like other aspects of a culturally posited psyche are "the place in which the most minute and local social practices are linked up with a large scale organization of power." '[29]

The body plays a significant part in such investigations. Lupton makes a strong case for bringing the body back in to constructivist positions (Butler, as we have seen, has been accused of ignoring the materiality of the body in her work, putting all her emphasis on performativity and culture). Lupton argues that, not only are emotive experiences related to the body, but also our sense of self is inevitably intertwined with embodiment. She seeks to steer a course between constructivism and reifying the biological ontology of the body, arguing that experiences of embodiment, as well as the body itself to a certain extent, are 'constructed through and mediated by sociocultural processes'.[30]

This is illustrated through an exploration of the move from the notion of what she characterises as the 'open' to the 'closed' body. Our contemporary notion of an individualised body with borders tightly policed is linked to the idea of the individualised autonomous self and comes as the result of changes stretching from the Middle Ages to the advent of capitalism. In the Middle Ages the body was seen as open and porous. In an atmosphere of uncertainty and fear, little thought was given to the future and emotional expression was a lot more spontaneous and public. People were given to sudden changes of mood, impulsive violent acts were common and there was little regulation in relation to sensual and emotional expression. 'As a result impulses tended to be followed without thought for the need to control or moderate them.'[31]

The idea of emotional discipline began to emerge in Europe in the sixteenth and seventeenth centuries. There was a strong link between conceptions of emotion and embodiment, one example being the perceived link between bodily fluids and emotions as fluids. Love and hate could be transmitted as fluids via bodily orifices and exchanging bodily fluids through sharing a common cup or exchanging clothes or substances such as hair were thought to form a bond between giver and recipient.

A discourse began to grow around the body as possessing an inside and outside, as opposed to being a porous mechanism, and disdain for bodily products emerged with a corresponding set of self-censoring practices. The body became something to be managed and controlled, and a Platonic link was made between the disciplined body and the disciplined self. Both post-Reformation wings of Christianity bought into this idea. Protestantism focused on the 'Word of God' rather than images of his corporeality, with a clamp down on sensuality and emotional stimulation, whereas Catholicism characterised demonic possession as unruly elements residing within the body to be expelled and cleansed.

Elias claims that, during the sixteenth century, as life began to become more predictable and violence and an early death were not such prominent features, an obsession developed with the public deportment of the body in the notion of *civilité*. This involved behaviours 'directed towards self-control, the holding of oneself apart from others, the stifling of displays of bodily function and the regulation of facial expression, table manners, gestures, dress and the disbursement of bodily wastes'. Likewise expression of emotion became a lot more controlled and 'refined'.[32]

In the wake of the Industrial Revolution and the move to living in large-scale urban groups, greater internal regulation developed as external mechanisms of control, which had been successful in smaller communities, began to break down. Emotion came to demote an invisible feeling rather than its previous conception as a physical movement. Individual autonomy and ownership over ones' own body was prized and a growth in British and German medical texts linked the passions to bodily affliction. By the nineteenth century, fear and horror of unregulated bodies and emotions arising from such discourses crystallised into ideas of the grotesque. Darwin aided such ideas with his evolutionary account of emotions citing 'progressive mastery of tears' as a sign of advancing civilization and placing the English at the civilized apex because of their refined use of crying.

A counter-discourse emerged in Romanticism, which claimed that excessive rationalism and the stifling of the emotions were unnatural and distanced people from that which was essentially human. One example of this notion filtering into everyday life was the cultivation of fashionable melancholy by the French upper classes in the eighteenth century as denoting 'sensitivity of spirit and gentility'.[33] Reddy traces the political consequences of the parallel growth of sentimentalism among the middle and lower classes and links it directly to the outbreak of the French Revolution. He claims that the prevalent language of the Revolution was that of sentimentalism and that this language was ideally suited to the production of intense emotions which the populace had trained themselves to feel through contemporary letter-writing, novels and theatre.

Increased emotional control associated with Louis XIV's elaborate aristocratic honour code and ideal of courtly behaviour, as well as a mood of optimism in human affairs and improvability, led to the seeking of 'emotional refuge' in a growing number of salons and

Masonic lodges, as well as in sentimental art. These mechanisms provided an outlet for proscribed emotional behaviour and became important sources of critique and new ideas. Sentimentalism became allied to a utopian political ideology through, for example, the Manichean structure of the plots of contemporary novels and plays. It was a short step from the battles between good and evil expressed therein to identifying evil in the corruption of the upper classes and court, with the innocent victims being the poverty-stricken underclasses. Such an approach was utilised to great effect by lawyers in trials of the period:

> Putting sentimentalism to practical use in this way gave the Manichean plot structures of its literary genres a sinister new political import . . . While offering implicit support to calls for popular political participation, more than any abstract theorizing could have done, such a strategy also necessarily heightened concern about sincerity.[34]

This concern with identifying individual sincerity was later to inform the thinking behind the Terror.

Reddy breaks with social constructivism in his evaluation of the emotional regimes he studies. He claims that sentimentalism was a powerful tool of resistance and critique; its emphasis on true expression of natural feeling rendered it inflexible as a mechanism of rule, however. The idea that sentimentalism was a mistaken view of emotional expression can help explain the extremes of feeling expressed in the period, the couching, and justification, of political decisions in terms of feeling and the emotional frustration caused by the Terror as people tried to hide emotional expression forbidden by the state.[35]

To facilitate such evaluation, Reddy proposes an ideal of emotional liberty. This liberty entails the freedom to change goals and make decisions 'in response to bewildering, ambivalent thought activations that exceed the capacity of attention and challenge the reign of high-level goals currently guiding emotional management'.[36] Conversely, emotional suffering results from explicitly putting emotional goals in conflict. Reddy gives the example of people under torture who are torn between giving up a cause to which they are emotionally committed and the preservation of bodily health. On this conception, any political order will establish an emotional regime that may be assessed in terms of whether it promotes emotional liberty or suffering. A sliding scale is envisaged, at one end of which strict regimes require formal emotional performances, through state ceremony or love of monarch/country, and deviant emotions are policed, whereas liberal regimes use strict emotional discipline only in certain circumstances (armies, schools, certain times of year or certain points in a person's life). Individuals operate without induced goal conflict and the emotional regime may operate as an umbrella for many emotional styles. Complex emotional regimes such as capitalism, whilst avowing much freedom, actually curtail the emotional opportunities of many, for example those who are dependent on a single salaried position. Such a society leads to a proliferation of varying levels of emotional freedom amongst its strata, criss-crossed by many forms of emotional refuge in which to experience the relaxation, abandonment or reversal of emotional norms.

The evaluation of liberal regimes is complicated, however, by the question of when, and what type of, induced goal conflict is compatible with a notion of emotional freedom. Reddy points out that the reduction of emotional suffering to a minimum is an ideal that has implications for political action in the problem of inducing such suffering in the fight for transition to a 'better' society.[37]

Following on from the above discussion, the second half of this chapter will seek to analyse the emotions inspired by our own consumer society, using Zygmunt Bauman's concept of *unsicherheit* (postmodern discontent) as a foundation. This will begin the process of investigating the structuring of thought in our society, which will then be expanded in the next chapter on narrativity. Together, these discussions will form the platform for discussion in the final two chapters of the book in which the type of radicalism which may emerge, specifically on the psychological level, is investigated.

Feeling consumed

Bauman argues that, whereas modernity strove towards '*universality, homogeneity, monotony* and *clarity*'[38] the institutions which it inaugurated produced 'institutionalised pluralism, variety, contingency and ambivalence'.[39] It was the embracing of these latter results which changed the mood and direction of society and what were seen as the failures of modernity were hailed as the successes of post-modernity. Society can no longer be seen as 'movement with a direction', be it guided by 'universalisation, rationalisation or systematisation'.[40]

With the effective dissolution of the state into its component parts in terms of life decisions, Bauman sees the logical turn as being towards individual agency. This agent is studied in terms of his or her 'habitat', both as a field of operation and as a site of individual creation. Whereas the cultural environment tends to be seen in social thought as that which determines the meaning of an agent's actions, the notion of habitat is merely the social space which makes 'both action and meaning-assignment possible'.[41] Meaning itself is no longer an ontological given but merely something that is available from a range of options if the individual wants it.

In a vein much repeated throughout Bauman's work, the agent is seen in terms of a consumer, the habitat

> sets the agenda for the 'business of life' through supplying the inventory of ends and the pool of means . . . In so far as the ends are offered as potentially alluring rather than obligatory, and rely for their choice on their own seductiveness rather than the supporting power of coercion, the 'business of life' splits into a series of choices.[42]

The habitat is, therefore, presented as being a kind of catalogue in which the individual agent chooses from a wide variety of life options, each vying to make themselves more appealing than the others, in a process of identity construction which Bauman terms 'self-assembly'.[43]

Bauman characterises the habitat as a complex system with no centralised goal-setting agency, which seeks, as did the Enlightenment vision of 'society', to manage and coordinate the lives of the populace, being populated instead by a profusion of single-purpose agencies each concentrating on one small area of social life. This allows the individual agent a considerably increased degree of autonomy than was previously the case. The side effect of this, however, is that agents are more isolated in their own individual social spaces, the only common thread being that the habitat is viewed as a space of indeterminacy taking on shifting contingent forms, which are always susceptible to change at any time and for no apparent reason:

> The existential modality of the agents is therefore one of insufficient determination, inconclusiveness, motility and rootlessness. The identity of the agent is neither given nor authoritatively confirmed. It has to be constructed, yet no design for the construction can be taken as proscribed or foolproof. The construction of the identity consists of successive trials and errors.[44]

The idea of the life-project as used in liberal theory, seen in terms of a defined endpoint or, failing that, as a set means of progression, is replaced with a non-cumulative process of self-constitution that has no such a priori foundations. The only 'visible aspect of continuity' throughout the existence of an individual, as well as the only visible site of the effects of our self-assembly, Bauman posits as being the human body.[45] Consequently, in line with the trajectory already suggested by Lupton in the last section, what we do with our bodies becomes more and more important: what we put in, take out, change or cultivate through exercise and health regimes.[46]

In the absence of normative guidance from a central agency, what becomes important in life is not the merits of the separate elements which we choose to use in our self-assembly from the catalogue of the habitat, rather it is the availability and accessibility of these 'tokens of potential self-assembly'.[47] The former of these two necessities, availability, is defined, on the one hand, in terms of visibility and, on the other, utility. Tokens have to be seen in order to be potentially chosen, but they also have to be able to convince the individual that their use in the self-assembly process will be successful or satisfactory. It is at this point that expertise and mass opinion, or rather the perception of expertise, becomes important. In the absence of centralised normative authority, agents look around for possible guidance from any one of a number of sources, which set themselves up as having particular knowledge to guide the agent in certain areas. The difference between both expert agencies and mass opinion, as opposed to a centralised catch-all authority, is that the agent is free, as a consumer, to accept or reject the opinions offered.

Freud argued that society involves a trade-off between individual autonomy and security, the former sacrificed for the sake of gaining the latter. Bauman, however, sees the present situation as having reversed Freud's diagnosis, 'it is security which is sacrificed day by day on the altar of ever-expanding individual freedom'.[48] In the consumer society in which we now live, our autonomy is based on the idea of choice – free choice – in essence a choice so free that it is considered unnecessary, and even undesirable, to choose on the basis of some overarching moral or ethical framework. The problem is that, when robbed of secure foundations for choice, the act of choosing itself becomes a frightening and isolating experience, hence the reliance on expertise or mass opinion.

Bauman characterises these existential worries under the label of *unsicherheit*, a German word deliberately chosen in opposition to Freud's *sicherheit*, used in reference to the security end of the societal trade-off. In order to translate *sicherheit* into English, three different terms are needed: (1) security, that the world is fixed and reliable, that what we have worked hard for will stay in our possession and that the rules and procedures with which we are inculcated are sufficient to take us through life; (2) certainty, in reference to what we can say about the world and about putting our life-skills into practice; and (3) safety of one's self and environment.[49] These are, Bauman argues, the 'conditions of self-confidence and self-reliance on which the ability to think and act rationally depends' the absence of which will lead to 'the dissipation of self-assurance, the loss of trust in one's own ability and other people's intentions, growing incapacitation, anxiety, caginess, the tendency to fault-seeking and fault-finding, to scapegoating and aggression'.[50] *Unsicherheit*, therefore, represents the absence of security, certainty and safety, with the corresponding effects. We are left with a lack of existential confidence as we are forced to make choices whose outcomes are necessarily unclear and the responsibility for which is unavoidably our own.

There is no framework against which to measure and judge one's actions and formulate life-plans; consequently, we each must try to find our own. This is, however, not such a simple and liberating process as it sounds, as most of us have absolutely no idea how to imbue our lives with meaning and direction. We look around, therefore, at what others are doing. Other people always have a tendency to appear to be more 'together' and in control than we do, a point to which we shall return in connection with the work of Jacques Lacan. In our consumerised society also, there is no shortage of companies and service providers who seek to offer us their own particular frameworks. which we may sign up to for however long they hold our interest before moving on to the next one. The problem with these frameworks, however, is their inherent link to an economic system based on competition and acquisitiveness. What they offer may seem to be altruistic in purpose, as various advertisements and agencies tell us how better to lead our lives, but economic concerns are the driving force meaning that the needs of the consumer-individual are always a secondary condition following profit. The other problem with consumer frameworks is their very profusion. The consumer freedom of choice turns rapidly into the existential nightmare of choosing when faced with a profusion of different options with no base from which to judge between them except the superficialities of consumerism.

In the consumer society, the idea of shopping begins to seep out of actual shops and into the very fabric of the way we live. 'Whatever we do and whatever name we attach to our activity is a kind of shopping, an activity shaped in the likeness of shopping. The code in which our "life policy" is scripted is derived from the pragmatics of shopping.'[51]

> We 'shop' for the skills needed to earn our living and for the means to convince would-be employers that we have them; for the kind of image it would be nice to wear and ways to make others believe that we are what we wear; . . . for ways of drawing attention and ways to hide from scrutiny; for the means to squeeze the most satisfaction out of love and the means to avoid becoming 'dependent' on the loved or loving partner . . .[52]

In shaping the consumer identity, society has moved away from the traditional model of the panopticon style so much in vogue in modern critical social theory in which people are conditioned to internalise certain disciplines by the feeling that they are being watched, effectively learning to police themselves.[53] As Bauman points, out the institutions of panopticism are useful only in 'training people in routine, monotonous behaviour, and reached that effect through the limitation or complete elimination of choice; but it is precisely the absence of routine and the states of constant choice that are the virtues (indeed the "role prerequisites") of a consumer.'[54] The ideal consumer should be willing and able to continually change his or her habits and routines, embracing each one on a purely temporary basis without commitment. Ideally, also the environment in which the consumer operates should be able to fulfil his or her desires instantly (as well as creating other ones), 'requiring no protracted learning of skills and no lengthy groundwork; but the satisfaction should end the moment the time needed for their consumption is up, and that time ought to be reduced to a bare minimum.'[55] These attributes of consumerism apply to shopping for identity as well as for products.

Bauman sees this consumer desire for consumable meaning as having acquired the qualities of an addiction:

> The more you do it, the more you need to do it and the unhappier you feel when deprived of fresh supplies of the sought after drugs. As a means of quenching thirst, all addictions are self destructive; they destroy the possibility of being ever satisfied.[56]

The promise of a well-adjusted life within a settled and secure self-identity therefore recedes into the distance as the existential life-project begins to seem like a journey without an end.

To sum up Bauman's conceptualisation, it can be said that the consumerisation of society has lead to a situation in which one seeks to construct one's identity through the consumer methods of 'shopping around', which permeate all the other levels of our lives. The fact that each person has to go through this process individually and under different conditions, as well as the changing face of social phenomena such as work, means that the traditional frameworks of solidarity, which might serve to underpin our sense of who we are, are undermined. We are divided from one another rather than uniting in order to find some sense of existential security.

Can we really say, however, that contemporary consumerism has made anxiety the dominant affective condition? If we go back to Lupton's socio-historical analysis discussed above, we find that she claims there has been a split between the body and the self in modern times. The self is held to be under threat from the influence of alien invasions of bodily emotions. We are 'flooded' with emotion, 'overcome', or bodily pain is externalised as a demon or monster outside of ourselves. There is a growing contradiction as time goes on, however. As the importance placed on 'knowing oneself' increases, there has been a turn to getting in touch with one's emotions. It is a testament to how far the divorce between body and self had been affected that such a notion would take such a hold.

Lutz explains that emotion has come to be placed in opposition to estrangement or disengagement from life. It is seen as more honest, authentic and human. 'In contemporary Western societies, the individual's understanding of the emotional self is an important aspect of ideas of the "real" or "true" self.'[57] This true self is something which involves some work on the individual's part to bring out.

One example of this idea was the Escalon Institute that taught people how to express their inner self and the Human Potential movement that grew out of its ideas. The claim of these movements was that one could go through various processes to strip away societal conditioning to uncover a 'true self' with which one could then live in accordance.

The Human Potential movement was superseded in the early 1970s by the ideas of Werner Erhard and his Erhard Seminars Training (est). Est conducted workshops in which people were told that the conception of an inner core of self, which had formed the basis of Human Potential, was merely another limitation and that one could be whatever one wanted. Est taught attendants, among them movie and rock stars, directors and parades of celebrities, to strip down the layers of the socially conditioned self to leave a tabula rasa on which one could create oneself anew.[58] Erhard's philosophy was that the self was not an individual personal phenomenon but rather represented the universal context upon which creative spontaneous being, not based upon the individual as ego or mind, could be born.[59] The more fixed one's identity the less experience of which one is capable[60]; for Erhard, the general problem for people was that they identified not with the self as matrix or context, but rather with one element or definition within it.[61] These ideas were a mixture of concepts drawn from 'Maxwell Maltz and Carl Rodgers, Zen, Subud, Scientology, hypnosis [and] Gestalt'.[62]

The message of est was that nothing mattered but the individually created self and hundreds of thousands went through the process in the early 1970s[63] for a range of reasons: 'to shed weight, shyness, phobia; to improve energy, self-image, appearance [and] love life'.[64] The original idea of challenging state power through individual transformation was lost and it was seen as more important that people be happy in themselves.[65] Yankelovich estimates from his research that in 1970 around 3 to 5 per cent of the American population agreed with these ideas but that by 1980 the figure had grown to around 80 per cent.[66]

It is undoubted that the individual experiences a greater degree of autonomy in relation to the habitat contrasted with former models of society. We have to be aware of two corollaries to this presumption, however. The first is what Miles calls

> 'the consuming paradox': the fact that in terms of our individual experience consumerism appears to have a fascinating, arguably fulfilling, personal appeal and yet simultaneously plays some form of an ideological role in actually *controlling* the character of everyday life. In effect, consumerism is at one and the same time, psycho-socially constraining *and* enabling . . .[67]

In other words consumerism, in theory, operates as a mechanism for completely free choice among the essentials of life, the notion that has been worked up into the market populism that we saw earlier. The fact that the items on offer are seen as essentials of life is an ideological operation of consumerism, however, as are the mechanisms by which we choose between them. The second corollary is that individual choice is presented as unavoidable, another ideological mechanism, with the emphasis on the individuality of the choice. If such choice is an exercise in individual self-creation then no one can help you be yourself. The various guides available in the habitat – magazines, consumer groups and television programmes – are all aimed at the already savvy and discerning consumer and, given the fact that they are niched to separate lifestyle groupings, one has to make a choice to begin with in selecting which are the relevant guides to one's situation.

The idea of niching gives an idea of the co-original process that is involved in consumer groupings, wherein the market creates groups and then tailors products towards them. Gunter and Furnham point to four ways in which the total market can be segmented. Firstly, we have what they call 'Physical Attribute Classification', which breaks down into geographic and demographic segmentation and, secondly, we have 'Behavioural Attribute Classification', which divides into product use and benefit segmentation and psychological segmentation on the basis of personality inventories or lifestyle analysis. Given the problems with the relatively superficial data of the physical attribute grouping and its inability to explain why two identical households exhibit radically different patterns of consumption, researchers turned to a deeper understanding of market segmentation by introducing the idea of lifestyling.

A lifestyle is defined as that pattern or construct by which people live and spend their time and money and which helps them interpret and control their environment. In its original form, psychographics linked lifestyle with the value system of the consumer but whereas the values of a specific set of consumers are fairly rigid the lifestyle patterns which reflect them are more malleable and open to change. The creative forces behind lifestyles are the 'cultural transfusive triad' (referring to institutional influences such as family, religion and school) and early lifetime experiences (referring to 'basic intergenerational influences such as depressions, wars and other major events').[68]

VALS (Values and Lifestyles) is one system of classification which utilises Maslow's needs hierarchy to assign people to one of nine segments on the basis of values and lifestyles. Maslow's influence is also found in the underlying belief that people are constantly improving themselves during their lifetime, a process which in turn influences their values and lifestyle choices. The VALS segments reflect this, comprising an upward momentum through the broad categories from Need-Driven through Outer- and Inner-Directed phases to the Integrated phase (the first three being subdivided to make up the nine categories). The Integrated phase is one of psychological maturity in which one fully realises one's own potential. In consumer terms, Need-Driven people are at the bottom of the hierarchy, comprising those who live in relative poverty with a consequent narrowing of choice and psychological goals. The greatest portion of the market is represented by the Outer-Directed segments who generally buy on the basis of what others will attribute to their choices. The Inner-Directed groups represent a smaller share of both the population and the market, being more individualistically directed in their consumption choices, but are important in that they may be 'trend-setters or groups through whom successful ideas and products trickle up'. In demographic terms, the Inner-Directed group is the fastest growing with the Outer-Directed group holding steady and the Need-Driven diminishing.[69]

A new system has been developed by Stanford Research Institute (SRI), updating the original VALS to deal with the fact that the link between values and lifestyles seems to be weakening. The reasons for this weakening have been presented as manifold by SRI, including the increasing diversity of the population, the globalised economy and a decline in consumer's expectations for the future. 'Combined with the increasing diversity of products, distribution and of media, values and lifestyles had become too fragmented to predict consumer behaviour.'[70]

The new system seeks to uncover stable psychological stances rather than fluid values or lifestyles. It classifies subjects along two axes, the vertical representing their resources (including education, income, self-confidence, health and intelligence) and ranging from minimal to abundant, and the horizontal representing their self-orientation. Self-orientation refers to whether they are principle-orientated (guided by their view on how the world should be), status-orientated (guided by the actions and opinions of others) or action-orientated (guided by a desire for activity, variety and risk taking). Each of these orientations is then subdivided by the vertical axis into two segments, one with high resources and the other with low. The six segments are, unlike the segments in the first VALS, roughly equal in size.[71]

What does this shift from the original VALS to the new version represent in a broader sense? It may be remembered that the Inner-Directed group was the fastest growing segment in the original system. The growth of this group could be said to account in a lot of ways for the breakdown of the first VALS system and the need for an updated version. The Inner-Directeds are the most individualistic of the segments, ranging from the fiercely individual *I-Am-Me* of around 20 years old through the *Experientials* who, as the name suggests, seek personal experience of many areas of life, to the *Societally Conscious* group who have a highly developed social morality and seek to improve the world.[72] The triumph of this segment of society could be seen as the reason why there is a weakening in the link between values and lifestyles and a growing fluidity in both.

By 'triumph' I am not alluding to any quasi-Marxist idea that the Inner-Directed group be seen as the new bourgeoisie. Rather this triumph could have come about through the tailoring of consumerism towards the defining characteristics of this segment. The growth of emphasis on individual identity would seem to support this and, although the whole VALS system can be seen to rest on a very individualistic Maslowian foundation, it extols the more militant version of individuality of the Inner-Directed group in that one should be true to one's self and stand out from the crowd, proud enough to ignore what everyone else says. The marketing of individuality is important not only for the Inner-Directed segment of the population but also the Outer-Directed who will fuel consumerism by buying to keep up. This idea also feeds into that of market populism with the market being seen as the ultimate democratic tool from an immediate individual point of view, with the consequent neo-liberal distrust of any form of institutional interference in personal choice. The war cry of consumer capitalism at the minute is that of individuality amongst diversity.

We can now look at some of the ways in which consumerism seeks to promote its ideology. This is an ideology that must operate on two fronts. Firstly, we must accept individualistic self-creation as a legitimate psychological fact (we must accept that our choice of jeans in some way feeds into who we are on a psycho-social level) and, secondly, in the competitive arena of the market place, we must be convinced that a particular product is to be preferred over the others on offer.

Harris suggests we must discuss consumerism at the most basic visceral level.

> Shoppers and moviegoers do not know capitalism from the standpoint of Hegelian dialectics and Althusserian Marxism, of plummeting prime interest rates and spurts of growth in the Gross National Product, but rather from the perspective of the sensations caused by the vibrant colours of labels, the enticing rhetoric on packages, and the dewy-eyed beauty of actresses in romantic comedies.[73]

It is at this level that we must begin our analytic of consumerism's impact on the individual, at 'this moment of engagement, of seduction, the very instant our neurons begin to fire.'[74] Harris defines what he refers to as the 'aesthetics of consumerism' as standing in opposition to the sensuality inferred by the traditional usage of aesthetics. Consumer aesthetics are made to be 'ascetic and cerebral, incorporeal illusions designed to stir up dissatisfaction, to provoke restless longings that cannot be fulfilled.'[75] They represent an artistic form manufactured for a specific purpose outside their presentation through aesthetic media. This purpose is, of course, to sell products and in advertising; this is achieved through building up mythologies of how clean one's house should be and what car one needs to drive to be defined a certain way.

Of course the mythologies can never be translated into the mundanity of the everyday world. The unlikely scenario in which product *x* does actually fulfil our dreams is unthinkable from a market perspective, because why then would we buy product *y*? Hence, there is the need for consumerism to manufacture desire and discontent and to keep them both insatiable.

This is a very subtle balance to strike in the public mind, however. The consumer ideology rests on the premise that capitalism can insti the psychology of individual self-creation and must hold out i various products as the means of doing so. What is to stop people adopting the first half of this ideology and jettisoning the second? If we begin to believe that we are all individuals engaged in self construction, why would we need the artificial props of the marke place with which to create our identity? Advertisers must constantly battle against the cynicism that they themselves have helped create: if we believe in individualism too much we will stop buying on the basi of self-discontent.

> One of the primary functions of the aesthetic of consumerism is to provid us with an emotional cushion, a form of camouflage, a credible disguis for a culture that refuses to admit the truth about itself, that sel righteously insists on its own anti-consumerism even when enjoying th luxuries and conveniences of mass production.[76]

Consumerism must present its products as standing outside (o even against) what is regarded as the mainstream of a vastly com mercialised culture. As consumers buy the various products on offe in massive, generic stores they must, to some degree, believe tha rather than being coerced to do so by what everyone of right min knows is the insidiousness of the advertising industry and the herc like demands of consumer culture, we are asserting our individualit against the system. 'Consumerism has created the perfect disguise fc conformity: rebelliousness.'[77] We must be convinced that our sense c individual self is brought into being through the purchase of mas produced goods fitting us into mass-produced consumer lifesty moulds (of which the 'rebel' is probably the most popular, both o the part of the consumer and the market). But this process must b made to look like we are in control and that we have chosen to fulfil ourselves in this fashion. In Chapter 1, it was claimed that our conscious self is our 'user illusion' of ourselves; to extend this we can claim that consumerism is the user illusion of our conscious self and operates in much the same way.

A useful tool in analysing how consumerism sells its desired aesthetics is provided by Robert Goldman. Goldman presents a framework for examining adverts derived from the Marxist idea of the commodity form. In essence, what an advert does is to remove an activity from the social context that gives it meaning and reterritorialise it in a different meaning framework. For Goldman, adverts recontextualise the social meaning on to products to enhance their exchange value. 'Ads arrange, organise and steer *meanings* into *signs* that can be inscribed on products – always geared to transferring one meaning system to another.'[78] Corporations discovered at a certain point that their goods were not selling on the basis of their use value alone because of the danger of product saturation in a culture in which people could conceivably acquire all that they *needed*. The growing sophistication of marketing on the basis of desire meant that products had to acquire an external exchange value aside from their quantification in financial terms. This has resulted in a wider range of products than ever before being seen as status symbols or as defining people in terms of certain other social categories (in terms of 'cool', for example).

In order for this to take place, the product must be seen in terms of the meaning frame on which its marketing is based:

> The semiotic reductionism necessary for producing a currency of commodity-signs involves transforming complex meaningful relations into visual signifiers. It then turns the relationship between the signifier and the signified into one of equivalence, so that the visual signifier can be substituted for the signified of the product.[79]

The social meaning frame of wealth is transposed on to a Rolex watch in such a way that not only does the watch actually come to signify wealth, but in some ways to be wealthy necessarily entails ownership of that particular watch.

As said earlier, Goldman interprets consumerism from a specifically Marxist standpoint. He claims that consumerism, or more specifically the commodification of all things and actions that go with it, justifies the bourgeois public sphere by reinterpreting the proletarian public sphere in its own terms, effectively plundering the latter for its meaning frames and then selling these back to the proletariat at the level of consumer products. 'Individuality is now derived from the goods people consume and how they appear.'[80] Whether or not one agrees that this is a result of the machinations of the middle classes for the purposes of establishing an ideological hegemony in the cultural sphere and reproducing wage relations at the level of culture, consumed individuality is certainly the stage we have reached.

Indeed, I am wary of a Marxist slant that would place too much emphasis on class in that it minimises the effects of consumed identity for social stratifications other than class. There are a lot of groups in society who are excluded from the consumer framework: the 'flawed consumers' in Bauman's parlance. They are left in the position of being fed consumer ideology through having their cultures mined for meaning frames to sell products, but not having the means to buy back these identities because of their economic position. It is the 'new' middle classes who are the ones who form the bulk of actual consumers of the products and are able to buy into consumer lifestyles. Economically less able elements in society can only buy into the desire but not its material fulfilment. Those who can seek material satiation of desire face a different problem in their inability ever to reach satisfaction, with the resulting lock into seeking more/other goods. These groups, the new middle class and the underclass of flawed consumers, are outside the traditional Marxist class template in that their identity is not linked to the means of production but rather to patterns of consumption.

The problem is that it is not the product that we consume but the sign, therefore it is not primarily the production of the commodity that concerns us, rather it is the consumption of the sign. To get access to the sign, however, we must buy the product. Good examples of the way this process links into our previous discussion on consumer aesthetics are provided by Roland Barthes. In one example, Barthes describes the use of foam in detergent adverts:

> As for foam, it is well known that it signifies luxury. To begin with, it appears to lack any usefulness; then, its abundant, easy, almost infinite proliferation allows one to suppose there is in the substance from which it issues a vigorous germ, a healthy and powerful essence, a great wealth of active elements in a small original volume. Finally, it gratifies in the consumer a tendency to imagine matter as something airy, which is sought after like that of happiness.[81]

Barthes referred to the arbitrary connection between signified (the product) and signifier (the images associated with it) in consumer aesthetics as the creation of a mythology around the product. The mythologies can be changed in line with marketing demands, one example being his discussion of the move from a mythology built around speed to one concerning the 'relish of driving' in Citroën adverts.[82]

The theorisation of the commodity sign is given a Marxist slant in the early work of Baudrillard, with the idea that the capitalist move to mass production is achieved by the final subsuming of use value by exchange value in terms of the latter taking on the arbitrary form of a Saussurean sign.[83] This fluid exchange value, because it is no longer tied to a product in anything other than the purely symbolic sense, is able to seep out into social relations, in effect commodifying them.

Goldman posits three ways in which the commodification affects society. Firstly, it universalises social relations by imposing on them universal market standards and codes that quantify human qualities, abstracting them from their context. 'Abstracted individuals and relationships are those in which means (consumption) and ends (whatever consumption yields) have no relation other than that provided by the commodity.'[84] In adverts, we see this exhibited by social exchanges which seem to revolve solely around the product and which seemingly derive their meaning from it. The friendly conversation only made possible by a specific brand of coffee, for example:

> Commodified relations have no clear end, no specific aim: why one would want to acquire the quality 'sexy' is not the point. Sexiness is separated from the total social situation of which it is really a part and situated within a new context provided by the commodity.[85]

Commodification also serves to atomise social relations. It has the effect of disconnecting patterns and bonds of social exchange and reframing them within the context of a specific product. The consequence of this disconnection, or subsumption of use value by exchange value in Baudrillard's terms, is that things come to be seen on equal terms as interchangables, which can be substituted for each other at will. We can change our mood whenever we like with the simple use of an air freshener whose scent will either invigorate or relax us. The process works for individuals as well, dislocating them from the social frameworks from which they once gained meaning and then presenting the catalogue of interchangeable, personally tailored possibilities to fill in the gaps left by atomisation. In the context of perfume, Goldman points out how smell has been divorced from its natural context and used as a second order signifier attached to a variety of moods, experiences and personal qualities.[86] In advertising, the personal pronouns used in the text and speech of adverts hold out the promise of what he calls, after Adorno, a pseudo-individuality to every consumer both individually and at the same time: the consumer, as one among many, is promised the means to become an individual.[87]

Lastly, the prevalence of the commodity form in society has a reifying effect. Different parts of the body are presented in isolation in advertising, demanding their own unique attention to make them stand out on their own. Events and experiences are also reified and sold as individual items mediated by a particular product. 'Advertisements thus separate the intrinsic qualities of being human from actual living humans. The link can be restored only by the purchase of the commodity.'[88]

We can see how these three elements interlink in the process of selling pseudo-individuality. For an advert to work it must posit a relationship between a single unit of a mass-produced product and any one of the many consumers who come in contact with the advert. It must separate the individual consumer from all of their personal history and context in order to promise that the product will have a uniform effect on all who buy it. All the units in a manufacturing run of the product are identical and the problem that advertisers face is to market the same product to many individuals who will read the advert in different ways. The particular part of life in relation to which the advert frames its meaning is atomised and reified, as is the potential consumer, and then the experience between them is universalised. The social nature of individuality is denied through the presumption that one can achieve it through purchasing a series of consumer products.[89] The polysemic nature of adverts, the fact that because of the ultimately arbitrary connection between signifier and signified, they can be interpreted in different ways by different consumers, does not militate against the strategies of advertisers. Rather if consumers can draw an individual message then this is even better for a marketing strategy based on diversity and individualism. As long as it is these two ideas that come across, the consumer can fill in his or her own meanings.

We have now a basic grasp of the mechanics of consumerism: the idea of the aesthetic, its manufacture of individuality and its contradictions, and the mechanic of the commodity form, both in terms of the commodification of human qualities and events and its wider repercussions for individual selves and social relations. As was stated earlier, adverts are the mechanism by which the market manufactures and communicates desire to the individual consumer.

The effect of consumerism is to hold out to the consumer a consumable persona. This is through both a network of linked goods providing the props for a certain lifestyle and the promise that a single product can change one's whole life. Through the reframing of meaning, one buys not a jar of coffee but sophistication, desirability or sociability; fundamental shifts in self-identity.

One way this can be theorised is through the concept of the 'persona' in its etymological meaning of a mask. In the context of his discussions on postmodern tribalism, Shields identifies a 'reflexive configuration of the body and psyche'.[90] Whilst this is certainly a form of individualism, he argues that it is set apart from the neo-liberal variety by its connection to 'expression, body-centredness, and . . . a social and spatial milieu.'[91] He analyses this 'logic of identification' primarily through the medium of spatial connection to certain sites of consumption, but his comments hold in general terms to the commodified self:

> A *logic of identity* is replaced by a more superficial, tactile *logic of identification*; individuals become more mask-like *personae* . . . with mutable selves . . . Their multiple identifications form a private *dramatis personae* – a self which can no longer be simplistically theorised as unified, or based solely on an individuals job or productive function . . . Consumption for adornment, expression and group solidarity become not merely the means to a lifestyle, but the enactment of a lifestyle, these *personae* are more like spiders at the centre of social and stylistic webs of their own making which extend the body in space, rather than the autonomous, disconnected and monadic ego-centred identities of bourgeois individuals. It is thus that one may properly argue that the reliance on group-imposed and endowed personal identifications represents a breakdown [in] individualism even in the midst of the motion towards identification.[92]

What we have left behind is the idea of stability and continuity of selfhood. The dissolution of many social ties and networks can be tied to the globalisation of consumer culture and the spread of the idea of diversity and individuality, which have an effect of undermining community ties and positing transcendental bases of identification through consumerism. This can be theorised, not as the disappearance of the situated self, but as the multiplication of the sites of situation in relation to which the self must be constructed. Bauman claims that postmodern consumer society disrupts the temporal flow of life through a focus on instantaneity, in essence performing Goldman's three operations of universalisation, atomisation and reification on the idea of time and linearity as are performed on society.

The above discussions can now lead us to an understanding of how, through the commodification of time and society, we have reached a point of commodification of self-identity in which the effects of universalisation, atomisation and reification on the self can be seen as manifest in the idea of the persona. The situational self is split in terms of the multiple and fragmented sites in which it must relate to others. In some ways, this is akin to the ideas of theorists such as Goffman, with his positing of the self as a series of social roles, and Gergen, who sees the self as a plastic, situationally adaptable entity.

This would correspond with our earlier discussions of what the conscious self actually represents. It was suggested in Chapter 1 that the self be seen as the situational projection of an essentially nonconscious mind. This manifests itself in consumer society as the persona, related, on the one hand, to a multiplication of sites of reference and, on the other, to consumerism's reterritorialisation of meaning. In the consumption of different products, we are fitting a variety of different personae. Some products even facilitate this multiple persona aspect within themselves: mobile phones with interchangeable snap-on faces for the 'sophisticated' or 'playful' look, for example, or the car that can bring out different elements of one's personality as the situation requires. When one multiplies these effects across the number of items and brands we consume, the number of personae we buy into are quite numerous.

At this point, we can summarise the effects which consumerisation has on self-identity. First is the fragmentation of core sites of communal and traditional identity through the prevalence of commodity culture and the effects that the commodity form has. Second is the substitution of these sites with the market and the various products it holds out, Bauman's habitat. This entails the inculcation of a new form of identity construction, with reference to products framed with meaning in a brand structure in such a way that the actual product falls by the wayside and its symbolism takes over as the primary exchange value. The mining and selling back of cultural meaning by brands has the effect of further fragmenting cultural identities and transplanting them to the arena of consumerism. The presentation of these branded identities leads to their equivalence in the catalogue of consumable possibilities and has the effect of endowing us with multiple partial identities or 'personae'.

We have come from a point wherein the VALS system was able to identify different personality types and market products accordingly to the current situation in which one element of the VALS hierarchy has come to be valorised in the concepts of individuality and diversity. It is within the matrix of manufactured diversity that the contemporary sense of self is formed, as a reflection of the habitat in which it finds itself. Presented with a catalogue of equally viable possibilities we end up with a self which is a catalogue of fractured personae, seen either in terms of their relation to different products or using concatenations of different products as props for shaping personae to deal with various situations. All three – selves, products and social situations – have become commodified and operate under the logic of the commodity form, the first as personae, the second as branded symbols, and the third as stages for the deployment of the other two.

Like Bauman, Langman feels this commodification of self induces negative psychological effects and emotions. She claims that the 'compartmentalization, decentering and enfeeblement of diverse expressions of selfhood' lead to feelings of fragmentation and isolation, which she crystallises in the form of panic and envy.[93] Panic is the result of moments of anxiety caused by reflection on the emptiness and loneliness of commodified gratifications of selfhood. This corresponds with Bauman's analysis of the individual nature of the responsibility for one's choices in consumer society and the resulting existential angst, especially in terms of unguided choices regarding identity.

Langman sees postmodern envy not in terms of coveting another person's goods but in coveting their sense of subjectivity. This idea connects to the discussion in the next chapter on Lacan and the idea of the mirror self as a way of conceptualising the search for a unified self amidst others who seem far more together. The advent of consumerism and commodification can be seen to play into these feelings by promising quick-fix solutions in the form of personae that one can step into or out of.

On a more general level, we can analyse the conception of self that consumerism works on as an essentially reflexive one. It was claimed previously, that the perfect consumer is one who can be relied upon to follow every trend that comes along and to forget the previous one in the process. We will encounter the horizontal nature of consumer-lived time in the next chapter. The effect of the commodity form on the idea of time, as well as mechanisms of capitalist production, converge along with the effects of consumer-meaning construction on self-formation, to give us a reflexive picture of self.

We can now bring together the ideas of this chapter with the idea of self built up in the previous discussions, in order to critique the effects that the logic of consumer capitalism has on our sense of self. The idea of reflexivity rests on a sense of self-identity that is essentially malleable and constantly monitoring and readjusting itself in line with external situations. These externalities can be the views of others, expressed or perceived, significant or otherwise, as well as objective and non-judgemental sources of non-normative information that change our patterns by stimulating reflection.

In *Modernity and Self: Self and Society in the Late Modern Age*, Antony Giddens theorises this reflexivity as being a reflection of the institutional reflexivity of modern society. He claims that modernity functions to disembed many of the taken-for-granteds of previous times, illustrating his point with the separation of conceptions of space and time from each other, the disembedding mechanisms that separate social interaction from locale and institutional reflexivity utilising constant streams of information about the world.[94] He also points to a 'sequestration of experience' by late modern institutions, which serves to shroud existential questions relating to identity and life through the creation of internally referential systems in civil society and administration that preclude any overarching moral framework acting as an orientation point for evaluation.[95]

In terms of self-identity, Giddens proceeds from 'the premise that to be a human being is to know, virtually all of the time, in terms of some description or another, both what one is doing and why one is doing it'.[96] He does, however, introduce the concept of 'practical consciousness', a subconscious understanding of everyday tasks which serves to bracket off anxiety from everyday life and which is part of a reflexive self-monitoring of action. This practical consciousness leads to a state of ontological security.[97] Whereas, however, practical consciousness is built up through habit and routine in early infancy, which leads to a sense of trust in others, for the self to become fully rounded in later life it must learn to act creatively.[98]

On an existential level, we are forever plagued, Giddens claims, by the looming threat of meaningless because we encounter central life questions within the framework of the internally referential systems mentioned above. These systems, though they offer technical solutions to life's problems, offer them from a non-normative perspective that does not provide a unified framework with which to assess our entire life. One of the threats to the self in late modernity is that of fragmentation. However, Giddens does not hold this to be a particularly pressing concern. 'A person may make use of diversity in order to create a distinctive self-identity which positively incorporates elements from different settings into an integrated narrative.'[99] He also points to the unifying effects of modernity through the collapsing of temporal space and the globalisation of abstract systems (media of exchange and systems of technical knowledge).[100] Giddens sees self-identity as being a constantly created reflexive project which takes the form of a trajectory through life (not in the Hegelian sense but in the sense deployed in self-help literature that one must 'keep going'). A continuous sense of self is maintained through a reflexive autobiographical narrative that utilises the material of social and cultural environment:[101]

> A person with a reasonably stable sense of self-identity has a feeling of biographical continuity which she is able to grasp reflexively and, to a greater or lesser degree, communicate to other people. That person also, through early trust relations, has established a protective cocoon which 'filters out', in the practical conduct of day-to-day life, many of the dangers which in principle threaten the integrity of the self.[102]

What we have in Giddens' assessment is the belief in a positive narrative resolution to the sorts of existential dilemmas presented in the foregoing discussion and with the individual encountering the contemporary world in the form of a reflexive narrative. Giddens believes that there is still the possibility inherent in our society to arrive at a coherent vision of selfhood based on the idea of self garnered from the profusion of self-help literature which has saturated Euro-American culture.[103]

What the analysis of the latter half of the present chapter has given us, however, founded on the basis of Bauman's *unsicherheit*, is a set of tools for a deeper set of claims. The reflexive self expressed as a trajectory in need of constant monitoring is not the way in which we deal with consumer society; it is the form of self which consumerism specifically holds out to us as an ideal type. Giddens is right to examine the existential problems which modern society creates through its sequestration of experience and disembedding mechanisms. What he fails to do, however, is to critique the type of self-identity which grows out of this situation, a fact, due in part, to his failure to engage the prevalence and effect of consumerism in contemporary society.

Both Bauman and Giddens agree that modern existential angst is engendered by contemporary forms of freedom. What Bauman adds to the equation is his identification of this freedom with the freedom of the consumer market, which has come to present itself as the ultimate type with the advent of market populism and diversity marketing.

At every step of the way, we find the market operating on both sides of the equation, both manufacturing desire and the supposed means to its satisfaction. It performs the function of both destroying old formations of meaning and stepping into the vacuum thus created to provide new ones. It creates the sense of lack through the creation of desire and its existential imperative, holds out the promise of fulfilment through its products and then ensures that the cycle never ends through making sure the latter cannot ease the former but merely exacerbates it. As Judith Williamson puts it, consumerism creates 'a real need – but [which is] falsely fulfilled: in fact sustained by its perpetual unfulfilment'.[104]

The very philosophy that lies behind the self-help literature which Giddens alludes to, is based on that of individualist self-actualisation – which the present market formation was built on and which had its roots in movements such as est.[105] The existence of self-help literature is a good example of the way in which the market creates the existential imperative of individual responsibility for self-formation, and then creates products to facilitate the process. Lasch comments that in the face of anxiety people now seek 'peace of mind under conditions that increasingly militate against it'.[106] The idea of therapy has moved out of the psychologist's office and into the book shop and the talk show. Both problem and solution now obey the logic of the commodity form and post-Freudian therapists now advocate mental health through 'the overthrow of inhibitions and the immediate gratification of every impulse.'[107]

What we have at the end of this chapter is the means to analyse more closely how the process of conscious self-creation, based on the means of articulation available in our background culture, can lead to the condition of *unsicherheit*. One of the primary reasons for this eventuality is the fact that our contemporary background culture is governed to a large extent by the market, which has come to act as the mediator of other cultural formations and which acts on an imperative of individual self-creation itself. Unlike other cultural formations such as the historical community or religion, the market does not exist for the purpose of helping people make sense of their world. It exists to make people money. Rather than help with self-identity by providing crutches for individual and social meaning, it serves the interests of the consumer market to inculcate the imperative of the individual self and then market products towards it that work on the basis of a perceived Lacanian lack at the heart of our individual existence. The information in this chapter has provided an account of the context in which this situation has come about and some of the mechanics by which it perpetuates itself.

The contemporary form that the idea of the individual self takes and the way in which it is deployed in the world are both market constructs and it is for this reason that the condition of *unsicherheit* is created. We do not need the overly conscious totalising conception of identity which the market holds out to us and which causes within us the experiences of desire and lack. We experience lack precisely because, in the consumer context, it is an artificially constructed idea which we do not necessarily need and which the way in which we function mentally may indeed preclude. As well as this, the functioning of a profusion of products, each holding out overlapping and often contradictory matrices of meaning, serves to frustrate the enterprise of conscious identity formation in line with market imperatives when we do act on the feelings of lack and desire.

The market can be seen to both extol a certain form of totalising commodity-biographical whole-life story whilst simultaneously frustrating its construction. The type of reflexive narrative that Giddens suggests is still too reliant on the conscious self-actualisation model of human functioning to assuage the effects of *unsicherheit* since it still, to a large extent, facilitates its emergence. What the combination of the nonconscious ideas in the first chapter and the analysis of consumer logic in the present may point to is that *unsicherheit* may not be overcome through any type of conscious narrativisation of our lives, be it autobiographical or commodity-biographical, totalising whole-life story or reflexive narrative.

If the function of a 'self' is to allow us to make sense of the social world in a way that facilitates our movement through it in terms of relating to our environment, we may see how consumer ideology frustrates this process. Consumerism creates the idea that we must have a consciously created and constantly monitored sense of individual self, which it then provides the tools to create. These tools, however, through the processes described above, all vie through meaning totalisation to stretch their product concepts across our entire life and self-definition. The result is a profusion of horizontal definitions that frustrate the idea of a conscious unified identity on the basis of which these products are bought. The self-help literature to which Giddens refers seeks to help us toward this unification but does not ask the question of whether the problem lies in the frustration of unified self-identity, or one's self-identity going off course, or whether it lies in the very fact that this is an artificial dream in the first place. The fact that consumerism works not on the fulfilment of desire but its exacerbation only serves to add to this situation.

Giddens is right that the self is reflexive, but this reflexivity extends only to the conscious entity and not what should be the reflexive relation between the conscious and nonconscious elements of our mentality. This reflexivity, following Norretranders, should accept that we do not need to be consciously self-inventing all the time. *Unsicherheit* lies not in the fact that we have not found the right product yet (as consumerism tells us), or that we must look to our inner authentic self and not artificial props such as products or the opinions of others (as the self-help people tell us), but that all such attempts are artificial in the sense that the self is a construct and not a mental inherency. The reason for suspicion of consumerism lies not in that it frustrates authenticity, which without its intervention we would be able to attain, but that it manufactures the idea and then leads us into spirals of self-perpetuating desire trying to achieve it.

This chapter has served to introduce another level to the psychological picture we have been building up. Emotion and affect are also useful concepts that link together societal influence and nonconscious processing and conditioning of action. In the next chapter, we shall again switch the focus back to conscious self-identity, without however losing sight of the nonconscious processes that underlie it.

Notes

1. James, 'What is an emotion?' and *The Principles of Psychology*.
2. For a good summary of the problems with James' position, see Dixon *From Passions to Emotions*, pp. 214–16.
3. LeDoux, *The Emotional Brain*, pp. 47–8.
4. Ibid. pp. 50–1.
5. Damasio, *The Feeling of What Happens*, pp. 67–8.
6. Ibid. p. 281.
7. LeDoux, *The Emotional Brain*, p. 19.
8. Ibid. p. 164.
9. Damasio, *The Feeling of What Happens*, p. 41.
10. Damasio, *Descartes' Error*, Ch. 8.
11. Damasio, *The Feeling of What Happens*, pp. 43–7.
12. Ibid. p. 51.
13. Darwin, *The Expression of the Emotions*.
14. Cited in Goldie, *The Emotions*, p. 87.

15. Dixon, *From Passions to Emotions*, p. 18.
16. Goldie, *The Emotions*, p. 89.
17. LeDoux, *The Emotional Brain*, p. 118.
18. Goldie, *The Emotions*, p. 90.
19. For examples of all these problems, see ibid. p. 91.
20. Dixon, *From Passions to Emotions*, Ch. 4.
21. Dixon, *From Passions to Emotions*, p. 246.
22. R. Harré quoted in Lupton, *The Emotional Self*, p. 16.
23. Ibid.
24. Kitayama and Markus, *Emotion and Culture*, p. 5.
25. Ibid. p. 6.
26. Ellsworth, 'Sense, culture and sensibility' in Kitayama and Markus, *Emotion and Culture*, pp. 26–7.
27. Many early social constructivists in the anthropology of emotion such as Michelle Rosaldo and Catherine Lutz explicitly draw on Schachter and Singer.
28. Geertz, *The Interpretation of Culture*.
29. Lutz, *Unnatural Emotion*, p. 7, quoting Dreyfus and Rabinow, *Michel Foucault: Beyond Structuralism and Hermeneutics*, p. xxvi.
30. Lupton, *The Emotional Self*, p. 32.
31. Ibid. p. 72.
32. Ibid. p. 77. See Elias, *The Civilising Process*.
33. Ibid. p. 82.
34. Reddy, *The Navigation of Feeling*, p. 172.
35. Ibid. p. 210.
36. Ibid. pp. 122–3.
37. Ibid. p. 127.
38. Bauman, *Intimations of Postmodernity*, p. 188 (author's emphasis).
39. Ibid. p. 187.
40. Ibid. p. 188.
41. Ibid. p. 191.
42. Ibid. p. 191.
43. Ibid. p. 191.
44. Ibid. p. 193.
45. This can be seen as quite a controversial claim, which does not receive much elucidation from Bauman. It may be, however, that the discussion on the fluid nature of the self, contained in the present work, serves to give it a plausible psychological base.
46. Bauman, *Intimations*, p. 194.
47. Ibid. p. 195.
48. Bauman, *In Search of Politics*, p. 16.
49. Ibid. p. 17. It would be interesting, but beyond the scope of this book, to investigate the relationship between *unsicherheit* and Alvin Toffler's 'future shock', 'the shattering stress and disorientation that we induce

in individuals by subjecting them to too much change in too short a time'. Toffler, *Future Shock*, p. 4.

50. Bauman, *In Search of Politics*, p. 17.
51. Bauman, *Liquid Modernity*, p. 74.
52. Ibid. p. 74.
53. The prime example being the discussion of panopticism, in Foucault, *Discipline and Punish*, pp. 195–231.
54. Bauman, *Work, Consumerism and the New Poor*, p. 24. It may be suggested, however, that the distinction is not as clear-cut as Bauman makes it since Foucault could argue that the panopticon may create an autonomous individual since it functions on the idea of utilising free choice in order to get individuals to discipline themselves through their own actions.
55. Ibid. p. 25.
56. Bauman, *Liquid Modernity*, p. 72.
57. Lupton, *The Emotional Self*, p. 89.
58. For personal accounts of the experience of est training, see Rhinehart, *The Book of est*, and Frederick, *est*.
59. Bartley, *Werner Erhard*, p. 181.
60. Ibid. p. 182.
61. Ibid. p. 184.
62. Ibid. p. xix.
63. Bartley quotes the statistic of 132,000 people having graduated from E.S.T. training by 1978 with a further 41,000 graduates expected by the end of that year and an expected 50,000 in 1979. Bartley, *Werner Erhard*, p. xiv.
64. Ibid. p. xv.
65. Lasch cites the experiences of ex-sixties radicals, such as Jerry Rubin of the Yippies, in the seventies, as they moved from communal calls for societal change to concentrating on personal therapy for their individual benefit. Lasch, *Culture of Narcissism*, p. 44.
66. *The Century of the Self, episode 3, 'There is a policeman inside all our heads'*, television programme, Curtis.
67. Miles, *Consumerism as a Way of Life*, p. 5. Miles uses 'psycho-social' in a slightly different way than I do to emphasise consumerism as a bridge linking the individual and society. It is an interesting parallel, however, in that he also advocates a sociology of lived experience to study the phenomenon, although not in the methodologically extended sense that I have outlined. With his view of consumerism as potentially enabling or fulfilling, Miles also has a more positive view of the consuming process than do I, the argument of this work is that consumerism presents itself as such but cannot be so because of its internal tension between its existential imperative and its mechanics of fulfilment.
68. Ibid. p. 65.

69. Ibid. p. 74.
70. Ibid. p. 80.
71. Ibid. pp. 81–2.
72. Ibid. pp. 75–6.
73. Harris, *Cute, Quaint, Hungry and Romantic*, pp. xiv–xv.
74. Ibid. p. xv.
75. Ibid. p. xix.
76. Ibid. p. xxi.
77. Ibid. p. xxiii.
78. Goldman, *Reading Ads Socially*, p. 5 (author's italics).
79. Ibid. p. 6. This is, of course, the process described by Barthes in his *Mythologies*.
80. Goldman, *Reading Ads Socially*, p. 17.
81. Barthes, *Mythologies*, p. 37.
82. Ibid. p. 89.
83. Baudrillard, *The Mirror of Production*.
84. Goldman, *Reading Ads Socially*, p. 24.
85. Ibid. p. 24.
86. Ibid. p. 27.
87. Ibid. p. 29.
88. Ibid. p. 31.
89. Ibid. p. 56.
90. Shields, *Lifestyle Shopping*, pp. 15–16.
91. Ibid. p. 16.
92. Ibid. p. 16.
93. Langman, 'Neon cages: shopping for subjectivity', in Shields, *Lifestyle Shopping*, p. 68.
94. Giddens, *Modernity and Self*, pp. 16–21.
95. Ibid. pp. 145, 149–55.
96. Ibid. p. 35.
97. Ibid. pp. 36–7.
98. Ibid. p. 41.
99. Ibid. p. 190.
100. Ibid. pp. 189, 27.
101. Ibid. pp. 52, 55.
102. Ibid. p. 54.
103. Ibid. pp. 76–80.
104. Williamson, *Decoding Advertisements*, p. 9.
105. The roots of the idea of the *aesthetic* creation of self can be traced back further to such concepts as Baudelaire's Flaneur and early nineteenth century English dandyism. Featherstone, *Consumer Culture and Postmodernism*, p. 67.
106. Lasch, *Culture of Narcissism*, p. 42.
107. Ibid. p. 43.

4

Endlessly Repeating Ourselves: Narrative and Self-Repetition

With our satanic question ever in sight, one of our main concerns must be the possibility of change. To think differently, for creative thought to occur, there must be change: at the psychological level and then projected out into the world. The question of breaking out of the confines of the influence of genetic mental structure and socialisation is also a question of how patterns of thought may change. This then is the relation that the present chapter bears to the rest of the book: our experience of time is the experience of change, primarily in terms of linearity, through autobiographical narrative with regard to ourselves and historical narrative with regard to the outside world.

The present chapter shall use the notion of the circularity of time at the microlevel of mental action (as per Libet), and build up to the folded nature of memory and narrative constantly going back and reinterpreting the past in light of present and future circumstances. The question then becomes whether such circularity can somehow combine with linearity to help us effect change at the political level. It is in this regard that Deleuze's concepts of difference and repetition will be discussed at the close of the chapter.

The neuropsychological material in Chapter 1, along with that on the emotions in the last chapter, combine to give us a model of mental temporality which is in many ways counterintuitive to our ideas of the relation between thought and action. In Chapter 1, Libet's studies indicated that conscious thought followed an action instead of initiating it. This was expanded upon by Gazzaniga and Le Doux's study of P. S. in which the linguistic left hemisphere of the boy's brain invented an explanation for an action carried out by the other hemisphere:

> We all feel that the conscious verbal self is not always privy to the origins of our actions, and when it observes the person behaving for unknown reasons, it attributes cause to the action as if it knows but in fact it does not. It is as if the verbal self looks out and sees what the person is doing and from that knowledge interprets a reality.[1]

Gazzaniga later characterised this function as being that of an 'interpreter', a device that creates the illusion of conscious control by interpreting present actions in terms of past events and memories. As previously highlighted, the location of this device in the linguistic side of the brain shows its intimate connection with language and marks it out as a distinctly social function.

This can be linked to the discussion of emotion in the previous chapter. Again, we have the idea that some feelings and actions are beyond conscious control, that the neurobiology of emotion, with its physiological and neurological effect, serves to greatly influence our thought and action. This was linked to our social environment, through the idea that different societies have different emotional structures and regimes, before an examination of what emotional regime may underlie contemporary consumer society: the existential imperative to individual self-creation through consumption.

We have, therefore, a picture in which nonconscious functioning, one major aspect of which is emotion, initiates thought and action that the conscious mind then seeks to retrospectively understand through the medium of language. This chapter will take this a step further to investigate the structure within which linguistic understanding is deployed. The primary structuring mechanism will be that of narrativity, although the traditional linearity of narrative will be questioned given the complicated relays involved in mental temporality. We interpret the present using the past and are constantly reinterpreting the past using the present; both are also reinterpreted and projected into an anticipated future. A complex layering consequently takes place folding back and forth over itself with many levels of reinterpretation.

One can use the thought of Jacques Lacan as a conceptual pivot between the affective social analysis of the end of the last chapter and the concerns of the present as stated above. Writing at a time when existentialism held great sway in French intellectual thought, Lacan opposed the inherent Cartesianism of the existential movement. Claiming that his work represented a return to Freud, he disagreed with the idea of a conscious and autonomous rational actor and came to argue for the situation of the human subject in society through the mechanism of language.[2] For Lacan, it is through language that we become constituted as subjects and there is an explicit connection, therefore, between the social and individual worlds.[3] Lacan may be seen as attempting to fuse the phenomenological subject with the concerns of structuralism. The idea of structures gave Lacan a different way of theorising the task of interpretation without putting an undue emphasis on a free subject as the base of such analysis.

In the realm of individual analysis, Lacan's great claim is that the unconscious is structured like a language. Hence, it is through an awareness of language that we are able to think creatively about the world and to enter into the dialogical relationships of social relations as well as the monological task of reflecting upon our own individuality. Language is also that which shapes the social world in which we carry out these relations in terms of shared culture and laws. It is the interaction of the child with this linguistic social reality, and the interpenetration of the former by the latter in terms of the formation of mental structures, which cements the tie between the individual and the social. In an important characterisation of Lacanian thought, the individual can be seen to 'mirror' the social.

In terms of its relationship with existentialism, this conception seeks to embed the individual in the social world in a much more direct and deterministic way than the 'situatedness' of Sartre and Heidegger. Lacan differs from these thinkers not only in the relationship of the individual to the social, however, positing as he does a very different sense of self to the existentialists. Sartre, in *Being and Nothingness*, argued that consciousness can never be fully aware of itself. As soon as we locate one of our attributes and claim that it in some way constitutes who we are, we have objectified ourselves. He therefore claims that we should view the self as more than a list of attributes or characteristics, as something that both transcends and binds these disconnected phenomena. Lacan also argues that we can never see ourselves as any one of our attributes. His reasoning turns however, on the argument that we will end up being bound into an 'infinity of reflection' in which we can never come to understand the original perceiver, always seeing ourselves as reflected by others.[4] On one level, this means that we are tied into a cycle of self-definition in terms of the way in which we believe ourselves to be perceived by others. In other words, as in Hegel's Master and Slave dialectic of self recognition, we can never be a fully 'finished' self because we are always dependent on our interpretation of others' interpretation of us. We are always aware of, and act according to, an imaginary gaze

Lacan sought to marry the ideas of psychoanalysis with those of structuralism by positing a subject that was a creation of societa forces. Lacan takes the most rigorous reading of Freud's geneti human subject in that there is no pre-existent *quidditas* to act as platform for self-formation. His principal project, therefore, is t 'show how what appears to be our central reality, our "selfhood", is actually constructed through a series of shifts in which we become inserted into the symbolic order of culture'.[5] For Lacan, the self is the product of social forces, most specifically as a function of language. This is illustrated through his idea of the mirror stage of development, which seeks to counteract essentialist conceptions of the ego. Lacan claims that an infant between the ages of six and eighteen months begins to recognise its reflection in a mirror and comes to identify this reflection as its 'self'. The infant regards the reflection as having more complete control over its body than it really has and thus posits the image as an ideal that forms the basis of future development. The identification of the self with the mirror image constitutes the first attempt at achieving unity of selfhood through identifying with what are seen as more complete others or, once within the symbolic realm, with powerful archetypal images, such as nationalism, that serve to gel the disparate elements of self together with a definite focus.

The concept of 'identification' is an important one in Lacanian thought.

> The identification of oneself with another being is the very process by which a continuing sense of selfhood becomes possible, and it is from successive assimilations of other people's attributes that what is familiarly called the ego or personality is constructed.[6]

The concept of identification is deepened with the linguistic mechanisms by which the subject is actually formed. Linguistic or symbolic systems are the means by which we mediate our intersubjective relations with others. Whereas the initial identification takes place in the realm of the imaginary, for the subject to achieve social reality it must enter the linguistic or symbolic order and the constraints and rules that are inherent within it. This repression of the limits of the imaginary identification in being forced to adhere to the logic of the realm of language, as well as the loss of the undifferentiated symbiosis between the mother and child experienced in the pre-mirror stage, inevitably causes an irreducible trauma or 'lack', an awareness of separation which, through a circular process, the self must seek to obscure through identification with more 'complete' others. This is the lack which language and the symbolic order are used to mask.

Lacan's explanation of the process by which the subject attains social reality draws heavily, as do other structuralists, on Saussurean linguistics, with the subject entering language as a signifier that is barred from access to a stable signified or fixed meaning outside the contingencies of language itself. The upshot of this complicated process is quite a different vision of the self than that envisaged by phenomenology. For Lacan, the influence of language is not as a means of articulation, as phenomenology would have it, but rather as a means of formation. There is no self to articulate before language effectively creates one, through imposing the perimeters of linguistic rules around our imaginary identifications. The self is robbed, therefore, of its essential core by means of which the human agent is meant to primarily engage with the world on a reasoned basis amenable to explanation. The waters become muddied, however, when the self is presented as a collection of distorted images thrown together to obscure the fact that we have no intrinsic selfhood, and brought to reality, as in Nietzsche, only through encountering the social rules to which we must adhere in order to express this incoherent bundle to others. The ideal of reasoned engagement with the world is rendered severely problematical as engagement with the world is in the service of an inherently irrational, or, at least nonconscious, process.

As we have seen, the idea that language serves to structure mental life is also shared by the thinkers encountered in Chapters 1 and 3. Damasio, for example, claims that whereas the self cannot precede the existence of emotions it can precede language. Given that language is a system of symbolic representation, for the self and consciousness to be born solely out of it would 'constitute the sole instance of words without an underlying concept'.[7] He indicates evidence from patients suffering from global asphasia, a total breakdown of all language functions rendering understanding of oral or visually presented language impossible. Such patients seem to have the ability to internally construct and then communicate thoughts without the use of language.

In response to the criticism that such patients may retain the use of some language-related functions in the brain, meaning they are not altogether deprived of linguistic ability at all levels, Damasio points to the case of Earl, who underwent radical surgery to deal with a fatally malignant brain tumour leading to the removal of the entire left hemisphere of his brain. Even in the absence of the side of his brain housing linguistic ability, Earl was able to make use of a few expletives and a repertoire of gestures and expressions to attempt to answer, or indicate his opinion on, questions put to him.

Damasio therefore draws a distinction between core consciousness a simple biological phenomenon not linked to language, memory attention or reason, and a more complex extended consciousness

These two forms of consciousness are linked with two different 'selves'. Core consciousness gives rise to a core self arising out of 'the sense of a single, bounded, living organism bent on maintaining stability to maintain its life'.[8] It is a transient phenomenon triggered by any object which causes a change in the neural patterns which represent the state of the organism at any given time.[9] As the environment changes, it impacts on our internal stability triggering core consciousness and, given the multitude of objects around us which may affect internal change, it seems continuous.

In contrast, extended consciousness gives rise to the autobiographical self, which is inextricably linked to autobiographical memory and the events of the individual's own life. Whereas the core self is as relatively static throughout life as the core neural patterns upon which it is founded, the autobiographical self changes throughout life and is constantly remodelled on the basis of new experiences. It is this extended, post-language consciousness which Damasio sees theorists such as Dennett and Varela as discussing. His primary point is that the brain has a narrative ability that precedes language and which adheres in its function to map internal and external changes over time. Indeed, he claims that such a narrative ability *must* precede language and points to Dennett's multiple drafts model of consciousness, Gazzaniga's left-brain interpreter and the philosophical puzzle of intentionality, as evidence of this inherent predisposition to storytelling.

What we come to call our 'self' is largely based on the building and remodelling of autobiographical memory. Damasio suggests that a lot of this work is done nonconsciously although neuroscience is so far in the dark as to how.

The story of consciousness

Dennett claims that we are always spinning stories, telling tales as a tactic of self-protection, self-control or self-definition. He refers to the illusion this presents to the listener as being like a centre of narrative gravity. The implied unity of self that this projects is, however, nothing but a theorist's fiction,[10] a user illusion in Norretranders' terms. He asserts that the form of our user illusion, which Norretranders ties explicitly into self-identity, actually changes the 'wetware' of our brains. This user illusion can only be a social construction, an idea which Dennett articulates with the aid of Dawkins 'memes', units of cultural transmission the successful of which replicate through passing from mind to mind. 'The most striking differences in human prowess depend on the microstructural differences induced by the various memes that have entered them and taken up residence'.[11] Whether or not one agrees with this characterisation in terms of memes or the simpler and narrower term 'ideas', the political relevance is apparent. It is the political operations of power/knowledge and cultural transmission that reproduce and implant these ideas and hence condition the narrative identity that underpins conscious thought.

In his short article 'The biographical illusion',[12] Pierre Bourdieu points to a narrative articulation of self, between interviewer and interviewee for example, which unfolds as a series of life-events that are not necessarily chronologically ordered,

> but which nevertheless tend or pretend to get organised into sequences linked to each other on the basis of intelligible relationships. The subject and the object of the biography (the interviewer and the interviewee) have in a sense the same interest in accepting the *postulate of the meaning* of the narrated existence . . . So we may assume that the autobiographical narrative is always at least partially motivated by a concern to give meaning, to rationalize, to show the inherent logic, both for the past and for the future, to make consistent and constant, through the creation of intelligible relationships like that of the cause (immediate or final) and effect between successive states, which are thus turned into *steps* of a necessary development.[13]

Bourdieu goes on to claim that the modern world acts on us in such a way as to try to give integration to the agglomeration of our individual sensations, practices and representations:

> but this practical identity reveals itself to intuition only in the inexhaustible series of its successive manifestations, in such a way that the only manner of apprehending it as such consists perhaps in attempting to recapture it in the unity of an integrative narrative (as allowed by the different, more or less institutionalised, forms of 'speaking of oneself,' confidence, etc.).[14]

One example he gives of such an integrative measure in society is that of the proper name, which seeks to create a fixed actor in the social world through the life-span. Bourdieu's aim in this example is to trace how the official representation of self, as tied into the phenomenon of the proper name in social and legal terms, comes to intrude on any other private representation we may hold. In other words the social/legal view of the individual, fixed within the social network fo life through a name, posits the taking up of a successive series of positions in that social world, which in effect become the trajectory of the agent through life and implants within us the notion that we should relate to our lives as history. This is of course an example that works better for men in our society, many women changing their name upon marriage.

The idea that the narrative format is socially constructed is interesting on a number of levels, both in terms of what it means for our self-creation and for the question of whether contemporary society can still sustain narrative identity. In the following pages, the idea of narrative will be divided into the components that can be seen to make it up: time, place and the way in which life-stories are put together.

The first issue to take up is that of time. Mark Freeman claims that 'the *history* one tells, via *memory*, assumes the form of a *narrative* of the past that charts the trajectory of how one's self came to be.'[15] This is a good illustration of the way in which time must be conceived for the idea of a narrative to operate, that is in terms of linear historicity. Even if we look at a different conception of time, we can see how the narrative technique can facilitate the unity of selfhood.

In Chapter 69 of *Being and Time*, Heidegger puts forward a rendering of time as a threefold horizontal unity of past, present and future. This is contrasted with the traditional linear conception of time as a sequence of moments in which future is experienced as present before disappearing as past. The way in which Heidegger sees the '*ecstatico-horizontal unity of temporality*'[16] being played out in authentic human existence is through the stretching of *Dasein* across the span from birth to death. To do this one must accept the 'thrownness' of one's birth and connect it in a very immediate (horizontal) fashion to the projection of one's mortality into the future. This basically means an acceptance of the conditions of one's birth, a realisation of the world-historical time one is born into with the particular opportunities and restrictions thus afforded, and a conception of one's own personal historicisation within that world: the conditions of one's birth, geography, social networks, and so on. Heidegger articulates this as *Dasein* handing down its 'heritage' to itself.[17] He goes on to claim that since authentic Being is Being-towards-death and since Being is essentially a 'futural' enterprise in that every decision must be made in the knowledge of the possibility of an unknowable death, this connects the past and future in such a way, through the present decision, that it is this future orientation which gives to the past its meaning.[18] In other words, being is a capturing of the past circumstances which have led to the present moment, for the purpose of future projection.

We therefore come to a notion of time as an entity so closely connected as to be viewed as horizontal. This stands opposed to the traditional view of time in terms of what Heidegger calls 'datability' – 'the "now", the "then", and the "on that former occasion" . . . [which] have a seemingly obvious related structure'.[19] This arises from the fact that inauthentic *Dasein* is forever concerned with the present-to-hand, that with which we are at the minute surrounded, which is viewed as appearing and disappearing from the future to the past. We are, in a sense, dislocated from our past and future by the fact that they have either ceased to exist or do not yet exist and are, therefore, somehow not our own. What authentic being calls for is, on a simple level, the re-appropriation of our selves as historical entities through whom time does not merely flow, but who are composed at any given moment by the essentially real presence of our past and future.

I would suggest that the only viable way of occasioning this re-appropriation in any meaningful way is through the articulation of our lives as narrative. Even though the articulation of our lives may involve some degree of linear sequencing, there may be no other way in which we can gain the requisite appreciation of the intimate connection which past, future and present hold, and achieve 'authentic historicality'.[20]

A notion of time that may be easier to grasp in terms of our everyday experience is that of Paul Ricoeur. In the third book of *Time and Narrative*,[21] Ricoeur looks at the opposite poles of objective cosmological time, on the one hand, and subjective phenomenological time, as per Heidegger, on the other. He comes to the conclusion that neither can be understood without reference to the other. Cosmological time finds it necessary to posit a contingent subject in order to perceive and measure it, and phenomenological time needs to refer to the objective pre-concept of time in order to find its definition.[22] Ricoeur seeks to bring both these poles together in the idea of a third dimension of time, that of narrated time. This narrated time is subjectively created by the intersection of history and fiction, in terms of the life-stories we each tell about ourselves. One example of this phenomenon is the calendar within which our subjective experience of everyday life is connected to cosmology.

Discussions of the nature of phenomenological time may seem to be overly metaphysical, though when we come to investigate Ricoeur in more detail we will see that he sought to promote lived experience over metaphysics. For us to construct our narratives, however, we must do so within the confines of the world in which we live, which means, at the most basic level, within the conceptions of time and space that we experience. How then does the idea of historicality in our lives relate to the kind of contemporary world in which the last chapter situated us?

In *In Search of Politics*, Bauman makes the point that within consumer society the focus tends to be on autonomous agents who experience life as a series of sensation-seeking moments, which cannot be shared with others in a community beyond the fact that everyone is involved in the same pursuit. 'The resulting decomposition of community finds its correlate in the fragmentation of life into its constituting units. The life-process of every agent tends to be split up into a series of episodes, each episode being in principle self-contained and self-sustained.'[23] As Adorno and Horkheimer put it 'Individuals are reduced to a mere sequence of instantaneous experiences which leave no trace, or rather whose trace is hated as irrational, superfluous, and "overtaken" in the literal sense of the word.'[24] Bauman argues that a linear conception of time used to derive its meaning from the sequential experience of stages, with the next anticipated, and the last interpreted, in the light of the present. Now, however, we seem to have a horizontal conception of time, not in Heidegger's sense but in that 'time spans are plotted beside each other, rather than in a logical progression; there is no preordained logic, in their succession; they can easily, without violating any hard and fast rule, change places – sectors of time-continuum are in principle *interchangeable*.'[25]

Elsewhere this idea is explained in terms of the notions of consumerism and 'liquid modernity' – '"instantaneity" means immediate, "on-the-spot" fulfillment – but also the immediate exhaustion and fading of interest'.[26] Moments in time no longer gain their meaning within a frame of linear expression, in terms of past experience and future projection, but are, rather, expected to be internally meaningful without any outside reference beyond the present moment.

In a later work, however, Bauman seems to extol the virtues of narrative identity as the means by which individuals seek to unify their lives in meaningful terms. 'Life stories are ostensibly guided by the modest ambition to instill ("in retrospect", "with the benefit of hindsight") an "inner logic" and meaning into the lives they retell.'[27] Unfortunately, Bauman does not go into very much detail about the construction of these narratives, nor about the way in which they are articulated, despite the fact that the very idea is problematised by his other recent analyses of society. If we take the way in which time is conceived as outlined in the previous paragraphs, the projection of a coherent identity back across time would seem no more desirable than possible. In *Liquid Modernity*, this point is made quite explicitly:

> Identities seem fixed and solid only when seen, in a flash, from outside. Whatever solidity they might have when contemplated from the inside of one's own biographical experience appears fragile, vulnerable, and constantly torn apart by shearing forces which lay bare its fluidity and by cross-currents which threaten to rend in pieces and carry away any form they might have acquired. The experienced, lived identity could only be held together with the adhesive of fantasy, perhaps day-dreaming. Yet, given the stubborn evidence of biographical experience, any stronger glue – a substance with more fixing power than easy-to-dissolve-and-wipe-out fantasy – would seem as repugnant a prospect as the absence of day-dreams.[28]

Indeed, in the consumer society of liquid modernity we are actively encouraged to resist unification of our episodic lives.[29]

Some sense of this creeps into the type of narrative alluded to in *The Individualized Society* in the re-rendering of the Marxist maxim as 'people make their lives but not under conditions of their choice.'[30] This is expanded in terms of the background conditions of life remaining relatively unquestioned:

> The process of individualization which affects the 'conditions' and the life narratives alike needs two legs to progress: the powers setting the range of choices and separating realistic choices from pipe-dreams must be firmly set in the universe of 'conditions', while the life stories must confine themselves to toing and froing among the options on offer.[31]

One of the presuppositions to discussing our sense of selves in terms of narratives is that we must be able to conceive of actions as 'texts'. I do not necessarily mean this in the Derridean sense that there is nothing outside the text. There are some interesting ideas in certain interpretations of this claim however. If one goes along with Moran,

> texts are not just books or pieces of writing in the usual sense, but complexes of meanings which relate to other such complexes [then] . . ., even *events* . . . may be treated as texts and their manner of being constructed may be examined by the kind of reverse engineering which Derrida calls 'deconstruction'.[32]

Rather, I am thinking of Ricoeur's more positive angle in that we seek to bring meaning to our actions in the only way that we know how, through speaking and writing. It is a simple but persuasive argument to ask in what other way we can bring our cognition to bear on our activities without actually articulating anything about them. On this notion, Madison cites Ricoeur's concern with motive – 'in order for a motive to have explanatory force, it must be given in the form of a small autobiography.'[33] He then links this back into the notion of temporality with another citation from Ricoeur in which he discusses the effect that the introduction of a third party, who will consider consequences as well as motive, will have on the perception of action. This allows us to see the action as detached from the agent, as more like the Derridean idea of text as speech detached from speaker:

> Detached from its agent, a course of action acquires an autonomy similar to the semantic autonomy of a text. It leaves its mark on the course of events and eventually it becomes sedimented into social institutions. Human action has become archive and document. Thus it acquires potential meaning beyond its relevance to its initial situation.[34]

Although this can be connected back to Dennett's concept of heterophenomenology in Chapter 2, what is interesting here is the idea that it is at this point that our narrative, and hence our existence, becomes 'temporally aware'. We are slotted into a conception of time in which our past is used to account for the motives via which, when we act, there are future consequences. It is this idea that Ricoeur is trying to get at in his idea of narrated time.

Central to the conception of narrated time is the idea of 'emplotment', 'an "arrangement of the incidents" which reorganises the concept of reality by staging a kind of creative imitation',[35] which Ricoeur borrows from Aristotle's *Poetics*. Ricoeur goes on to examine emplotment in terms of Aristotle's three stages of *mimesis*: a pre-understanding of the world and action, the creation of the plot in words or symbols and the application of the plot by a translation of the narrative into the creation of a life-world in which the reader can move. As Ricoeur puts it, these three stages constitute 'a *prefiguration* of the field of practice, a *configuration* of the text, and a *refiguration* of the world of living acting and suffering through the appropriation of the text.'[36]

We come then, via Aristotle, to a notion of narrative as comprising a beginning, a middle and an end in which an action is given meaning through the place it plays within the overall story. 'Plot is what makes action *intelligible* (it is what "holds together circumstances, ends and means, initiatives and unwanted consequences"). It is, in short, what makes for *understanding, meaning*.'[37] Madison makes the point that anti-novelists who refuse narrative emplotment may in fact better reflect the actual lived experience of a life which has no set beginnings or ends, and hence no middle, and which is experienced rather as a collection of overlapping episodes. He then goes on to claim, however, that, given the teleological structure of life, narration is the best means of understanding it.[38]

Another version of narrative construction is given by Charles Taylor. Taylor expands the idea we encountered in Chapter 2, of humans as self-interpreting animals, into an account of self-formation in *Sources of the Self*, arguing that we weave the disparate strands of our various interpretations into a coherent narrative with which we create a unified self. Taylor's thesis rests on the proposition that we must find some way of both identifying and orientating our lives towards, some conception of 'the good'. Our lives therefore represent a 'quest',[39] a process of elucidation and internalisation which involves us extracting our moral conceptions from within our background culture and using them to render our lives meaningful. Smith defines Taylor's core organising principle as the idea that a 'person is a being for whom things matter',[40] or, as Taylor himself puts it, 'we are selves only in that certain issues matter for us.'[41]

Self-interpretation is not a neutral enterprise 'since interpretative disclosure always takes place by way of articulating a contrast.'[42] We can only make interpretative decisions about the issues that matter for us, including their selection, through a process of discrimination and ranking, constructing a hierarchy of personal importance. This is only possible with reference to the common source of meanings and articulation that we find in our background culture and shared language. The kind of self-interpretation that Taylor is talking about is an inherently social operation, which depends on ready access to an understood and articulatable culture for nourishment. Indeed the claim is made more strongly in terms of both the cultural and personal frameworks in which we operate and of the strong evaluation by which we do so. Frameworks, for Taylor, are sets of 'qualitative distinctions' in which we think, feel and act and which have a greater claim on us than the others on offer in society. The goals and standards that these frameworks establish for us are the means by which we judge our subjective desires and choices; they are the 'strong evaluations' by which we judge our actions:[43]

> I want to defend the strong thesis that doing without frameworks is utterly impossible for us . . . that the horizons within which we live our lives and make sense of them have to include these strong qualitative discriminations. Moreover this is not meant just as a contingently true psychological

> fact about human beings . . . rather that living within such strongly qualified horizons is constitutive of human agency, that stepping outside these limits would be tantamount to stepping outside what we would recognise as integral, that is, undamaged personhood.[44]

It is through the process of conversation with significant others who share our frameworks that we are able to construct a self by way of a process of articulation of our feelings and desires:

> I am a self only in relation to certain interlocutors: in one way in relation to those conversation partners who were essential to me achieving self-definition; in another in relation to those who are now crucial to my continuing grasp of languages of self understanding . . . A self exists only within what I call 'webs of interlocution'.[45]

Smith identifies Taylor's argument as being tied into a 'phenomenological argument of what life would be like under conditions in which a horizon of strong evaluative distinctions were unavailable.'[46] It is the absence of such possibilities for orientation that Taylor uses to explain crises of identity. An individual suffers an identity crisis when they are unable to make the strong evaluative choice between different forms or modes of life on a normative level. It entails an inability to choose one form of life as 'better' than another given that one has lost contact with the frameworks which lend the necessary evaluative tools for such distinctions. In such a case, the life of the person concerned seems devoid of any inherent meaning, given that its meanings cannot be tied into any normative cultural background.

Given Bauman's claims about the profusion of moral horizons and the absence of an overarching evaluative framework with which to judge their respective merits, the only way for us to mentally 'survive' may be to learn to live with contingency. Taylor, however, disputes this claim: 'the force of the identity crisis is just that the question of what is really of more or less importance, worthwhile or fulfilling *demands* an answer even if we are not in a position to give one.'[47] Thus the frameworks from which we draw our strong evaluative decisions are inescapable, in the sense that they help to provide answers to questions that pre-exist for us. These questions have a necessary pre-existence because the answers to them construct our identity as human agents. Communal frameworks provide the base from which we construct our moral identity, which, in turn, provides the base from which we deal with the situations we encounter in everyday life. To do without either of these components, communal or personal, would render us devoid of an identity or personhood. 'The notion of an identity defined by some mere de facto, not strongly valued, preference is incoherent.'[48]

Rosen sees Taylor's argument as running parallel to Heidegger's claim that 'the "question of Being" has been suppressed by modern man's "fall" into inauthenticity – in other words modernity has been cut off from the kind of deep questioning which alone would enable it to understand itself.'[49] In Taylor's analysis the dominant vision of the constitutive good is disengaged reason. This vision of disengagement not only causes problems in the sense that in order to live up to it, individuals are required to disengage themselves from the very frameworks which would render their lives meaningful, but it also fails to provide a solution to those problems since denial of frameworks obscures the nature of society's identity crisis.

It may be that Taylor falls prey to the same problems that plague phenomenology. As Smith illustrates,

> Taylor's justification for the inescapability of horizons of strong evaluation does turn on the *conscious* state of the person in an identity crisis: strongly evaluated motives must be conscious, as must be the 'stand' by which . . . the self wins back its identity.[50]

It is indeed one of the postmodernist charges that the self-interpretative vision of identity 'presupposes a reflective and consciously situated "I" for whom the question is inescapable'.[51] Taylor's arguments therefore may operate only for a certain type, or one facet, of self.

Richard Rorty seeks to marry the hermeneutic stance with some vision of the unconscious by an appeal to some of Freud's conceptions. Rorty believes that the 'disengaged, controlling, disciplining, instrumental stance of the self' is represented by the Freudian ego.[52] He also claims that Freud enables us to set our constructed life stories on a much more contingent basis. This is achieved through the move from a grand, unifying narrative to a collection of small narratives to cover all of one's actions, including those that cannot be accounted for by the strong evaluations of Taylor's conception. These tie in with those actions, nonconsciously initiated, which require retroactive justification – as seen in the P. S. experiment.

Rorty constructs self-interpretations 'not, *pace* Taylor, transcendentally and ontologically, but naturalistically and pragmatically. Furthermore, it is just the attitude of affirmation towards the contingency implied by such construal that characterises normative orientations in a post-modern culture.'[53] He attacks the supposed unity of Taylor's narrative by pointing out that in order to ascribe a particular desire or belief to a person, it is always neccessary to relate it to the narrative whole of that person's web of beliefs and desires; in a conception like Taylor's, the self must be understood holistically. The fact is, however, that some of our beliefs and desires are contradictory. The way in which Rorty deals with this incoherence of selfhood is by positing a network of 'quasi-selves', each with a set of desires and beliefs for different situations so that an act seemingly in contradiction with one set would be fitted into another. These different quasi-selves form part of a causal network moulded by the individual specifics of our upbringing. Over the course of our lives, therefore, several mutually incompatible mini-narratives of strong evaluation are formed, of which only one is capable of examination by introspection at any one time.[54]

It could be argued that this conceptualisation of self-formation chimes in more coherently with what has been said about the relation between the conscious and unconscious portions of our mental life. As the small fraction that is our conscious mind strives to make sense of a contradictory external world, as well as an internal life that operates with a lot of information that is not available consciously, the answers it comes up with are bound to contradict each other on occasion. There is also the fact that given the source of our narratives, our cultural environment, one might expect the structure as well as the content to be mirrored. Rorty's plurality of narratives would therefore appear to be the more legitimate product of the incommensurable fragments of modern society than Taylor's unified whole. If, as Norretranders claims, the aim of the endeavour is purely pragmatic, to help us make sense of both the inner and outer worlds, there would seem to be no reason why the justifications we present should all fit neatly in to one single narrative. Indeed, when one takes on board the work of Freud, it would seem that our minds, both conscious and unconscious, are just such a bundle of inconsistencies, interdependent across the conscious divide. We, as human agents, are however able to operate coherently in a very complex world and not be overly troubled by our mental fragmentedness. We must therefore operate with some unifying factor, a user illusion, that gives the impression of unity and coherence that helps us survive in everyday life.

Rorty's conception may also better fit in with Lacan's vision of how a self is attained. Rorty claims that the desires and beliefs of a person are never fully accounted for and are always open to reinterpretation. 'One can pragmatically adapt to the contingencies of self-hood by self-creation through self-description.'[55] This then opens up the possibility that instead of searching for one's true essence as a person, one could, through moral reflection, investigate the many different facets that go to make up one's individuality. The concept of self, therefore, would be defined less by Taylor's unity and more by a Lacanian conception in which 'self' is merely an umbrella term for a collection of different quasi-selves formed and articulated through language.

I do not believe that is an entirely satisfactory way to go however. Taylor's idea of selfhood through strong evaluation seems to break down on two levels. Firstly, it can be argued that contemporary society simply does not provide the necessary frameworks of meaning to facilitate this type of self-construction. Secondly, in line with Rorty's criticisms as well as our own previous psychological discussions, the phenomenological notion of a conscious unified self is disrupted by the introduction of evidence that devalues consciousness' role in our mental lives. Rorty's alternative of numerous quasi-selves only available to introspection one at a time may go too far in the opposite direction in that he claims, for example, that we 'see ourselves as centerless, as random assemblages of contingent and idiosyncratic needs rather than as more or less adequate exemplifications of a common human essence'.[56]

One advantage that Rorty cites of his conception over Taylor's is that it can cover all the actions in our lives, right down to the smallest.[57] This is achieved through the fact that if one of our actions cannot be posited to fall within one particular conception of self, then it is conceived as belonging to a different quasi-self with its own web of desires and motives.

It is indeed important to view identity in a non-exclusive way instead of positing the self in the autobiographical way discussed earlier and which Taylor can be seen to extol. In taking account of the minutiae of our daily lives, it seems inherently counterintuitive to claim that actions are carried out by different quasi-selves. It is counterintuitive, given what was said earlier, that we could each give an account of our actions if asked and that we can develop these accounts at various levels of depth, projecting the underlying foundations of current actions back in time and linking them to networks of desire and motivation. It could be said that all our mini-narratives can be slotted into place within an overall meta-narrative as they are articulated in terms of ever increasing abstraction from everyday life and are called upon to articulate longer and longer spans of time containing more and more events.

This can be seen as analogous to Ricoeur's idea of emplotment, as well as having the hierarchical structure favoured by functionalism as described in Chapter 2. As we seek to account for more and more of our lives in one go, we do so in terms of a retrospective emplotment that is seen as leading up to the time of telling. Rather than seeing our various actions in terms of the expressions of different quasi-selves, we can see them as being amenable to articulation in terms of many mini-narratives, which we can then link together in order to make sense of them in relation to each other rather than seeing them as unconnected in terms of our sense of self. They would therefore exhibit a provisional linking together as opposed to an essential one. This relational articulation is then the meta-narrative, the life story as written from the point of view of the time at which it was consciously reflected upon. This then is the difference between the provisional meta-narrative and the strong evaluation that Taylor bids for. Whereas the latter is seen as a relatively stable mechanism of articulation, forever enmeshed within a particular framework and only cognisable through one set of concepts, the meta-narrative is wholly contingent on the current circumstances of the telling. Contrary to Taylor, the meta-narrative can and does change with the motivation particular to the telling. It is a utilitarian device, a function of the left-brain interpreter, as seen in the P. S. experiment. We are constantly re-evaluating and rethinking our identity, shifting it about within the social spaces we inhabit, always encountering new situations that require an assimilation that may alter its plot. The self as it unfolds over a life is not just one plot with many twists and turns, which can and do contradict each other as occasion necessitates as long as it keeps the action moving with surface coherence. Indeed, it cannot be said to 'unfold' at all in terms of some Hegelian trajectory towards self-realisation. Neither is it one story told from the perspective of different characters. It is a story that can switch actual plots in the middle of telling. As the narrator of Beckett's *The Expelled* comments at the end of his tale, 'I don't know why I told this story. I could just as well have told another.'[58]

This notion better reflects the psychological evidence discussed in Chapter 1. The idea of meta-narrative and mini-narrative can be seen to fulfil the same function as does the 'user illusion' view of consciousness in that it provides justification and unification where there may not have been such before for the purpose of orientation. In the same way as P. S. consciously sought to explain why he had pointed to the things he did and to connect them in a coherent explanation, we each seek to do the same at a multitude of levels in our daily lives, from the most mundane description of what we have done today to relatively complex articulations of how our present position in life fits in with 'who we are' and 'where we want to be'.

This conception of narrative can also facilitate the different conceptions of time that were described earlier, given that it is an entirely contingent articulation. We can therefore see it as operating within the concept of Ricoeur's narrated time in that the meta-narrative and mini-narratives both conceive themselves in terms of the subjective time-spans that they are called upon to cover and articulate with a consequent depth and emplotment. Given the episodic nature of consumer-based time, mini-narratives and inherently reflexive meta-narratives may be the only way that narrative identity can be sustained in contemporary society.

Excursus on community

Given the ideal of hedonistic individualism exhibited in consumerism, as well as the importance put on communal frameworks in ideas of narrative identity, one must ask what social formations are available in the individualised society. One coalescence is the idea of the neo-tribe, and the consumer tribe in particular.

Neo-tribes can be characterised as present-orientated non-instrumental sociations with ritual-based associations, relative closure against outsiders and a constant self-monitoring of group identity.[59] In the contemporary context, Shields identifies them as being 'short lived flashes of sociality . . . whose only sanction against their members is exclusion if and when their interests change from those of the group. Membership is thus short-term and even multiple.'[60] Shields connects this new form of sociality to the new form of personae in self-identity. The freedom to try on and easily change personae is facilitated by multiple, fluid group identities wherein social roles, in Goffman's terms,[61] can be switched and supported; one can move from the office to the home to the gym with a switch of identity to suit each context. The enactment of different roles requires different social stages and different supporting casts, as well as the different props which consumerism now seeks to offer us.

Herein, we see the connection between the contemporary notion of individuality and contemporary social frameworks. The idea of authentic individuality, which in existential terms could only be played out on an individual level, free from the constrictions of

Heidegger's *das Man* and the objectifying gaze of Sartre's 'third', takes on a new social dimension. The consumer imperative of individuality and authenticity, for all its dressing in atomistic language, must be seen in terms of social roles that require fluid social platforms for their performance. The self is no longer an instrument for self-fulfilment but takes on the form of the spectacle, as we have seen in the use of the gaze in marketing. In consumer terms, products are sold on the basis of self-fulfilment but this can only be enjoyed in the sight of others. The actual fulfilment comes in the public consumption in selected arenas such as the home, the work place, the bar or club. The implicit message of consumer ideology is that there is no point being fulfilled if no one knows it. The self must be a conspicuous process of achievement, a fluid and mutable social self.

In existential terms, rather than being objectified by the gaze of the other we are made solid by it. We are all movie stars now in that we are taught not to exist if the camera is not on us. Indeed, in some ways we do not even need the 'other' to be a real person. Through the processes of spatio-temporal distortion inaugurated by globalised consumerism, combined with the ever growing pervasiveness of the technological and mechanical in our lives, especially as a mediator of communication, we have succeeded in disembodying not only time and space but the subjectivity within it. As we communicate over greater distances, increasingly we hear each other's voices through the plastic of the receiver or words made up by pixels on a screen. One result of this process is to open the way for what Langman calls the 'other of the imaginary'. She claims:

> In the age of television, we learn to see Others as if our eye were a camera. Role-taking and -making are less based on words than images. Taking the role of the other is now to imagine that we are being seen via camera by the larger audience of home viewers. The larger audiences, persons or groups to which self-presentations are now directed may not exist in reality, but in hyper-reality.[62]

In the cases where the audiences and the support for the playing out of our social roles are real people, they are increasingly organised in terms of transient tribal subgroups. One good example is the experimental groups used in Sulkunen's study of the new middle classes. Sulkunen studied groups of regulars in three bars in Helsinki. The groups of pub-goers he studied had all the hallmarks of a tribe in Maffelsoli's terms: they were loosely based, transient voluntary groups of people with a very limited agenda, in this case drinking, which the group rarely moved outside and which other life roles, such as family life, were not allowed to intrude upon. The idea of the tribal in this sense is that of the contemporary tribe, rather than the traditional anthropological sense that represents something into which one is born and which conditions all areas of life, the former having no instrumental purpose outside a very limited context. It is for this reason that membership must be multiple: we need one for work, one, or maybe several, for our home life if we have an extended family that only gather for specific occasions, and several for different leisure contexts.

Neo-tribes can also have a geo-ethnic organisational impetus as a response to globalisation processes and to the culture of consumer individualism. Geo-ethnic tribes, such as those Horsman and Marshall identify,[63] are one response to the perception that the globalisation process is driving political and cultural sovereignty further and further away from the peoples and locales where it was once located. They are therefore defined by common language, geography, religion, ethnicity or shared experience and are usually mobilised against an other. In more abstract and functional terms, they are organised along the lines of whatever they feel is threatened and against those whom they feel pose the threat. In this sense, some contemporary neo-tribes outside the sphere of consumption, and sometimes specifically organised against it, can have an instrumental purpose, although this is usually limited to a single issue or group of issues which imposes upon different people a homogeneity they would not otherwise possess and which is dissolved as soon as the threat is passed.

Bauman identifies several more social formations in conditions of liquid modernity – the peg-style, the cloakroom and the aesthetic communities. These three are not altogether separate entities but are better seen as elaborations on a theme. In *In Search of Politics*, Bauman uses the term 'peg-style community' to identify the effect of consumer individualisation on social bonds. Given that consumerism presents the idea that the responsibility for self-formation, and the consequences of our failures in that area, as in all others, are inherently individual and do not lend themselves to communal articulation, we are stripped of the possibility of coming together to find communal solutions to our problems. A peg-style community is a situation wherein a collection of individuals come together briefly to hang their individual worries on a social peg around which the group is organised. These pegs are public issues that can give the impression of the possibility of solidarity, examples being 'a prospect of recycling poisonous substances in the immediate neighbourhood or the release of an acknowledged paedophile from prison'.[64] The nature and actions of these communities are linked into the framework of *unsicherheit* in that, given the problems in pinning down the causes and solutions to uncertainty and insecurity, emphasis comes to rest on issues of unsafety. As discussed in Chapter 3, those feeling unsafe can quickly look around and identify external problems, which can then be addressed in the hope that their resolution will bring the lacking peace of mind. This is the electioneering work of governmental party politics in which, over the years, travellers, single mothers, immigrants and more broadly rising crime rates, problems in the health service and fear of cultural and legal submersion in Europe have all been major platforms in political campaigns. The problem is that these surface issues, the easily identifiable pegs, do not cut to the root of the feelings of *unsicherheit*; after each peg is dealt with, another must be found.

In terms of the communal aspect of these communities, they would seem to share the transient nature of the contemporary tribal formations discussed above. They are single-issue formations that form and dissolve in as fluid a manner as any in the liquid modern context. The term 'cloakroom community' is used in *Liquid Modernity* to describe how these groups form around a single spectacle, like theatre-goers who collect in one place (the theatre) to watch an event and whose numbers can be counted by the number of pegs taken up by their coats in the cloakroom. This change in terms draws attention to the single-mindedness of the people who join together in such a manner; like theatre-goers, their attention is captivated and directed towards the single spectacle playing on the stage at the time:

> Cloakroom communities need a spectacle which appeals to similar interests dormant in otherwise disparate individuals and so bring them all together for a stretch of time when other interests – those which divide them instead of uniting – are temporarily laid aside . . . Spectacles as the occasion for the brief existence of a cloakroom community do not fuse and blend individual concerns into a 'group interest'; by being added up the concerns in question do not acquire a new quality, and the illusion of sharing which the spectacle may generate would not last much longer than the excitement of the performance. Spectacles have come to replace the common cause of the heavy/solid/hardware modernity era . . .[65]

For Bauman these types of social formation serve to spread and dissipate social energies instead of coalescing them into the form of community they are seeking to replicate or replace.

These ideas are given a fuller exploration in *Community*, this time, following Kant, under the tag of the 'aesthetic community'. The aesthetic community is held in contrast to the ethical community, which is built on long-term commitments and durable rights, which can in turn be used as a platform when planning the future. The aesthetic community, however, is one that seems to build on the all-consuming consumer ideology: all commitments are short-term and liable to foreclosure and the community itself a fluid entity in terms of aims and composition. Given the emphasis on individual freedom, it must be open enough to join and leave at a moment's notice.

In an extension of the idea behind the cloakroom community, Bauman discusses the role of the entertainment industry in creating spectacles and cults of personality around which such communities can be formed. This ties in with the points made in Chapter 3 about the search for role models to offset the individualised responsibility for ordering one's life. In liquid modern terms, the entertainment role model seems to be the perfect pivot around which such movements can form:

> To serve the purpose, idols must be glittering enough to dazzle the spectators and formidable enough to fill the stage from wing to wing; but they must be volatile and moveable as well – so they quickly disappear into the wings of memory and leave the scene free for the crowd of would-be idols waiting their turn.[66]

In summary, the type of sociality that Bauman identifies as growing out of liquid modernity and the privatisation of *unsicherheit* are short-lived single-issue communities. In these, disparate individuals lump together their collected worries and hang them on a public issue which they can join together to fight, or a phenomenon generated by the entertainment industry, although these may be one and the same wherein celebrities adopt issues and envelop them in the cult of personality. These communities are not long-term and have no ethical commitments; they have, in the spirit of consumerism, 'bonds without consequences'.[67]

In some ways, one could suggest a parallel between the types of community described by both ideas of neo-tribalism and Bauman and Giddens' characterisation of the 'pure relationship'. In the latter, the intimate relation is dependent entirely on itself and its perpetuation is contingent on the satisfaction gained by the parties involved. The ties in the pure relationship are entirely voluntary and entered into with freely chosen individuals. For Giddens the pure relationship may be durable and enduring and in that way different from contemporary forms of community we have discussed. I believe, however, that the conditions behind it are similar. At the base of both is the idea that the satisfaction of the individual is primary to all social or intimate ties, which can be dissolved at a moments notice if the former conditions are not fulfilled. In this way, relationships, whether they are intimate ties between two people or wider social ties, are inherently dissolvable and easily replaced. We know that we always have other options. Social lives come to be conducted in terms of shopping around and consumer ideology. Social ties are now subject to planned obsolescence. Doubtless this is also to do with increased mobility due to which durable ties with any degree of longevity may only be conducted electronically from a number of different locations in the world; those we meet face-to-face we may not be around for long and therefore, may not have sufficient time for social investment in.

The philosophy of neurological temporality

Two passages from Nietzsche's *Beyond Good and Evil*:

> By far the greater part of conscious thinking must still be included among instinctive activities, and that goes even for philosophical thinking . . . 'Being conscious' is not in any decisive sense the *opposite* of what is instinctive: most of the conscious thinking of a philosopher is secretly guided and forced into certain channels by his instincts.[68]

> 'I have done that,' says my memory. 'I cannot have done that,' says my pride, and remains inexorable. Eventually – memory yields.[69]

Freud cites the latter passage as the most exhaustive and impressive portrayal of the influence of affective factors on memory.[70] Both together are a good illustration of the co-original relay between the conscious and nonconscious, acting from one direction to the other in each passage. The nonconscious and affectual stimuli influence conscious thought at the highest levels and the conscious mind shapes and reshapes memory. The idea of time links into this as change presupposes a notion of the temporal. Temporality on the conscious level is expressed in terms of narrative, as we have seen, but it is harder to extrapolate a theory of time in relation to the nonconscious and then to link this with the former.

Herein we have a problem, which can be linked back to the material covered in the last chapter. There the question lurked in the background of how one could think in an original sense given the influence of environment on both the conscious mind and the emotions. This can be seen as the question of psychological change on the social spatial level. We will now have to address the question of change on the temporal level of mental apparatus.

Augustine suggested three temporal levels: the present of past things (memory), the present of present things (direct perception) and the present of future things (expectation).[71] These have an essentially mental reality and their perception, comparison and calculation belongs to the realm of consciousness.[72] This accords with both Kant's conception of time as a mental category and Freud's placing it within the secondary process of the preconscious as one of the ways in which the influence of the external world patterns thought.

One way of understanding time in relation to the nonconscious is through Bergson's concept of pure duration. Bergson argued that we conceive time in spatial terms, as a continuous line of discrete moments[73] connected by way of forward causality. This spatialisation still infuses contemporary description with the post-Einstein metaphor of travel in time as a fourth dimension. Pure duration, on the other hand, resists such spatialisation by positing a series of qualitative changes melting into and permeating one another. There is still movement as in the linear metaphor, but there is no serialisation of moments. Rather than thinking of the self as a series of distinct states linked in a unidirectional causal series, which Bergson argues is deterministic, we should conceive of the self as an uninterrupted flow with some acts springing from the totality rather merely than just the previous link in the causal chain. Such acts Bergson considers to be the exercise of free will.

Linked to the idea of pure duration is that of pure memory.[74] Bergson sees memory as the point of interaction between mind and body. On one level there are motor mechanisms and habits; these do not include a mental representation of the past but a purely physical learned response. Outside this lies pure memory, an infra-conscious total record of all life events that is essentially spiritual in nature, existing outside the brain but able to filter through it. Although a dualist, Bergson differs from others of this view in that he understands the union of mind (as pure memory) and matter as occurring on the temporal level of pure duration rather than on the spatial level, as in the Cartesian pineal gland for example. In his later book *Matter and Memory*, Bergson came to the view that what lies behind the concept of duration is that the past exists in as real a way as the present. Every present act contains within it the accretion of the past as memory in a noumenal unconscious. For Bergson the unconscious was nothing more than this vast virtual storehouse of memory.

The concepts of pure duration and pure memory may afford a way of conceiving time in relation to the nonconscious. Libet's experiments allow a re-conceptualisation of the neurological question of conscious/nonconscious interaction away from the spatial to the temporal plane: not 'where' in the brain, but 'when'. The retroactive mapping of conscious awareness that Libet identifies seems to problematise a straight forward narrative scheme, and Bergon's nonlinear temporality may present an alternative. (The latter, however presents the danger of circularity and the absence of originality that we shall have to address in due course.) Gazzaniga and LeDoux's P. S. experiments indicate the spatial nature of consciousness. It operates in terms of symbols and language, deployed in linear narrative fashion, in its search for cohesion in mental life. This is then mapped onto actions initiated by the nonconscious, which does not seek to make sense of the external world in the same way. Operating in terms of motor responses, the reactive nature of the nonconscious means that it does not use spatialisation, in Bergsonian terms, in the same narrative way as the conscious. Nor is there a sense of temporal linearity beyond pure reactivity.

If the nonconscious can be said to have mental 'content', other than patterned responses that are purely neurophysical, it is in the form of memory. Connolly uses Deleuze's image of nonchronological 'sheets of past'[75] to illustrate how memory can be seen to operate outside linearity:

> One shape it assumes is that of a rapidly mobilized set of virtual memories, assembled in nonchronological order from different periods in your life as, say, you encounter a disturbing situation. For example, you hear a man walking at a fast pace behind you on a dark city street. Virtual memories from different events in your adulthood, childhood, and adolescence might be mobilized quickly to help organize your perception and operational response. Since it takes the form of a virtual sheet, the memory does not become an explicit recollection.[76]

In such affectively imbued situations, the response initiated is an assemblage of virtual memory from different moments from one's past, which hover below consciousness creating an affective patterning within which conscious and physical responses are deployed. Such an assemblage of virtual memory can be seen in terms of Bergson's pure duration and memory. We must be careful however, in that

Deleuze used memory in the same way as Bergson, positing it on the virtual but not actual levels and thus projecting it out of the material realm. We may embody the concept however, in the neural memory trace and in the hardening of neural pathways over time.

Given the plasticity of the electrical connections arising from the brain's wetware, sheets of past are folded and refolded into each other in response to present situations and the interaction of conscious and nonconscious. This creates new associations between disparate memories from various points in one's life that may again be redeployed in future situations. Herein we can see Augustine's conceptualisation of three temporal levels all existing in the present. The change in a memory through present conscious thought or association with present situations can be conceived of as a change in Augustine's present of past things. Nothing has changed but the present perception of what happened and its changed projection into the future.

As indicated above, the use of Bergson' nonlinear pure duration and the influence of present thought and action by assemblages of virtual memory may introduce an unwanted degree of circularity into mental processes. This circularity has already reared its head in Libet's retrospective consciousness and the link between consciousness thought, affect and social environment. Do we think in circles, and if so, what does this mean for originality in thought and free will?

Stuck in a moment that you can't get out of?

Circularity of thought would prevent the formation of new and original concepts and hence, foreclose any critical political potential. A linear-based narrative mode of thought would overcome such fears but, as we have seen, such conceptions place too much emphasis on the role of consciousness as well as facing obstacles presented by our background culture of consumerism, and postmodernity in general, which push towards the fragmentary and episodic. Even in narrative conceptions pure linearity is problematised by the reliance which a narrative conception of self must have on memory and culture. These constant 'references back', which are necessary for a narrative to present any semblance of coherence over time and in the social context of its being understandable to others, again introduce a degree of circularity.

A set of concepts that may help weave together the ideas of circularity and originality whilst not privileging the conscious and allowing a primary role for memory, affect and nonconscious processes may be found in Deleuze's repetition through passive synthesis.

Given Deleuze's admiration for Bergson, on one level *Difference and Repetition* argues for a dualist view of reality. Reality is not only composed of actual things, but also of a virtual realm that lies beyond the actual. The virtual is composed of pure becomings or intensities. In this side of reality, the emphasis is more on processes than concrete *things*. This is a concern which runs throughout the work and which renders Deleuze so useful in the present context. The actual object is an expression of the pure becomings or intensities of the virtual, and the latter connects to the actual through the sensations experienced by an individual coming into contact with an actual object. The existence of a realm of fluid processes and becomings, never actualised or solidified in that realm, is important for Deleuze to be able to suggest how circularity can still give rise to originality.

Deleuze outlines three processes of repetition that enable a reciprocal determination between the virtual and the actual. Repetition is that which allows actual things to acquire fixity in the world we can perceive and intensities in the virtual to come into relation with each other. The three different cycles of repetition are also linked to three syntheses of time, which help to explain how they come about. The first repetition is that of habit. What we conceive of as our 'self' acquires fixity through constant repetition of small psychic and behavioural events. For Deleuze, in the repetition of a habit the past is synthesised or contracted into the present as a behaviour orientated towards the future. This synthesis is seen as passive in that it occurs in the mind but is not an active operation carried out by it. In explaining this, Deleuze cites Hume's idea that in a series of AB, AB, AB the mind acquires the habit of expecting B after A, because when A happens it is retained in the mind when B appears. This retention is not an active process, like the generation of memory, however, but is passive, with the mind in this instance being likened to a photographic plate that retains the image of A as B appears. (We can also think back to Freud's use of the image of the mystic writing pad to illustrate unconscious traces and, on the more material level of the nonconsious, the image of water running in channels). Through repetition the mind begins to expect the occurrence of B after A as it synthesises all the previous instances of their occurrence upon the present appearance of A.[77] For Hume, the imagination is the function which links the members of a series into an expectation or habit. For Deleuze, the imagination, 'or the mind which contemplates in its multiple or fragmented states', performs the more radical role of drawing something new, a difference, from repetition.[78] Between any repetitions there will be a myriad of differences, and since this order of repetition functions as a contraction of time (both past and future) into the present moment, these differences too will be synthesised into the expectation or habit. This process of acquiring habit is a nonconscious process more akin to behavioural conditioning than to the formation of memory:

> These thousands of habits of which we are composed . . . thus form the basic domain of passive synthesis. The passive self is not simply defined by receptivity – that is, by means of the capacity to experience sensations – but by virtue of the contractile contemplation which constitutes the organism itself before it constitutes the sensations.[79]

Such a conception can be linked back to the material of Chapters 1 and 3 in that the passive synthesis that forms habit can be seen as the laying down of neural pathways and the imbuing of certain actions/objects/situations with a somatic marker that is reactivated at their next encounter. These constitute the systems that underlie 'larval' selves, described by Deleuze as dissolved selves.

Whereas the first synthesis of time is concerned with the present moment connected forward and back, the second involves the connection between the present and the past through the passing of the former into the latter. The passive synthesis of habit, and the active synthesis of memory formation in which memory traces of what has just happened are formed in the present moment, are both predicated on a passive synthesis in memory. This second passive synthesis makes use of Bergson's pure past as a means to explain how the present becomes past. In order to become past, the present must already have an element of the past in it. When the present passes, it becomes part of a pure past that will be part of any future present moment (since any present must contain an element of past). Therefore, the totality of the pure past, comprising all moments that have past, forms part of any present moment; it is synthesised in the present moment. As in the passive synthesis of habit, the present moment is a contraction. Rather than being a contraction of distinct occurrences, however, the second synthesis of memory is a contraction of the entirety of pure past, which forms an integral part of the present.[80]

Deleuze passes on to a discussion of repetition within a life, which serves to show how continuity can be preserved through the succession of discrete moments. Each present moment replays the past, a process conceived of not as determination but as destiny:

> [This] . . . implies between successive presents non-localisable connections, actions at a distance, systems of replay, resonance and echoes

> objective chances, signs, signals and roles which transcend spatial locations and temporal successions . . . What we live empirically as a succession of different presents from the point of view of active synthesis is also the ever-increasing co-existence of levels of the past within passive synthesis.[81]

The difference between determination and destiny can be brought out using the Buddhist conception of dependent origination. This is a process of psychological and moral becoming, illustrated as a process of twelve steps leading through consciousness, to the sensing of an object and the latching on to that sensation which causes changes in our mental life and consciousness. In such a way a repeated action becomes a habit, a habit hardens into a personality and, by virtue of a certain personality, a person will put themselves in certain situations (a destiny). The process is deterministic in that each of the twelve steps is founded on the former, but there is always room for an outcome other than the next step. In Buddhist terms, the most important intervention would be the cutting of the link between sensing and repeated craving of an object or sensation, thus not allowing a habit to form. For Deleuze also, the passive syntheses of habit and memory condition the present moment; one can reshape the past, however, by connecting to the pure past through reminiscence. This is not like the voluntary bringing to the surface of the active synthesis of memory that replays past moments. Rather this is an involuntary mechanism (Deleuze cites Proust's recollections of Combray) which looks beyond past moments to the pure past, playing (rather than replaying) pasts in a form that never actually were. Hence, we can plasticise our past and change the foundation of the present moment. It is also true that, though the present is conditioned by the past, a range of options will always be presented in which a range of responses can be played out to any given situation.

It is in such a way that the future is produced by means of the third passive synthesis and repetition. Although the past is present in both the previous two syntheses as habit and in pure past as memory, in the third synthesis there is a disruption of the perfection of the foregoing circular form and it is this disruption that allows the creation of the new future. One can bring back in the notion of the virtual to help explain this. Even though the present moment is fundamentally conditioned by habit and memory we still possess the possibility of relating differently to each memory or habit under present conditions. Through this different relation, we are constantly reshaping the content of memory, refashioning habits and imbuing both with new affectual resonances. A sheet of past can serve to combine different memories in new ways, creating a different collage hovering just under consciousness as a foundation for action.

An example from the last chapter can be used to illustrate this. In Damasio's work with David, the latter was able to pick out the photograph of the researcher who had been most friendly towards him 80 per cent of the time. On the one hand, this illustrates the affective markers laid down by their interactions through the passive syntheses of habit, then hardened into memory. These syntheses are good illustrations of passivity since David was fundamentally unable to actively synthesise experiences to form new memories. In addition, however, one may suggest that without the third synthesis David's selection rate would have been 100 per cent. If the present moment of each selection was founded on the first two syntheses, there would have been little way in which the habits of interaction and pure past they facilitated would have not resulted in the recognition of the friendly researcher. The third synthesis allows a break in such a circle making possible the 20 per cent error margin David exhibited. Different sheets of past could have been formulated in the second synthesis, thus changing each in the repeated series of selections. This could be added to the possibility of different reactions to the same sheets of past through different relations to the virtual intensities in each of the series. On a fundamental level it is not the same thing that repeats for Deleuze but the possibility of difference.

It must be pointed out that Deleuze himself was not amenable to linking his project to 'scientific' research, as, for him, science did not present a fully realised account of reality.[82] Science, for Deleuze, works only in the field of the actual, neglecting the necessity for the virtual realm, which he posits to account for change. There are, however, definite linkages between the concepts outlined above and the material that forms the core of the present work.[83]

On the one hand is the nonconscious nature of the three levels of passive synthesis. Individual consciousness was not, for Deleuze, a major player in the formation of identity and was of little concern to his work. Indeed given that *Difference and Repetition* is not a work on the philosophy of mind, but an argument for a certain vision of the whole of reality, the first two syntheses of habit and memory do not necessarily have to take place in a mind at all, but can refer to any process. They can be usefully applied to the human mind however. In the first synthesis, repeated series lead to the laying down and strengthening of particular neural pathways. The concept of passivity is particularly useful in this regard when one recalls the amount of nonconscious processing which goes on below conscious awareness. Most of our sensory information is passively synthesised and imbued with affectual markers. These can become nonconscious, automatic processes and subroutines carried out in reaction to certain situations.

Likewise, the second synthesis can illustrate how each present moment is built upon a foundation of all that went before it. Each time we react, consciously or nonconsciously, or a random thought crosses our minds, this is the result of all that has gone before: all the building up of neural pathways, the biological and instinctual inheritance. In Chapter 1, when the backwards referral of consciousness was first introduced, the example was given of the reaction of snatching one's hand from the fire when burnt and then feeling the sensation of pain (one can also think of losing balance, regaining it, feeling the rush momentary fear and then thinking 'I almost tripped'). At that stage, the point was made that it is of little use to us to have to go through a process of conscious computation first, before withdrawing our hand. We would have been more badly burnt because of the time that was lost. Deleuze's incorporation of pure past into the second synthesis suggests the immensely deep and complex foundation of such a momentary action. The biological honing of c-fibres, neurochemistry, message-carrying chemicals in the bloodstream and muscle reaction and control down the ages can be combined with the instinctual knowledge of the burning quality of fire learned over a lifetime of individual experiential and cultural ingraining, aside from any deeply engrained inherited reaction (such as fear of the dark or of the noise from behind). These have all been founded, in turn, upon slight variations in environment that have caused and refined them as well as the line of biological vessels within which they have been passed down. The instant reaction of the present moment, in this very material sense, can be said to synthesise the whole of the past.

The present action will then further refine and add to this past. The particular neural pathways which led to the signal to remove the hand will be strengthened as the body learns to speed up the process to further reduce damage on the next occurrence, for example, and the stock of memories will be added to as 'that time I nearly burnt myself' becomes part of the past in its own right. The next time the situation occurs the same mental process will initiate. The circle of situation and reaction will be repeated, but it will be different because of the enhanced pathways and the additional memory, as well as any other differences in context (a different fire in a different place, maybe the other hand this time, having just watched the *Towering Inferno* on television or the influence of other context-dependent neurochemicals on the action of those controlling the reaction).

The temporal structure of Deleuze's ideas allows a conceptualisation of how circularity and the microlevel of interaction between nonconsciousness and consciousness, as per Libet, can be combined with a degree of linearity through the repetition of difference. This linearity, on the level of consciousness, can be conceived of in narrative terms and, on the nonconscious level, as changes in neurophysiology and neurochemistry. As stated, this is very much a materialisation of Deleuze's position, however, and one that he would have been keen to resist since it engages primarily with the actual side of reality.

In order to engage with the virtual we must revisit some of the discussion from Chapter 2. One of the main issues to engage in terms o the virtual is the fact that Deleuze argues that we are the product o virtual events we can never fully control. The chance for originality comes for him in the possibility of counter-actualising, or 'vice dicting', previous events, playing them in different ways, and in hi critique of Descartes. Deleuze suggests that Descartes' predicate of th thinking self is insufficient to explain the individuality of differen people with the same biological and mental structures. As Cartesia thought is substance dualist in nature, separating mind and brain Deleuzian dualism posits a virtual layer of reality lying behind th mind itself, with the interaction between the virtual and the min being the site of originality. The interaction between the two take place based on the individual's reaction to the intensities that mak up the virtual. This reaction takes the form of affect and sensation Different intensities can become layered upon each other, creating i turn layers of affect and sensation that accompany each thought i consciousness or nonconscious process. The originality and differenc of a thought or process therefore comes from its intimate and evolv ing connection with the virtual intensities of which it is the produc on the actual plane. As can be seen, this connection introduces a flu idity into the realm of the actual which means that mental life is a ever-changing, never complete, process.

In terms of the present project, this can be connected back to th material of Chapters 1 and 3, with the nature of affect changin the conscious-nonconscious loops of Libet, Gazzaniga and LeDou The abstraction that Deleuze makes of the virtual, however, lea us to ask what lies behind affectual reactions and points to the somewhat unknowable quality. With this in mind, let us turn to Bauman's concept of *unsicherheit*, the feeling of postmodern anxiety and discomfiture identified in the last chapter. Using the assemblage of theoretical tools now at our disposal, we can further fill out the picture of its functioning. *Unsicherheit* can be conceived of on a number of levels. We have previously identified it as a result, on the cultural level, of the mismatch between the demands of consumer society for individual self-creation and the consumer method of doing this, which functions only to constantly manufacture desire. We can also identify it in the disruption of coherent whole-life narratives by the segmentation and fragmentation of time that contemporary society inspires, leading to a frustration of the explanatory function of consciousness so well exhibited by the P. S. study. Our present mode of social life may, therefore, have created an emotional and structural regime that produces *unsicherheit* as an affective mental response. Whether or not one commits to the transcendental elements of Deleuze's world view, the affective sensation loops connecting the virtual nature of this regime to the actuality of processes in mental life and the Foucauldian shaping of bodies and responses are a useful way of characterising such a result.

Notes

1. Gazzaniga and LeDoux, *The Integrated Mind*, pp. 149–50.
2. Lacan, *Écrits*.
3. Ibid. pp. 1–9.
4. Ibid. p. 148.
5. Frosh, *Politics of Psychoanalysis*, p. 131.
6. Bowie, *Lacan*, pp. 30–1.
7. Damasio, *The Feeling of What Happens*, p. 108.
8. Ibid. p. 136.
9. Damasio characterises these neural patterns as a proto-consciousness existing below the level of consciousness, a tripartite division that draws reminiscence of Plato and Freud.
10. Dennett, *Consciousness Explained*, pp. 418, 429.
11. Ibid. p. 207.
12. Du Gay et al., *Identity: A Reader*, pp. 297–303.
13. P. Bourdieu, 'The biographical illusion' in Du Gay et al., *Identity: A Reader*, p. 298 (author's italics).
14. Ibid. p. 299.
15. Freeman, *Rewriting the Self*, p. 33 (author's italics).
16. Heidegger, *Being and Time*, §69:411.

17. Ibid. §74:435.
18. Ibid. §74:438.
19. Ibid. §78:459.
20. Ibid. §74:437.
21. Ricoeur, *Time and Narrative, Vol. 3*.
22. Stevens, 'On Ricoeur's analysis of time and narration', in Hahn, *The Philosophy of Paul Ricoeur*, p. 503.
23. Bauman, *In Search of Politics*, p. 77.
24. As quoted in ibid. p. 77.
25. Ibid. p. 78.
26. Bauman, *Liquid Modernity*, p. 118.
27. Bauman, *The Individualized Society*, p. 8.
28. Bauman, *Liquid Modernity*, p. 83.
29. Christopher Lasch, in his *Culture of Narcissism*, p. 30, claims 'to live for the moment is the prevailing passion – to live for yourself, not for your predecessors or posterity. We are fast losing our sense of historical continuity, the sense of belonging to a succession of generations originating in the past and stretching into the future.'
30. Bauman, *The Individualized Society*, p. 7.
31. Ibid. p. 7.
32. Moran, *Introduction to Phenomenology*, p. 453.
33. Ricoeur, as quoted in Madison, 'Ricoeur and the hermeneutics of the subject', in Hahn, *The Philosophy of Paul Ricoeur*, p. 83.
34. Ricoeur, as quoted in ibid. p. 84.
35. Kemp, 'Ethics and narrativity', in Hahn, *The Philosophy of Paul Ricoeur*, p. 373.
36. Ibid. p. 373.
37. Madison, 'Ricoeur and the hermeneutics of the subject', in Hahn, *The Philosophy of Paul Ricoeur*, p. 85 (author's italics).
38. Ibid. p. 85.
39. Taylor, *Sources of the Self*, p. 52.
40. Smith, *Strong Hermeneutics*, p. 37.
41. Taylor, *Sources of the Self*, p. 34.
42. Smith, *Strong Hermeneutics*, p. 37.
43. Taylor, *Sources of the Self*, pp. 19–20.
44. Ibid. p. 27.
45. Ibid. p. 36.
46. Smith, *Strong Hermeneutics*, p. 39.
47. Ibid. p. 39.
48. Taylor, *Sources of the Self*, p. 30.
49. Rosen, 'Must we return to moral realism', p. 187.
50. Smith, *Strong Hermeneutics*, p. 45.
51. Ibid. p. 45.
52. Ibid. p. 45.

53. Ibid. p. 41.
54. Ibid. p. 42.
55. Ibid. p. 43.
56. Rorty, *Essays on Heidegger and Others*, p. 155.
57. Ibid. p. 161.
58. Beckett, *First Love and Other Novellas*, p. 67.
59. This definition draws on general aspects identified across the literature as for example in Maffesoli, *The Time of the Tribes*; Shields, *Lifestyle Shopping*; and Sulkunen, *The European New Middle Class*. Although the definitive text on neo-tribalism can be regarded as Maffesoli's, I have chosen to concentrate on the more practical applications of his theories.
60. Shields, *Lifestyle Shopping*, p. 15.
61. Goffman, *The Presentation of Self in Everyday Life*.
62. Langman, 'Neon cages', in Shields, *Lifestyle Shopping*; p. 56.
63. Horsman and Marshall, *After the Nation-State*.
64. Bauman, *In Search of Politics*, p. 48.
65. Bauman, *Liquid Modernity*, p. 200.
66. Bauman, *Community*, p. 69.
67. Ibid. p. 71.
68. Nietzsche, 'Beyond Good and Evil', in *Basic Writings of Nietzsche*, p. 201.
69. Ibid, p. 270.
70. Freud, *The Psychopathology of Everyday Life*, p. 198 fn 1.
71. Augustine, *Confessions*, p. 235 (ch. XI xx, 26).
72. Ibid. ch. XI xiv, 21
73. Bergson, *Time and Free Will*.
74. Bergson, *Matter and Memory*.
75. Deleuze, *Cinema 2*, pp. 95–122.
76. Connolly, *Neuropolitics*, p. 97.
77. Deleuze, *Difference and Repetition*, pp. 70–1.
78. Ibid. p. 76.
79. Ibid. p. 78.
80. Ibid. pp. 81–2.
81. Ibid. p. 83.
82. For most extensive analysis of the sources of Deleuze's view of the unconscious, see Kerslake's excellent *Deleuze and the Unconscious*.
83. For an account of the connections between Deleuze and affect on his own terms, see Massumi, 'The autonomy of affect', in *Parables for the Virtual*.

5

Psychological Revolt

Having constructed a conceptualisation of the mind and its connection to its surroundings as well as having painted a picture of the present environment it finds itself in, the psychological possibility of critique remains to be examined. It is easy to state that the mind is shaped wholly by a combination of neurophysical parameters and social experience, but the very fact that one feels so resistant to this idea shows the merits of deeper examination. Consciousness rebels against the notion that its limits can be so circumscribed and the artistic, cultural and philosophical labour of our species is a record of our attempted transcendence of such limits. The question is also of the utmost political importance. If one cannot adequately think outside the socio-political matrix into which one is born, we are left with little alternative but passive acceptance or partial critique.

Beginning with the following discussion of the possibilities for critique on the conscious level, the next two chapters will, therefore attempt to begin sketching how, given the foregoing material, we can actually attempt to think differently.

The potential of the personal conscious

A useful starting point in this regard is the work of Jean Baudrillard both in terms of his analysis of society and in the perceived negativity of his conclusions for resistance. Baudrillard's thought moved from Marxism in the late sixties to a gradually more semiological conceptualisation of consumer society.[1] His later writing utilises the concept of 'hyperreality': nothing in consumer society has any referent or reality outside itself, existing only in the constant stream of distortions and images and displaced meanings which make up the ever-expanding communications networks of the contemporary world.[2] As Poster points out in his introduction to a selection of Baudrillard's writings, this presents a problem for critique since there is 'no one dominating, nothing is being dominated and no ground exists for a principle of liberation from domination.'[3]

This problem can be underlined with reference to the pessimistic conclusions to which this led Baudrillard in *Fatal Strategies* and 'The masses: the implosion of the social in the media'.[4] In the latter, the only form of critique which is espoused on the part of the masses is silence in response to the non-communicative bombardment of information by the media. The masses 'disappear', 'turn themselves into an impenetrable and meaningless surface' behind which they parody and reverse that which is delivered to them through the media.[5] Baudrillard likens this strategy to that of a child who responds to an adult's injunctions to behave with 'infantilism, hyperconformity, total dependence, passivity, idiocy' thus responding to the totality of the opposing system better than a subjective response which deals with only one facet of it.[6] The masses, therefore, utilise the strategy of taking on the characteristics of the object rather than the subject and of 'refusal by over-acceptance'.[7]

The question must be asked if, through my own characterisations of the human condition in contemporary society, I have not also closed off the avenues of critique through positing the self as a reflection of its surroundings. One of the themes that has pervaded throughout this work is that of a fluid and mutable self which is open to change. Rather than using this as a mechanism to disappear into the social matrix, to use fluidity to present a meaningless surface in a strategy of resistance by over-engagement, critical possibilities abound in a positive articulation of fluidity. Consumer society becomes its own gravedigger when it sells us the idea that change is not only possible but also desirable.

The first critical question concerns the reason for resistance. If the self is nothing more than a mutable reflection of its environment, why should we privilege one set of social meanings over another? If the aim of the self is to ease social life, then surely the best course of action is to embrace the prevailing societal modes of self-articulation, since it is these modes of being which present the best hermeneutic chance of facilitating social understanding through shared meanings? The answer to both of these questions lies in the argument given above, that the existential imperative that lies behind the consumer identity is in contradiction to its proposed articulation through the market. It is a marketing technique that, when deployed with the other techniques examined in Chapter 3, serves to heighten and exacerbate desire rather than leading to the self-realisation promised. This is the frustration and uncertainty that leads to *unsicherheit* as Chapter 3 concluded. As we have seen in the last chapter, it is also a state of affairs that, although experienced by most, does not lend itself to communal articulation because of its existential individualist base.

On this foundation, the reasons for resistance are manifold. We should be critical of the existing state of affairs, on the one hand, because it makes those of us who live within it unhappy and uncertain, as evidenced by increases in anxiety disorders. The economic and social functioning of the system also condemns those outside it to exclusion and poverty. Aside from these very real issues, we should also question any system that presents itself as the only alternative, which seeks to mould our self-articulations and which claims that there is no other way of life.

In the face of the discussions in the previous chapters, there is the added consideration that the society in which we live in some ways conditions our sense of self through providing it with the social frameworks with which we create our identity. These social frameworks will also govern the way in which we relate to other people and to ourselves and, therefore, are of an extremely important political nature. The foundation of a psycho-social analytic should be to explore the relations between these factors, how society conditions identity, how identity conditions social relations and how these relations in turn form politics. The thread that runs through the analysis I have presented is that of fluidity and change. Repeatedly, the point has been made that we live in a society that is fluid and dynamic and constantly on the move. This aids the response to one of the most important questions which a psycho-social analytic throws up – what are the conditions of possibility for a particular societal, thought or political structure to change?

The idea of change must be examined in terms of societal structure thought and interpersonal relations given the co-original matrix that they form. One way of examining the potential therein is through Deleuze and Guattari's *Anti-Oedipus*.[8] In this work, the two investigate the connection between capitalism and the psychoanalytic structure of the Oedipus complex as an explanation for psychological repression. Ostensibly, the book functions as a critique of psychoanalytic categories, with the Oedipus complex prime among them, but given the density and subtlety of the thought contained therein, there are several lines of investigation that may be deemed relevant for our purposes.

One of the main themes of *Anti-Oedipus* is the constrictions which prevailing modes of thought and action place upon both the individual and social formations. Deleuze and Guattari paint a picture of the unconscious as a collection of 'desiring-machines' which may be plugged into both each other and the machines of the sociality. This machinic way of theorising the world is based upon the notion that the latter is an inherently fragmented entity – 'we live today in the age of partial objects, bricks that have been shattered to bits and left-overs'.[9] Any idea of totality or unity in the world is seen as peripheral and imposed outside these fragments. One reason for the fragmented nature of the world may be the operations of capitalism, which a large part of the book explores. Capitalism is presented as a schizophrenic process that deterritorialises and renders fluid much of what in previous societies had been fairly rigidly demarcated.[10] This happens on the economic, social and ultimately the psychological fronts in that capitalism is said to produce schizophrenic individuals.[11]

The idea of the schizophrenic is one of the most subtle and complex in *Anti-Oedipus*. In one sense, it serves as a way of analysing the particular psycho-social moment we find ourselves in under capitalism; in another, there seems to be a valourisation of the schizophrenic as in some way holding the key to revolutionary potential; and, finally, there is a repudiation of this notion and a claim that it is the schizophrenic process, not individuals with that clinical tag, which holds the potential for revolution.

The underlying characteristic of schizophrenia in Deleuze and Guattari seems to be the ability to think differently, to break out of the strictures of the prevailing modes of thought and operation, to open up the possibility of new conceptual territories. The idea of liberation for them is centred on the prominence of desire in their work (at one stage it is asserted '*there is only desire and the social, and nothing else*').[12] Goodchild explains that desire is inherently revolutionary in that it affects and changes everything in society and that nothing stands outside it. It is productive in a way that other bases for action are not:

> All fixed orders of society, including conventions, institutions, and impulses, that provide a framework for possible social relations, but which themselves remain unaffected by what happens, are instances of antiproduction. When desire is present, however, it exists as a process that changes the connections and social relations of society, transgressing all boundaries.[13]

Desire, therefore, is a productive force that can be harnessed by the will to change in order to effect transformations in society. This is until it runs up against the operations of capitalism, however. Capitalism functions on one level to liberate flows of desire by its process of deterritorialisation, but does so within confined limits, straining to keep the deterritorialisation process reined in.[14]

The problem is that not only does capitalism produce schizophrenics but it also operates to repress them, since the schizophrenic process contains elements that would push deterritorialisation to its limits and unravel the capitalist framework:

> They [the schizophrenics] must reinvent each gesture. But such a man [sic] produces himself as a free man, irresponsible, solitary, and joyous, finally able to say and do something in his own name, without asking permission; a desire lacking nothing, a flux that overcomes barriers and codes, a name that no longer designates any ego whatsoever.[15]

Schizophrenia becomes a creative act of production against the repressive limits imposed by capitalism and the Oedipal interpretation of psychic functioning. 'The revolutionary path', therefore, may not be to withdraw from capitalism but to force it along the lines of deterritorialisation on which it already functions; to accelerate and complete the process, as it were.[16] The idea is to run away within capitalism; not to opt out of the capitalist framework, but to escape within it. Whereas one should not withdraw from the world market,[17] 'the revolutionary knows that escape is revolutionary . . . provided one sweeps away the social cover on leaving, or causes a piece of the system to get lost in the shuffle.'[18] The difference is that one must present an alternative by one's act of withdrawal, highlight the 'lines of escape'[19] along which one has moved, and not simply opt out in Baudrillardian silence.

Underlying all this is desire as a creative process. It seems essential to differentiate this productive liberated desire from the variation we have already encountered in Chapter 3, the artificially created and permanently exacerbated consumer form of desire that capitalism manufactures as a product of its operations. The latter is one of the ways in which desire is co-opted in order to disrupt the schizophrenic flow of desire that may actually lead to the creation of something new, which ties it up in the endless repetition of the old. Capitalism is a deterritorialising enterprise, which in the end is only partial. It replaces the networks it dissolves with the operations of capital as a limit on the social world that it produces. Schizophrenia on the other hand represents the 'absolute limit' of deterritorialised flows:

> Hence one can say that schizophrenia is the exterior limit of capitalism itself or the conclusion of its deepest tendency, but that capitalism only functions on condition that it push back or displace this limit by

substituting for it its own immanent relative limits, which it constantly reproduces on a widened scale.[20]

We can now begin to tie these ideas back into the work that has been carried out in previous chapters, before investigating how we might harness these ideas for the purposes of change. If we apply the theories of Deleuze and Guattari to the mechanics of consumerism, we could claim that the matrices of meaning presented by advertising, as well as the existential imperative underlying them, are ways of delimiting the forms of creative desire outlined in *Anti-Oedipus*. In the thought of Deleuze and Guattari this engenders a situation of schizophrenia, reflecting the schizophrenic process of capitalism's deterritorialising action. In Chapter 3, it was suggested that the result of consumerism on identity is the induction of a type of multiphrenia through the creation of different personae or the different mini-narratives of the last chapter before being tied together by a meta-narrative. On this surface reading, there may be parallels between the two conceptualisations, although they operate at two different theoretical levels.

The schizophrenic suffers from his or her fate under capitalism, not because of schizophrenia itself but because of capitalism's defensive reaction to it. This reaction is to try to block the flow of the schizophrenic process, 'it is the constrained arrest of the process, or its continuation in the void, or in the way in which it is forced to take itself as a goal.'[21] This too has resonances with what was suggested earlier as the cause of *unsicherheit*, the imposition of an existential imperative onto a process which does not work along those lines, instead being a primarily unconscious utilitarian construction, and the frustration of these existential goals by the consumerism which imposed it. Here too, we have the disruption of the process of living. This can be traced on one of two levels, either the disruption of utilitarian and fluid self-construction in line with constraints placed upon it, or the disruption of the fulfilment of that construction along societal lines.

In the context of what has been argued in earlier chapters, it would make sense to posit the second of these two options as the source of disruption. If we are claiming that the conscious self is a utilitarian enterprise that facilitates social orientation through its construction making use of the meanings found in surrounding culture, theoretically it would be possible to create a self in line with whatever culture one found oneself in, in our case consumer capitalism. The problem would then arise with the tension within that culture which frustrated such self-construction. This interpretation also falls closer to that of Deleuze and Guattari. For them, the self, or subject, is a tangential effect of the operations of desiring-machines of the unconscious and appears on the periphery.[22] There is no 'natural' self to disrupt at this early stage; that comes later in the interruption of schizophrenia's fulfilment.

Given these parallels, it may be useful to examine the remedies which Deleuze and Guattari suggest for the alleviation of our contemporary ills. As stated above, repeatedly in *Anti-Oedipus* it is claimed that resistance should come in the form of a completion of the process rather than withdrawal from it:

> The schizophrenic escape itself does not merely consist in withdrawing from the social, in living on the fringe: it causes the social to take flight through the multiplicity of holes that eat away at it and penetrate it, always coupled directly to it, everywhere setting the molecular charges that will explode what must explode, make fall what must fall, make escape what must escape, at each point ensuring the conversion of schizophrenia as a process into an effectively revolutionary force.[23]

Again, it is worth repeating that it is not the schizophrenics themselves who are deemed to be revolutionary, but the schizophrenic process itself. This decentred, fluid and partialising process must take hold at the molecular level. 'Molecular' is defined by Goodchild as 'flexible processes, whose nature may be affected by the process or its constituents; working according to specific interactions; often occurring in local or small scale situations', in contrast with 'molar', or rigidly functioning macro-processes, which proceed according to laws or statistics.[24] The question of how these resistances may be carried out is partially answered by Massumi, who suggests five strategies for resistance to create friction in the molar capitalist machine:[25]

- 'Stop the world': this constitutes introducing stoppages into the molar machine, either through 'tactical sabotage' or by introducing incremental improvements in the existing order in order to integrate on its terms.[26] These are to open spaces for the process of 'becoming', liberating the previously blocked flows of desire to reintroduce fluidity to thought and being.
- 'Cherish derelict spaces': in some ways this represents using the spaces thus created by stopping the world and 'forcing holes in habit'. These spaces may be geographical, such as those territories

referred to by capitalism as the 'third world' or ghettoes in the 'first world'. It may take the form of daydreaming, the privacy of one's own home, dissident anti-ideological politics, non-church religion, and so on. The important thing is that these spaces are interstitial, operating within the world in the spaces between conventions and orthodox territories.[27]

- 'Study camouflage': this is learning to pass as members of the social order to be resisted in order to effect incremental change. The danger is, however, that one may get tied in to operating along the molar lines which one is forced into through operating within the strictures of the machine to be resisted.[28]
- 'Sidle and Straddle': due to the dangers of the above reformist political change, one may be inclined not to see the dangers inherent in directly confrontational methods. These, it is claimed, may lead to the resistance defining itself purely in negative oppositional terms to that resisted, thus defeating its purpose of escape, and may also lead to a hatred of the enemy and 'microfascism'. The answer is therefore to 'sidestep', to operate from the sidelines and periphery.[29]
- 'Come out': 'Throw off your camouflage as soon as you can and still survive. What one comes out of is identity. What one comes into is greater transformational potential.'[30]

With these suggestions in mind, we can begin to build up a picture of how resistance can be carried out within a Deleuzian and Guattarian framework. The foremost point is that critique and action must operate on two levels. On the one hand, they are carried on within a specific locality, a specific site of micro-politics; they are always part of a machinic assemblage even though this may be what they are trying to resist. Within this assemblage an outside grows; new patterns of thought and action trace trajectories that break out of a particular system. Critique and action are, therefore, simultaneously from within and without.

There are dangers to these characterisations, however, which are pointed out in both *Dialogues*[31] and *A Thousand Plateaus*[32] and which all seem to amount to what is referred to as 'fascism', be it of a molar or molecular variety, the latter taking the form of more insidious micro-fascisms. We learn from Foucault that there will always be something which resists in any machine, however, and it is from this that one may draw hope. It seems also that this resistance will usually begin at the molecular level as a trickle, which later becomes a flow;

these flows amount to nothing, however, if they do not serve to affect and reshape the molar level.[33] These flows constitute nomadic war machines, mechanisms of disruption, erected along the boundaries of a given system, which impinge on it and disrupt its functioning.[34] This is a specific disruption rather than that which arises from the general functioning of machines in serving as breaks in the flows of that transmitted from previous machines.[35] In a way, it is the constitution and deployment of these war machines that most of the rest of this chapter will investigate, bearing in mind the warning that it is in the nature of the capitalist state to try and absorb war machines into itself.

The later writings of Michel Foucault may help to illustrate how, on an individual level, one may begin to utilise the suggestions drawn out of Deleuze and Guattari's work by Massumi. Deleuze and Guattari's positing of liberation as centred on the conception of desire can be seen as a response to Foucault's analysis of the operations of power. If we remain within the language of *Anti-Oedipus*, it can be said that Foucault's genealogies of how power operates to construct accepted truth in particular situations constitute ways of disrupting the machines in a given system from the inside. By showing the contingencies on which our visions of social and individual life rest and how they serve certain interests, Foucault opens up the 'derelict spaces' of which Massumi speaks, stopping the world by suspending our belief in it.

In one interview, Foucault identifies power as an essentially productive force, making the point that if it were purely repressive then no-one would obey it.[36] In the same interview, he claims that there are many different kinds of revolution[37] and that opposition primarily comes about through a reorientation towards the daily struggles of the ordinary people who are caught in the 'fine meshes of the web of power'.[38] The role of the intellectual in these struggles is to open up new interpretations of truth in specific areas, to perform, in Foucault's case, genealogies that show that things are not necessarily as 'naturally occurring' as the powers-that-be would have us believe. In essence, the intellectual's task is to present tensions and discrepancies and open up the way for alternative conceptions. There is a refusal in both Foucault and Deleuze and Guattari to indicate what form these alternatives may take, preferring instead that the people effected should speak for themselves.[39]

Deleuze can be seen to provide a critical context within which to situate Foucault's tracing of the capillaries of power, which flow through certain truth formations, and the ways in which these capillaries may be blocked. For him the idea of resistance is essentially a battle over truth.[40] In his interviews for gay magazines we can get a clearer perspective of how groups must begin to act and think in ways outside the hegemonic conceptions which oppress them. He claims that for the gay community the issue should not be a question of trying to integrate into a heterosexual framework of definition.[41] There is no 'truth' of sexuality to which one must conform but rather one must seek to create space for a multiplicity of relationships.[42] Homosexuals must, therefore, seek to absent themselves from hegemonic conceptions and create a uniquely gay lifestyle.[43]

This puts the emphasis for critique and political action very much on individuals and groups rather than in overarching political programmes. Foucault prefers to speak of the impetus for change relying more on social movements, whose relative lack of a set programme, far from being a drawback, is in fact an opportunity for political experimentation.[44] The danger of falling into a sedimentary form of thought and action is one of those outlined by Deleuze, whose concern is always to keep the lines of flight fluid and open, lest they fall into the 'micro-fascism' of habit and complacency.[45] Foucault puts this concern into a positive formulation of critique as aesthetic and productive rather than normative:[46] it is about the asking of questions and the creation of alternatives rather than the exposition of the new best way to live. Critique must serve to open up possibilities and multiplicities rather than closing them down.

There are problems that arise from Foucault's conception of resistance in its relation to the power nexus that it opposes. A lot of Foucault's later analysis goes into showing how relations of power and knowledge form us as subjects. The question arises of where resistance is to take hold if subjects' self-consciousness is formed by the system that they are to oppose, coupled with the assertion that no matter how we attack the formative system we cannot abandon it wholly.[47] Haber points to the fact that resistance in Foucault must always act within a power relation, to show how it is not a necessary fact that resistance will always lead to transformation. The immanence of critique to that which it resists will always leave open the possibility that it will be subsumed, another warning given by Deleuze and cited above in relation to the encompassing power of capitalism, and one that is present throughout Foucault's own work.

This co-option is made all the easier by the immanence of critique to the power structures it engages in ontological terms, since the individuals who carry out such critiques have had their frames of reference constituted by that power. There is a tension, therefore, between the Deleuzian injunction to think 'outside' power structures, echoed in Foucault's idea of an ethic of self-construction and in interviews in which he calls for resistance to take the shape of new forms of living, and the confines which Foucault's actual analyses of power place on critical possibilities.

We can frame this problem in relation to the picture of self built up in previous chapters. Again, the satanic question arises. If the conscious self is reflective of the society in which it finds itself, in our case Western consumerism, how then are we to form an adequate conception of that society and how to oppose it? If we accept that, to some degree, we have internalised the multiphrenic existential imperative of consumerism, how do we step outside it and, if we cannot, then how is resistance possible? How do we think differently?

I believe that there are a number of inherent possibilities to consider. The first of these will be explored in the next chapter but is worth mentioning at this stage. If the conscious self is that which mirrors society, then we should look to the unconscious to provide critical tools. This could be envisaged as operating in a number of ways. We could look to the pre-reflective instincts to form the basis of revolutionary action.[48] From a Deleuzian perspective, this may seem initially attractive in that it forms a line of flight out of the privileging of the conscious ego with its operation of reasoned thought, which may be seen as part of the Freudian/Oedipal construction of society. How well an instinctual critique could function is open to question, however. One major point is that it could not seek to justify its actions to others, as to do so would immediately engage the social/linguistic faculty of consciousness in using social meanings for the purposes of explanation. Such a critique may be inherently anti-social and may not work on a collective level.

The second alternative may fall prey to the same problem. One could use not the instincts but a form of analytic meditative absorption, such as that utilised in Buddhist philosophy. Therein one would try to disconnect oneself from forms of power/knowledge, to loosen their hold on the conscious mind by performing systematic genealogies on both external and mental phenomena until one comes to a sense of emptiness underlying everything. This could be fairly easily achieved in relation to consumer ideology; it takes little thought to come to the conclusion that one's choice of car has very little relation to other areas of life and personality except in the meaning matrices of consumerism. This would be an essentially experiential individual enterprise, however, with similarly limited communicability to instinctual pre-reflective critique. This is evidenced by the reliance in Buddhist philosophy on a primarily personal meditative experience of *sunyata* (emptiness) in order to grasp Buddhist ontology.

If we reject methods of critique that seek to either precede or step outside consciousness then we seem, at this stage, to be left incommunicado by the individuality of the experience. One must also be wary that such methods are open to co-option by consumer capitalism as they could be seen to fall within the remit of individual existential self-creation. One of the reasons Bauman gives for the anxiety of *unsicherheit*, it will be remembered, is the fact that responsibility is left to the individual and the worries that this throws up do not lend themselves to collective action. If we are to act collectively, does this not mean tying ourselves back into a social framework of communicability and therefore using the frames of reference that we seek to resist? One option may lie in the very structure of consumerism as characterised by Bauman's habitat. The multiple sites of identity may provide platforms for a profusion of internal partial critiques. We would then end up with a critical enterprise that took the rhizomatic form spoken of in *A Thousand Plateaus*, multiple lines of critique criss-crossing each other from different points of origin. The problem would be that none of these could provide a line of flight that could escape the system if they were to maintain a degree of justifiability on a communal level. We are, therefore, left with individualist critique, which may stand outside the system but which cannot be a communal enterprise, or a more socially orientated resistance that is merely a partial and not a thorough critique.

This may be to underestimate the creative capacity of consciousness, however; maybe it is in this capacity that Deleuze and Guattari's desire and Foucault's productive power provide us with hope. On the one hand, it may be that Foucauldian genealogy functions like a psychoanalytic exposition: once the subject is shown the contingencies on which current regimes of truth rest, the scales drop from his or her eyes and they are psychologically freed to pursue alternatives. This is a highly simplistic characterisation, however, and one that hinges to a large extent on belief in Freud's 'talking cure'. From the anti-Oedipal perspective, it is also suspect.

The other alternative is to find a median between the individual and society. This is where the social forms that contemporary society has caused to coalesce may be turned against the system that created them. If we work on a rhizomatic basis of critique sustained by tribes and peg-style communities, we may be able to bring a degree of outside inside. A group may be able to organically evolve perspectives on society that stand outside its hegemony to some degree, whilst still maintaining the capacity for social communicability within that group. The fact that group membership is both fluid and multiple may mean that the members of that group could communicate their ideas to other groups of which they are members to maintain a degree of understanding. This would be bolstered by the idea of co-originality: the self is not just reflective of society but feeds into its creation. Small changes in one, therefore, may have the potential to affect the other in a gradual process of change. At this point, it may be useful to turn to Bauman's concept of the *agora* as providing a site where this process could take place.

Bauman pointed to the image of the *agora*, the classical Greek marketplace, as an intermediary site of exchange, where the private concerns of the *oikos* could be translated into policy at the level of the *ecclesia*. Bauman's point is that, in the contemporary context, the *agora* has come under threat from the seepage of power away from the *ecclesia* and the colonising of the *agora* by purely private concerns, which, rather than being translated to the communal level, merely serve to underline the private nature of the concerns expressed and the individual responsibility for their solution.[49] The remedy for this situation is, in his eyes, to re-establish a situation wherein the concerns of private conditions are able to be expressed in public terms. In the parlance of the previous paragraphs this comes down to an issue of communicability, in which these concerns are able to be discussed and dealt with on the communal level, necessitating their re-description in terms which have social as well as personal meaning.

The issue of incommunicability is taken up by Hardt and Negri in *Empire*.[50] They look back to the period of proletarian internationalism – characterised as three waves: from 1848 to the 1890s, after the Soviet revolution in 1917 and, finally, from the Chinese revolution through to the spirit of the sixties worldwide – and claim that revolutionary action constituted chains of events, with action in one part of the world sparking off a reaction elsewhere.[51] This reactive quality was based on the 'translation' of struggles into the language of other proletarian observers worldwide and the recognition of a common cause. After a redefinition of the proletariat to include '*all* those exploited by and subject to capitalist domination',[52] the problem with revolutionary action in contemporary conditions is sa[id] to be the failure to communicate the common causes and adversaries of struggle to other potential sites of discontent. 'This is certainly one of the central and most urgent political paradoxes of our time: in our much celebrated age of communication, *struggles have become all but incommunicable*.'[53] The result of this, it is claimed is that individual struggles now travel vertically to the global level in order to effect change instead of spreading horizontally.[54]

Hardt and Negri are at pains to point out the potential of such a scenario, despite the fact that local activists no longer see themselves as fighting the same enemy. They suggest that the global level to which they must travel to stake their claim is itself this enemy, Empire. Using the Deleuzian idea of critique from the outside, Hardt and Negri suggest that, since one of the defining features they claim for Empire is its filling of all voids and its mastering of communicative language, there is no outside to Empire and that critique and resistance must be carried on from the inside.[55]

This strategy is an update of Marx's idea that the capitalist system will dig its own grave, that the tools of resistance can be found within the system. Deleuze and Guattari also embrace this idea with the suggestion that one push certain elements to their limits within the system. As Hardt and Negri put it, 'the functioning of imperial power is ineluctably linked to its decline':[56]

> In the constitution of Empire there is no longer an 'outside' to power and thus no weak links – if by weak we mean an external point where the articulations of global power are vulnerable. To achieve significance, every struggle must seek to attack at the heart of Empire, at its strength . . . [T]he construction of Empire, and the globalization of economic and cultural relationships, means that the virtual center of Empire can be attacked from any point. The tactical preoccupations of the old revolutionary school are thus completely irretrievable; the only strategy available to the struggles is that of a constituent counterpower that emerges from within Empire.[57]

'his has repercussions for the nature of revolutionary strategy and Iardt and Negri spend some time discussing the relative disadvanages of localised struggle. They claim that to reify the local nature of ction, as in Foucault for example, is to run the risk of presenting a ılse dichotomy between the local and the global levels and of not ddressing what may be the constructed nature of locality. Given the eterritorialising nature of globalisation, the localisation of struggle ould play into the hands of the contemporary capitalist system, ffectively cementing the problem of the translation of action.[58]

Given the discussion presented in previous chapters, it may also be possible to found the idea of incommunicability on a less structural level and point to the impact of the mechanics of consumerism on the construction of identity. The operation of the existential imperative supported by consumable goods is to isolate individuals, leading to the fragmented socialities identified in the last chapter. This may be what underlies the localising tendency and the failure of translation of struggles.

Turning to the constitution and nature of the new proletariat, which they dub the 'multitude', Hardt and Negri posit its revolutionary potential as a group as residing primarily in its bioproductive capacity. As in Marx, therefore, revolution is seen to have its seat in the labour power of the revolutionary class. 'Living labour is what constitutes the passageway from the virtual to the real; it is the vehicle of possibility,'[59] labour being defined as the 'power to act'.[60] In an interesting twist, the idea is presented that Empire is constituted as a reaction to actions on the part of the multitude.[61] Herein lies the revolutionary potential, however, in that 'the well-known relentless dynamism of capitalism does not then reside in capital, but in living labour, that has at every step *forced* capital to reorganise.'[62]

The contradictions, thrown up in a position which posits Empire as a totality of horizons without an outside, are overcome for Hardt and Negri by the coupling of the creative potential of labour with the 'generative determination of desire'.[63] 'The entire conceptual horizon is thus completely redefined. The biopolitical, seen from the standpoint of desire, is nothing other than complete production, human collectivity in action.'[64] Desire is that which gives the creative and original impetus to labour and the closing chapters of *Empire* can be seen as suggestions and explorations as to how this potential may be further freed. In the language of Deleuze and Guattari, the project culminates not in suggesting what a counter-empire may look like or what specific activities may bring it about but rather in pointing to how the blockages to lines of flight out of the current system may be removed to aid the organic bottom-up generation of counter-empire by revolutionary practice.

One of the symbols of the dissension of the multitude is Deleuze and Guattari's idea of nomadism, this time rendered concrete in mobile labour presented as 'new barbarians' disrupting the disciplinary conditions to which they are subjected by simple desertion.[65] is recognised, however, that the practical experience of this rather romantic notion is 'a new rootless condition of poverty and misery', rather like Bauman's vagabonds. In the final chapter of *Empire*, three rights are suggested in order to open up paths of desertion and to allow the multitude to affirm its singularity. This latter is achieved

> by inverting the ideological illusion that all humans on the global surfaces of the world market are interchangeable. Standing the ideology of the market on its feet, the multitude promotes through its labor the biopolitical singularizations of groups and sets of humanity, across each and every node of global interchange.[67]

I would argue that this is a process made easier in some ways by the existential imperative of consumerism, which asserts the idea that we must create our conscious individuality but puts its own tools forward for the process. The question must be asked whether we can utilise our internalisation of this doctrine only in part and re-orientate the means of achieving it to some 'purer' form of construction. The discussion in previous chapters would lead one to believe that no form of construction is purer than any other, meaning that the difference in this case would be merely strategic. Given the a-humanism of the poststructuralist position on self-construction, however, this can be seen as presenting no great contradiction to Hardt and Negri.

The three rights claimed for the multitude in *Empire* are a right to global citizenship, a right to a social wage untied to labour productiveness and a right to a reappropriation of the means of production, which in the contemporary sense is taken to mean information and knowledge. The first of these serves to increase mobility and allow the flow of the multitude into new spaces to assert new freedoms. The second is in part a recognition that post-Fordist working practice and the move from industry to the service and communication sectors means that the working day is harder to limit and that 'the proletariat produces in all its generality everywhere all day long'.[68] If one's job consists of the production and manipulation of knowledge, it is hard to erect barriers in one's head between 'work thought' and 'leisure thought'; even the exercise of thought itself in any scenario could be seen as keeping the machine oiled. The social wage would also stand in opposition to the biased gendered nature of the family supported by the male wage earner and is claimed as a necessary corollary to the extension of universal citizenship. The right to reappropriation is a recognition that the machines of production are now people themselves.

The question arises of whether the extension of these three rights will do anything to ease our postmodern anxiety. Will they cure *unsicherheit*? It must be remembered that the ideas presented in this chapter are not extended by their authors to address this problem, they are answers to different questions, or in the post-structural sense the generation of questions and the creation of spaces from which to answer them. The Marxist answer to *unsicherheit* is a simple one: all our ills are the product of capitalism and once it falls we will be free to create better alternatives. This seems too easy an answer, however, given all that has been said about the nature of the conscious self. On one level, the analysis is quite correct, as we have identified *unsicherheit* as being one element of the emotion regime of consumer capitalism. In this conception, the means of self-construction are at odds with the existential imperative and this tension, as well as the inherent insecurity in contemporary society, is made manifest in a postmodern anxiety. *Unsicherheit* arises, not from capitalism itself but from a tension within the way in which a particular societal formation forms its inhabitants' idea of self. As such, a range of alternatives is open, from reform of the current structure to the call for a new one. The main point is that from a psychological perspective, as well as from many others, our current form of society has failed.

Given the theoretical ground we have covered in the preceding pages, it is time to turn our attention to the practical exposition of critique in today's world. In this regard, I have chosen to focus discussion on the multiplicity of ideas and practices brought together by the media term 'anti-capitalism'. The way in which such practices operate serves to throw into relief many of the theories we have been discussing as well as mirroring the characterisation of fragmented social and psychological formations in previous chapters.

The potential of the social self

The first striking feature of the anti-capitalist snowball is its make up. The protests and events that dot its calendar are made up of a dazzling array of different groups campaigning on a range of different issues. A meeting like the World Social Forum, convened to discuss strategy and options, did not seek to draw up a manifesto or impose any hierarchy of combined aims and methods. Each group remains autonomous within a web-like structure connected via the internet and various workshops and teach-ins. In this way, the movement seems to have the rhizomatic structure spoken of earlier. There are multiple points of origin, lines of protest and desired destinations from the merely reformist to the outright revolutionary.

This may be one of the strengths of the movement. The fact that it is a many-headed hydra, which grows organically, makes it a lot harder to predict or control. Klein sees this fragmentation as an outgrowth of 'fragmentation within progressive networks and changes in broader culture' as well as a response to the political reality of the failure of traditional parties.[69] She sees strength in the fact that 'it is so different from the organising principles of the institutions and corporations it targets. It responds to corporate concentration with fragmentation, to globalization with its own kind of localization, to power consolidation with radical power dispersal'.[70] This would seem to fulfil the criteria of Deleuzian and Gauttarian politics outlined in the last section. Multiple lines of flight present a myriad of alternatives, both in their principles and in their organisation, which serve to disrupt the system.

The question of how deep this alternative goes is another matter however:

> Like the Internet itself, both the NGO and the affinity group networks are infinitely expandable systems. If somebody feels that he or she doesn't quite fit into one of the thirty thousand or so NGOs or thousands of affinity groups out there, she can start her own and link up. Once involved, no one has to give up individuality to the larger structure; as with all things on-line we are free to dip in and out, take what we want and delete what we don't. It seems, at times to be a surfer's approach to activism – reflecting the Internet's paradoxical culture for extreme narcissism coupled with intense desire for community and connection.[71]

The problem lies in that this paradox may be one of the tensions that underlie our insecurity, begging the question of whether it should be mirrored in resistance. The other way of interpreting this is from the perspective that one should use the tools of resistance inherent in the system to disrupt it. Accordingly, the drive to individualism in consumer culture could be utilised in our mode of engagement with it, lending each the ability to sit as spiders at the centre of his or her own web of revolutionary activity. If, in Bauman's terms, our worries are incommunicable and this is the product of our psycho-social training, then the network form of protest may be the only one open to people at the conscious level, both in terms of strategically engaging the system and from the psychological perspective. It is the form we are most adapted to and can utilise to the best effect. In other words, one may aim to produce a society in which the social conditioning is unlike that which one has undergone and which one has used as a lever for change.

In terms of the communicability issue discussed above, network resistance may be one way of overcoming the need for social meaning, although it does not provide an ideal form of pure critique since it uses elements in the system and is still very much an internal critique, though one which seeks to escape.

If we go back to the social formations discussed in the last chapter, it would seem that the form that the anti-capitalist movement takes mirrors peg-style communities and neo-tribes to a large extent. This may be true of the former rather than the latter since tribes are relatively closed in terms of membership. Peg-style communities are open with fluid and multiple membership, which may be either short or long term. There are disadvantages to this sort of loose organisation, as Klein also highlights. There is a lack of structure at protests that undermines the strategies deployed at the events and a lack of goals to be pursued in between events. There is also no consolidation of gains or collective reflection on lessons learned outside of the individual groups that take part. Although the World Social Forum was an attempt to combat this, it had very little structural impact. Klein comments that given this situation a culture of 'serial protesting' is growing up within the movement as an attempt to keep up momentum.[72] Attempts to combat this, through such things as the WSF and the International Forum on Globalisation (a planned 'permanent convergence centre' in Washington), are faced with structural problems born of the very things that are the movement's strength.

This is an unresolved issue, Klein's opinion being that the movement has achieved so much already in terms of radicalising a generation that it should be left to run without the imposition of structure. The question in some ways turns into that of what the aims of the movement should be. If the only desired effect is to radicalise people who will then go off and disrupt the system in their own individual ways, then centralised organisation is not necessary. If the aim is rather some sort of revolutionary change, then a bolshevising of the movement becomes necessary and this attracts much resentment on the ground from other groups who see it as a hijacking of protest by 'governments in waiting' undermining the very critique itself.[73] Given the seeming intent of many of the groups involved to open up spaces for change (following the Zapatista idea of creating a world with the possibility of many worlds within it), this lack of organisation may not present a problem and may aid the idea. From a Deleuzian and Guattarian perspective also, it has the advantage of a rhizomatic organisation which strikes the system at many points and which allows people who experience oppression in different ways to speak for themselves. A monolithic movement may have structural advantages and may be able to act as a stronger lever for change but the changes it sought could never be as diverse and directly expressed as within a rhizomatic anti-system. From the strategic point of view, it also presents the system with a single enemy to attack and discredit instead of thousands. One of the speakers at the WSF, Atila Roque, summed up the point by claiming:

> We are trying to break the uniformity of thought, and you can't do that by putting forward another uniform way of thinking. Honestly, I don't miss the time we were all in the Communist Party. We can achieve a higher consolidation of agendas, but I don't think civil society should be trying to organize itself into a party.[74]

The rhizomatic structure also brings critique closer to the individual, who can participate at a higher level in a smaller group. This links us into the second point about the anti-capitalist movement, the link between the local and global levels of struggle. James DeFilippis presents a perspective from within the Globalise Resistance Movement, a broad socialist-based alliance. He claims that the current form of protest has given rise to large-scale groups in Internet-organised protests at multinational gatherings.[75] This leads, in his opinion, to a lack of connection with local groups and struggles and to community groups being relegated to the sidelines of protest.[76] One of the reasons he gives for this in America is the loss of radicalism on the part of community organisations, becoming by the 1980s:

> Community Development Corporations (CDCs), which basically build affordable housing, and in the case of larger ones, functionally act as community-scale Chambers of Commerce. In the process, notions such as 'community control' have been replaced by 'community-based assets', 'non-confrontational organizing' and 'social capital'.[77]

Given both the structure of the current anti-capitalist movement and the de-radicalisation of community groups, DeFilippis claims that there are three reasons why the former becomes a truly social movement by joining with the latter. Firstly, he cites the localisation of daily life and the primary experience of conflict at the local level.[78] Secondly, he argues that questions of scale in social relationships are not a natural outgrowth of the relationships themselves but a co-original element in both formation and outcome. By seeing local struggles as purely an expression of global issues, we devalue the former and the individuals who take part in them and accept too much of the rhetoric of globalisation and corporate placelessness.[79] The most important reason he cites, from a theoretical point of view, is that it is at the local level that real alternatives are constructed and experienced.[80]

There are many examples of these local alternatives. One is the Landless Peoples Movement in Brazil, an organisation that mobilises the poorest elements in society to re-appropriate fenced-off land for sustainable agriculture.[81] In Italy also, social centres are appearing in abandoned buildings, representing an alternative political system providing day-care and advocacy for refugees as well as social and cultural nexus points and meeting places for the planning of direct action. Klein quotes an estimate that there are 150 such centres operating in Italy, one, Leoncavallo in Milan, is 'a self-contained city, with several restaurants, gardens, a bookstore, an indoor skateboard ramp and a club so large it was able to host Public Enemy when the rap group came to town.'[82] Barcelona also houses many squatted social centres such as Miles de Viviendas (Thousands of Homes) which runs a pirate university and pirate TV station for the neighbourhood as well as other organised activities. One may also look to the campsites organised to house protestors at the 2007 G8 conference in Rostock for shorter-term social alternatives.[83]

From the point of view of a way out of *unsicherheit*, it may be that these alternatives on the local scale offer the possibility of a different experience of the social to that found in the consumer mainstream, thus assuaging some of the uncertainty and insecurity that is experienced there. Chances are, however, that the insecurity may be just moved to a different source. Given the hostile reaction of governments to any sort of alternative system within their borders it is likely that such projects will sooner or later come under attack by the state introducing elements of unsafety back into the psyche of participants in the schemes. The important point about the rescaling of conflict to embrace a more local level is, however, this opportunity for the *personal experience* of alternatives, as well as the very real practical benefits which may be accrued from local schemes working with those on the ground who need them.

Harking back to Hardt and Negri's arguments in the last section, we may be reminded of the necessity of not losing sight of the real structural cause of the unrest, in their terms, Empire, in those of the protesters, capitalism. Hardt and Negri claimed that local protest had the drawback of reifying the local and playing into the hands of the system. Protest, they argued, should leap to the level of the global and attack Empire at its heart. I think it may be said, however, in light of the preceding discussion, that the local has a definite part to play in critique and resistance, both in terms of the level at which people experience oppression and can therefore fight it for themselves (in Foucaultian/Deleuzian terms) and with a view of breaking out of the prevalent modes of thought which condition *unsicherheit*. The network form of protest, which serves to connect up many different sites and levels of resistance, may also be a way of overcoming the incommunicability of local struggle, Deleuzian 'micro-fascism' and defeat by isolation which may flow from the separation of points of protest. This indeed seems to be what has made the Zapatista movement so successful, with its extensive use of the Internet linking it into an international arena and to other forms of protest elsewhere. Internet alternative media sites such as Indymedia and Protest.net, as well as the common practice of specific group websites containing a long list of links to other groups, are examples of how news and activities from one part of the globe can be spread and linked to others in the networking of resistance. As these various struggles are translated on to a common level, the problem of communicability that Hardt and Negri see as a barrier to horizontal organisation is to a large extent overcome. It is important to realise, however, that it is not so much a question of a common language in which various sites of resistance are expressed. This is precluded, not just by the specific local circumstances that have led to their emergence, but also by the range of theoretical foundations that underpin these actions: anarchist, ecologist, Christian, humanitarian and socialist, for example. Rather, it is the positioning of these various struggles alongside each other in an intellectual space, be it the virtual space of the Internet or the immediate space of rubbing shoulders at a protest or meeting, which facilitates the construction of network resistance.

Network resistance also allows the various nodes along its span a degree of autonomy that they would not enjoy under a more hierarchical umbrella organisation. Not least among the reasons for this is the lack of a common language into which various localised conflicts would have to be translated and thus 'flattened' to some degree. The fact that each group can express itself in the terms that it finds most meaningful is another factor that precludes that which is resisted gaining an easy handle on the resistance movement. It cannot respond in a single language of denial, but must make its case on many levels, in many places and in many tongues. It also allows individuals within movements more autonomy to connect on a personal level, both with the system they are fighting and with the goals they hope to achieve.

This is an important consideration given the structure of the self that consumerism has produced. Rightly or wrongly (or maybe neither) we have been trained to regard ourselves as conscious individuals and we frame our thoughts and activities within this. It is also within this conceptualisation that we must look to find the tools of resistance to overcome the condition of *unsicherheit*. Whereas the economic, political and cultural conditions that the anti-capitalist movement seeks to overthrow may be amenable to rectification by a sharp change in the system, though even this is doubtful, the psychological conditions that the system engenders are not so easily overcome. It is relatively easy to change a government or a policy, but to change the way in which we relate to who we are and how we frame our thoughts, given that most of us are not prone or free to indulge in long bouts of introspection, is not an immediate process that will be achieved through a change in superstructure. As much as the structures of society lead to our sense of self, the same is true vice versa. At any stage, we can only frame societal structures in line with the meanings we have taken from our background culture. Self and society are a co-original process, with culture as an intermediary, and whereas society is a relatively artificial concept and easily malleable the other two are organic and only malleable in the longer term. A society can be overthrown in a day but the network of meanings that make up culture and the self are not amenable to such rapid change.

The anti-capitalist movement has the advantage of seeking to work on all levels rather than on merely the societal one as in traditional revolutionary enterprises. In many ways, it is not the state which is our problem but the interplay between state, culture and individual self. Through creating alternative spaces and modes of relation groups such as Reclaim the Streets and those discussed earlier in Italy and Brazil provide hints that things could be different to what they are. This in itself is a vastly important goal since one of the main conditioning factors in our society is the TINA perspective: 'There Is No Alternative'. In terms of the alternatives provided by the anti-globalisation movement, it can be said that, although they come from cultural concepts that are riddled with *unsicherheit*, they seek to provide an escape route out of it; it is this psychological condition that provides many in the West, who are not beset with the poverty of other areas, to seek change where they may not have otherwise.

The relation between self and society, with the latter split into culture and state, is one of the prime ways in which we may harness the Marxist idea that a system provides the tools of its own resistance

Whether it can be destroyed or not is another question. Its superstructure certainly can, though we may be wise to be more hesitant about the psychological imprints it leaves behind and be aware of them in order to build a true alternative.

Notes

1. Baudrillard, from *Le Système des Objets*, to *The Mirror of Production.*
2. Baudrillard, *Simulacra and Simulations.*
3. Poster in Baudrillard, *Selected Writings*, p. 6.
4. Baudrillard, *Les Strategies Fatales*, and Baudrillard, 'The masses: the implosion of the social in the media' in Poster, *Selected Writings.*
5. Baudrillard, 'The masses', in *Selected Writings*, pp. 213–14.
6. Ibid. p. 218.
7. Ibid. p. 219.
8. Deleuze and Guattari, *Anti-Oedipus.*
9. Ibid. p. 42.
10. Ibid. p. 34.
11. Ibid. p. 245.
12. Ibid. p. 29 (author's italics).
13. Goodchild, *Deleuze and Guattari*, p. 74.
14. Deleuze and Guattari, *Anti-Oedipus*, pp. 139–40.
15. Ibid. p. 131.
16. Ibid. pp. 239–40.
17. Ibid. p. 239.
18. Ibid. p. 277.
19. Ibid. p. 277.
20. Ibid. p. 246.
21. Ibid. p. 362.
22. Ibid. p. 20.
23. Ibid. p. 341.
24. Goodchild, *Deleuze and Guattari*, p. 218.
25. Massumi, *A Users Guide to Capitalism and Schizophrenia*, p. 106.
26. Ibid. p. 103.
27. Ibid. pp. 103–4.
28. Ibid. p. 105.
29. Ibid. p. 106.
30. Ibid. p. 106.
31. Deleuze and Parnet, *Dialogues*, pp. 137–9.
32. Deleuze and Guattari, *A Thousand Plateaus*, pp. 227–31.
33. Ibid. p. 216.
34. Ibid. pp. 230, 351–424.
35. Deleuze and Guattari, *Anti-Oedipus*, pp. 36–7.
36. Foucault, *Essential Works: Vol. 3*, p. 120.

37. Ibid. p. 123.
38. Ibid. p. 117.
39. Deleuze in Foucault, *Language, Counter-Memory, Practice*, p. 209.
40. Foucault, *Essential Works: Vol. 3*, pp. 131–2.
41. Foucault, *Essential Works: Vol. 1*, pp. 157, 160.
42. Ibid. p. 135.
43. Ibid. p. 165.
44. Ibid. pp. 172–3.
45. Deleuze and Parnet, *Dialogues*, p. 137–8.
46. Foucault, *Essential Works: Vol. 1*, p. 323.
47. Haber, *Beyond Postmodern Politics*, pp. 98, 97.
48. One would have to look to the instincts rather than Freudian drives as the latter are seen to be a social product.
49. Bauman, *In Search of Politics*, pp. 97–8.
50. Hardt and Negri, *Empire*, pp. 50–9.
51. Ibid. pp. 50–1.
52. Ibid. p. 53.
53. Ibid. p. 54.
54. Ibid. p. 55.
55. Ibid. pp. 58–9; on the link between Empire and the communications industry, see pp. 32–4.
56. Ibid. p. 361.
57. Ibid. pp. 58–9.
58. Ibid. pp. 44–5.
59. Ibid. p. 357.
60. Ibid. p. 358.
61. Ibid. p. 51.
62. Brown and Szeman, 'The global coliseum', p. 179 (author's emphasis).
63. Hardt and Negri, *Empire*, p. 387.
64. Ibid. p. 387.
65. Ibid. p. 212.
66. Ibid. p. 213.
67. Ibid. p. 395.
68. Ibid. p. 403.
69. Klein, *Fences and Windows*, pp. 20–1.
70. Ibid. p. 21.
71. Ibid. p. 20.
72. Ibid. p. 23.
73. This point is made on the Wombles website, an anarchist/libertarian group who form human barriers against riot police during many protests. www.wombles.org.uk/lessons.htm
74. Quoted in Klein, *Fences and Windows*, p. 201.
75. DeFilippis, 'Our resistance must be as local as capitalism', p. 365.
76. Ibid. p. 367.

77. Ibid. pp. 367–8.
78. Ibid. p. 368.
79. Ibid. p. 370.
80. Ibid. p. 371.
81. M. Gonzalez in Bircham and Charlton (eds), *Anti-Capitalism*, p. 153.
82. Klein, *Fences and Windows*, p. 225.
83. http://www.camping-07.de/content/view/11/138/lang,en/

6

The Political Nonconscious

In the previous chapter, we have looked at some themes concerning the role of consciousness in thinking differently. To similarly examine the role of the unconscious and nonconscious is, however, more problematic. The lack of insight we have into our mental life below the conscious level, and the seeming antithesis between mental functioning at such levels and social structures, makes the mapping of the former to the latter difficult. The problem has, however, already been addressed by theorists who have attempted to unpack the Freudian unconscious in political terms and it will be useful to canvas such attempts before moving on to examine how the foregoing neurological material on the nonconscious may be rendered political.

The prevailing theme that comes through such an exercise is the varying ways in which the relation between the 'instincts' and civilisation have been conceived. For Freudians civilisation represses the instincts, forcing their energy into less destructive channels. We must examine, however, whether such a vision can still be maintained with the move from conceptions of the unconscious to the nonconscious Not only have there been moves to reconceptualise mental life, but the society in which we live has also changed. The question must be asked of whether the old Freudian attitudes can still be deemed useful in contemporary consumer capitalist culture.

The problems of nonconscious politics

One of the foundational problems in trying to frame a politics o the nonconscious comes in assessing the interrelation between suc mental functioning and our social lives. The nonconscious either is fil tered through consciousness or directly encounters the world throug behaviours, speech acts and veiled thoughts, which are, by thei nature, difficult to investigate.

As we have seen, Freud suggested that civilisation comes abou as the result of a trade-off in which we repress some of our instinct in order to gain security from our primeval fears. 'It is impossibl to overlook the extent to which civilisation is built up upon the renunciation of instinct, how much it presupposes precisely the non-satisfaction . . . of powerful instincts.'[1] Society is constructed to curb instincts that would otherwise have destructive potential for the individual. For Freud, therefore, the reason for civilisation is a negative one: it is necessary for the perpetuation of human existence to curb our natural instincts by bringing them within the scope of an artificial order that must be necessarily repressive.[2] The constant stress that Freudians identify in society is due to the fact that the most powerful of the instincts suppressed is the Thanatos or death instinct. Thanatos manifests itself in our aggressive tendencies as an 'original self subsisting instinctual disposition', which poses 'the greatest impediment to civilisation.'[3] This is where the superego enters the picture as the mechanism by which society internalises its values into each individual, leaving the ego to mediate between its demands and those of the id.[4]

Possibly the greatest benefit of societal formation, on an individual level, is, therefore, the provision of security. Whether we agree with Freud or not, there is a case to be made for our fear both of the unknown element that resides within ourselves and of the unknown quantity that is the mental lives of other people. The laws and customs that regulate society are the panacea against these fears and are viewed as a necessary evil if we want to stay in control of our lives. This issue of control is an important motor of action, both in Freudian thought and in our everyday lives. As we have seen, however, the neuropsychological material discussed in Chapter 1, as well as that on affect in Chapter 3, points towards a conception of our mental lives in which conscious control is not a dominant force. Likewise, the discussion of contemporary society in Chapter 3 and the notion of *unsicherheit* problematises the Freudian ideal of mental control through societal structure, at least as regards the present form of the latter.

As we have seen already, Nietzsche rejects a valourisation of consciousness. He, like Freud, sees it as an outgrowth of the social aspect of our lives: a necessity born of our need to communicate with each other. He rebels however against the controlling influence it seeks over our mental lives, seeing it only as a superficial overlay of the uncommunicatable individuality that constitutes our essential nature. For Freud the connection between the individual unconscious and society comes in the transformation (sublimination) of individual sexual instincts into social goals. For Nietzsche, the process of sublimination is the misrecognition of an individual impulse as altruism; it is not a transformation but a masking. So, whereas for Freud society can be seen as useful in impeding our destructive impulses, for Nietzsche it is an illusion to be exploded in the search for authentic individual becoming.

The way in which society impacts upon our mental functioning, for Freud, is through the reality principle. This is the mechanism by which the conscious and preconscious, or in Freud's structural phase, the superego, are shaped by social ideas and concepts, the internalisation of which serves as the defence mechanism through which the unconscious is held in check and its desires subliminated. The form that the reality principle takes will therefore be predicated by the social ideas of the time and we must therefore investigate its curren form.

In twenties America there was a widespread social taboo agains women smoking in public. In a bid to overcome this and boost sale of cigarettes to women, George Hill, the president of the America Tobacco Corporation, hired a man named Eduard Bernays.[5] Bernay had recently set himself up in New York as a public relations counse a common enough sight today but a new idea in the 1920s. He ha come to the profession after being employed by the American gov ernment in the war to promote the idea, both at home and abroad that the US war effort was being conducted in order to bring democ racy to a troubled world. The success of this endeavour led him t consider whether the same techniques of propaganda could be use during peacetime for commercial means, and hence was born the pro fession of 'public relations'.

Bernays also happened to be the nephew of Sigmund Freud an believed that in his uncle's ideas lay the methods of mass persuasio that he needed. In line with these beliefs, he took the America Tobacco case and consulted a psychotherapist for advice. The thera pist informed him that for women cigarettes were a symbol of ma power and dominance and advised him to appeal to this unconsciou element of the female psyche in order to make them sell better. I other words, he should form an unconscious connection betwee smoking and challenging male power.

Acting accordingly, Bernays organised a ploy at the annual East Day parade in New York in which he hired a number of debutante instructing them to hide cigarettes under their clothes, join the parad and to light them up at a given signal. He then informed the press th he had heard that a group of suffragettes would be staging a prote during the parade by lighting up 'torches of freedom'. The story was a sensation, with the 'torches of freedom' caption being carried in many main newspapers. The sale of cigarettes among women began to rise and the taboo against them smoking in public was allegedly broken.

On a much wider level, however, the idea came to prominence that there was a far more effective way of selling mass products than on the basis of need and utility as had been done before. You could persuade people to behave irrationally and buy products they did not really need by appealing to their unconscious desires and feelings. Previously this had been the preserve of 'luxury' items. Cigarettes did not change women's position in society in any real way; the act of smoking now made them feel more powerful, however, and that was what made cigarettes sell. With Bernays' help products became symbols of how you wanted to be seen by other people in society. He established the idea that there should be an emotional connection between people and the goods and services they choose to use.

This was an important step in economic terms as well. At the time, American corporations were still engaged in the mass production of limited lines of products and were worried about the danger of coming to a point where supply outstripped demand, where people simply had everything they needed and stopped buying. The idea that you could link products to desire rather than need came as a revelation and, beginning in the early 1920s, US banks began sponsoring the creation of large department stores in major cities in which products would be sold in this new way. They hired Bernays to deliver the new form of buyer, the consumer. He set about inventing ideas such as product placement in films and paying celebrities to put forward the message that one bought, not out of need, but to express your inner sense of self to others. He has claimed, for example, that he was the first person to suggest to car manufacturers that they sell cars as symbols of male sexuality.[6]

It cannot be said, however, that it was followers of Freud in the advertising industry that first brought the idea of desire into marketing. Products had been sold on the basis of desire over need ever since there has been anything resembling disposable income. A basic acquisitiveness can also be traced back further, to the appropriation of luxury goods as symbols of power by rulers throughout history. In terms of more recent economics, two examples of marketing on the basis of desire preceding the twentieth century can be found in women's periodical magazines in the nineteenth century and the rise of arcades as places to shop in major European cities in the same period.

As regards the former of these two examples, Margaret Beetham claims that the main economic role of the women's periodical was to 'position its readers as consumers of commodities'.[7] There was a growth in advertising in women's magazines in the nineteenth century, as a means to keep prices down, and from the 1890s these advertisements were concerned with commodities, not as 'made objects but as objects with "value" ' not related to the utilitarian function of the product.[8] Walter Benjamin's and Rachel Bowlby's work on arcades also points to selling products on the basis of manufacturing desire. Bowlby points to the creation of spectacle in arcades and early department stores[9], and the creation of needs marketing and early branding around the turn of the twentieth century.[10] Benjamin points also to the World Exhibitions of the nineteenth century as 'places of pilgrimage to the commodity fetish' for the working classes that glorify the exchange value of commodities, pushing their use value into the background.[11]

These examples of desire marketing before the twentieth century are illustrative of the growth of the idea that one could sell products on the basis of a manufactured want rather than a need (for food, clothing or shelter). These early illustrations are still confined to a relatively small group of people, however: the magazines in Beetham's work were read by middle and upper class women primarily in the London area and arcades were places where the bourgeoisie came to stroll. With the growth of disposable income over time, desire marketing has been able to address wider and wider audiences, a process that is still ongoing today, to the point where one may say that the Western world has formed a consumer culture with the principles of consumerism expanding to take in an ever-increasing remit. Aside from the quantitative difference between earlier examples of desire marketing and our contemporary situation, there is a qualitative difference also in that consumerism has developed an existential imperative on which to base the manufacture of desire: that individual development can be aided by consumer goods.

The stock market crash of the 1920s ended the first major wave of consumerism in the US and, in the aftermath, people tightened their belts and went back to spending on the basis of need and utility. After Roosevelt's re-election in the 1930s and the expansion of the New Deal, which sought to control the laissez-faire capitalism blamed for the 1929 crash, major corporations banded together in the National

Association of Manufacturers to fight an ideological battle with the government by linking the idea of free business to that of democracy. Eduard Bernays, in his capacity as advisor during the 1939 World's Fair, managed to present the idea of free enterprise being able to fulfil the desires of the people far better than the politicians could.

The next major step took place in the 1940s with the research of Ernest Dichter, an old neighbour of Freud's from Vienna.[12] Dichter set up the Institute for Motivational Research to uncover the 'secret self of the American consumer' and set about applying psychoanalytic group-therapy techniques to various products. He was asked to apply his new idea of the focus group by the Betty Crocker company to discover why their new range of convenience foods, and in particular their cake mix, were not selling despite pre-launch research which had suggested that many housewives thought them a good idea. Dichter formed a focus group in which housewives free-associated about the cake mix and claimed to find that they had a sense of guilt about the image of ease used in the product's promotion. Dichter suggested to the company that they include in the instructions on the packet that the customer should add in an egg, claiming that this would be seen by housewives as a symbol of them adding their own labour to the process and thus assuaging their guilt. Sales of the product soared and Dichter went on to produce such famous slogans as 'the tiger in your tank' for Esso as well as the marketing of the Barbie doll with ideas from a children's focus group.

The idea that underlay the Freudian school of marketing was that one should sell to the unconscious desires of the populace[13] and its practitioners, like Dichter, believed that aligning yourself with particular products bolstered one's self-image and made people more stable, rather than the mass of seething urges in need of control that formed the Freudian image of humanity. In the sixties, however, the pendulum of popular opinion swung away from Freudian pessimism, from the repression of the self to its expression.[14] Dichter was one of the last great Freudians in advertising theory in this period as Freudianism waned and humanism gained the ascendancy. The idea that consumerism can be underpinned by the marketing of desire has, however, endured to be investigated by both Freudian political theorists, such as Marcuse, and those from a Marxist background who similarly explore ideas of commodity fetishism, like Baudrillard.

For non-Freudian perspectives, we may at this point revisit the discussions in Chapter 2 of the way in which the unconscious may be shaped by external forces. Ramachandran and cognitive behavioural therapists, for example, seek to use conscious action to vary unconscious patterns, whereas theorists from a phenomenological perspective, such as Dreyfus, Clark and Varela, privilege embodiment and the effects of language usage. Whether one sides with those who privilege conscious action or those who point to other factors in influencing thought, arguments can be made for the influence of consumerism upon our thinking.

In terms of conscious patterning of thought, one can point back to Bauman's points about the activity of shopping in Chapter 3. Therein he conjectured that the influence of consumer society had been to condition us in such a way as to lead to the use of techniques of 'shopping' through all areas of life, from the search for existential meaning to human relationships. Goldman makes a similar point in relation to the separation of the signified and sign in consumerism and the reorientation of human practices and qualities around a particular product. In relation to theories of embodiment it will be remembered that the third effect which Goldman posited that commodification has on society was the presentation of different parts of the body in isolation from one another, with the link between body and self only being restored through the medium of a particular product. If, as the phenomenologist theorists posit, thought is patterned through the experience of embodied living, then this effect of commodification will have an impact on such patterning.

For both Freud and Nietzsche, however, the relay between unconscious and society is a two way process. The unconscious is not passively acted upon but bursts out to shape societal structures and communal ways of behaviour. The best example of this process is contained in Freud's *Totem and Taboo* in which he investigates the ways in which unconscious drives and motives are played out in culture and religion. For Nietzsche, it is art and religion that present the social manifestations of mental forces and that are, for him, positive and negative, respectively. Another example may be the sublimination of individual behaviour in communal gatherings, be they religious, artistic or political. Therein the conscious of each participant may be dissolved into the emergent properties of the collective, giving rise to 'mob' behaviour.

Indeed, the desire upon which consumerism acts and which it seeks to expand and shape, in Freudian and Nietzschean terms, may be seen as an externalisation of libidinal desire or will. If such is the case then one must reckon with Freud's view that our desires may not be capable of fulfilment: 'It is my belief that, however, strange it ma sound, we must reckon with the possibility that something in the nature of sexual instinct itself is unfavourable to the realization of complete satisfaction.'[15] In such a view, consumerism would therefore play on an essentially unquenchable reservoir of desire. This can be linked with the idea of 'lack', which one finds in both Freud and Lacan. For Freud, there is always something lacking for the complete discharge of our drives, a discharge which can only come fully with death, and which can be attributed to something within the nature of the drives themselves. For Lacan, lack is felt at the mirror stage and then throughout life, as one feels an existential emptiness at the core of selfhood when confronted by other subjects and objects that appear to possess a control and completeness that the individual does not feel he or she possesses themselves.

The possibilities of nonconscious politics

Much of the political discussion of the nonconscious starts from the foundation of overcoming instinct. In a modern context, this can be traced back to a Kantian privileging of the conscious over nonconscious mental elements. As we noted in Chapter 1, however, the idea goes back further and can be seen in Plato's metaphor of the charioteer as conscious mental control.

In *Daybreak*, Nietzsche paints a picture of our relation to the world being a product of our drives. In aphorism 119, we are asked to imagine walking down the street and noticing that someone is laughing at us. Our reaction to this situation will not be conditioned by a conscious evaluation of the laugher's motive followed by an assessment of what would constitute a legitimate and strategic response on our part. Rather our reaction will result from the action of whichever one of our drives is in ascendant at that particular moment. This serves to explain both how different people will have different reactions and how the reaction of one individual will differ on separate occasions. Also in *Daybreak*, we find Nietzsche's therapeutic method for overcoming instinct. At aphorism 109, he gives six methods for such an achievement:

1. Avoiding occasions on which the instinct could be satisfied and allowing longer and longer periods between satisfactions to cause it to wither away;
2. If this is too hard to accomplish immediately, one can institute a regimen of control by which the satisfaction of the drive is limited

to certain times and places. After this is mastered one could then pass on to the method outlined above;
3. One may try to convert desire into distaste by deliberately gorging oneself with whatever the instinct desires;
4. One may create a mental link between satisfaction of the instinct and an unpleasant thought or sensation, thus causing the latter to arise when the former comes to mind;
5. Working upon the assumption that there is a limited pool of what Freud would term libidinal energy upon which the instincts can draw, one can use this energy to satisfy other instincts, lessening the tension and energy pushing for the fulfilment of the one we are trying to change; and
6. Finally, if everything else fails, we can attempt to consciously lobotomise the entire instinctual machinery as advised by Schopenhauer's successor Von Hartman.

It is interesting to note how many of these techniques have found their way into the repertoires of behaviourism and cognitive behavioural therapy. We must remember, however, that Nietzsche does not seek a valorising of conscious control over the nonconscious. In the *Birth of Tragedy*, in relation to Socrates and the idea of 'rationality at any price' leading to a consciousness devoid of instinct, he comments: 'To *have* to fight the instincts – that is the formula of decadence: as long as life is *ascending*, happiness equals instinct.'[16] When he posits his methodologies for overcoming of instinct it is not our conscious mind that seeks to exert control, it is merely the means by which a rival instinct seeks mastery over another and uses consciousness as a tool for that end. For Nietzsche any such application of technique to the self is merely the result of the instincts warring with each other under the surface of consciousness. Much of his work on morality is then an investigation of how one set of instincts has come to be privileged over another. He concludes that the 'herd instincts' are selected as a result of being those which conduce to social life and community.

As such, the only 'cure' for the instincts is to create a new set and for Nietzsche, this is the role of the Overman. In relation to Socrates Nietzsche has claimed that happiness equals instinct. By his ability to affirmatively answer the question of eternal recurrence (whether we can bear the thought of living our lives repeatedly, exactly as before) the Overman represents the new set of instincts which, through their fulfilment, will lead to a state of satisfaction and ultimately happiness. One of the major differences between Freud and Nietzsche, therefore is that the former sees contentment in reconciling the demands of the instincts with the demands of society through a functioning ego as a buffer, whereas Nietzsche sees happiness in the positive transformation of the instincts followed by a life lived in their satiation.

Nietzsche's pragmatic use of consciousness as a way to transform that that lies below it without seeking to privilege the former is also found in the psychological techniques of Buddhism. Buddhism teaches, in the formulation of the Four Noble Truths, that much of human life is unsatisfactory because we cling to objective and subjective entities that are ultimately subject to constant change. We desire to anchor our happiness to material possessions, for example, in the mistaken belief that the objects themselves and our reaction to them will have a degree of permanency that will bring us lasting happiness. The objects will eventually perish through the action of time and usage, however, and the self that seeks to relate to them will also change and mutate, resulting in differing reactions. Much of the unsatisfactory nature of life (be it on an intellectual or emotional level) can, therefore, be traced back to a mistaken reliance on permanency. Indeed, underlying this is the belief in the self as a solid entity that we should seek to bolster, coddle and protect. This essentially artificial mental construct is both that which desires and the existence of which is sought to be bolstered by the desiring of external entities. Buddhism posits a release from such an unsatisfactory state of affairs through a realisation of the empty nature of our self-conception leading to a reorientation of our relations with the external world. Such a realisation is to be effected by a combination of conscious work on mental processes, as well as attempts to dethrone consciousness, and the sense of self it creates, by switching it off through meditative experience. Thus, as in Nietzsche, consciousness is a tool to be used accordingly and eventually surpassed.

Buddhism deconstructs the self into five aggregates: feelings, the emotive element in human experience; perceptions; dispositions, which account for the absence of pure perception; consciousness, that which explains the continuity of the sense of self that is mistakenly thought to lie behind the dispositions; and body, the physical element. In Buddhist analysis, none of these five elements is eternal and unchangeable; neither do they stand alone, independent of each other. All change from moment to moment in a process of interlinked flux. What we think of as the self results from a privileging of the dispositions and consciousness. The dispositions serve to colour perception and to regulate our relation to feeling and body. The mistaken attribution of an essential thinker lying behind the separate momentary acts of consciousness is what leads to a sense of self, and this too is heavily conditioned by the dispositions. An understanding of the mechanics of psychology and of the inherent emptiness of both external and internal phenomena (in the sense of being subject to change) will, in Buddhism, aid the pacification of the dispositions and engender a greater sense of equanimity.

One way in which this is effected is through analytic meditational practice, within which one takes each of the five aggregates in turn and deconstructs it to find if a continuing sense of self lies therein. Another is through the Zen practices of seated meditation, during which one systematically stills the conscious mind, and meditative absorption within whatever mundane task one performs at a present moment. This latter can be linked to Norretranders' claim that we are in fact happier when we are able to switch our consciousness off and let the nonconscious take control. Citing examples ranging from virtuoso musical performances, to professional football, to washing the dishes, he shows how tasks are performed more efficiently when done unconsciously. The psychologist Lilly calls this the '+24' or 'the basic professional state' and describes it as the effect when we 'lose ourselves in practice'. 'The important part about +24 is the enjoyment and the automatic nature of what one is doing plus the loss of self-hood, and the absence of ego.'[17]

This fits in with our experience of many situations in life where there is a marked difference between carrying out actions with which we are familiar and those with which we are not. In the latter, there is a strained sense of awkwardness and clumsiness, of not being at home in your own shoes. The comfortable feeling of the former comes from not having to think about what you are doing, the discomfort of the latter in that you are trying too hard. Norretranders theorises this as being the result of differences of will between the conscious and nonconscious in which the conscious attempts to veto the actions initiated by the nonconscious. It is the resulting tension that leads to the discomfort. Feelings of comfort arise from actions in which the consciousness is content to sit back and let the nonconscious be in control. Likewise, in Buddhism the feeling of comfort arises from not filtering an experience through a sense of consciousness that seeks to bolster itself by clinging to the former despite its transience. Anxiety arises when the experience dissipates or changes, or when our reaction to it shifts, as in Nietzsche's analysis of whichever instinct is to the fore at that point in time.

Although Buddhism denies the existence of a substantial self, it does not claim that what we commonly think of as our personality is beyond description. The dispositions are causally conditioned and the other four aggregates are then coloured by the dispositions, thus leaving the stamp of a personality on our mental experiences. The fact that the aggregates contain no substantial essence and are shaped by the conditioning of experience is the means by which Buddhism can facilitate psychological change. The idea of conditioning is the cornerstone of Buddhist psychology. As the aggregates have no intrinsic essence they derive their form and content from the impact of outside factors and are therefore constantly changing. The unhappiness and unsatisfactory nature of existence, encompassed in Buddhism by the term *dukkha*, is the result of identifying with any of these fluctuations.

Through a process of consciousness working on the dispositions, leading to changes in the latter that will then lead to changes in consciousness itself and the other four aggregates, one's thought processes can be changed. Meditational work, when not focusing on analysis through the use of consciousness, can serve to try and directly impact on the dispositions. Often the two processes are used in tandem, with analytic meditation first being used to focus on a particular topic, such as the inherent emptiness of the aggregates, and then, once a conscious insight has been reached, analysis being switched off and the mind allowed to just absorb the insight without working on it any further. The emotions can also be harnessed, with Buddhists in the later Mahayana tradition using meditative techniques to inspire compassion. One forms a compassionate feeling, for example, and then slowly imagines it spreading out from the body to encompass friends, family, the surrounding area and then on to the whole world through a process of visualisation. Once this all-encompassing feeling of compassion is attained, one then lets the conscious visualisation process slip into the background and tries to merely experience the feeling at the visceral level. It is hoped that through this the dispositions will slowly be changed.

Western humanist or psychoanalytic-type therapies therefore are seen with suspicion from the viewpoint of Buddhist psychology since their main objective is to strengthen the ego. In later psychoanalysis, and in its development since the 1960s, the emphasis has been on strengthening the ego to act as a buffer between the demands of society in the form of the superego on one hand, and the influence of the unconscious id on the other. In humanism and person-centred therapy, the focus is likewise on the individual self as the nexus of both theory and practice. For Buddhism this will not solve the client's problems, as it will merely cement the identification with a fixed substantial self. When changes take place, therefore, through the conditioning effects of the dispositions and the fluctuating of consciousness, the cracks in this self-conception will appear. Such theories and therapeutic practices teach clients to cling ever more tightly to the very cause of their problems. There are of course schools of psychoanalysis, such as object relations and Lacanianism, which highlight the empty nature of the self-perception.[18]

One of the main sources of Buddhist psychology is a collection of writings called the *Abhidharma*, which, in its seventh book, the *Pattana* or the *Book of Origination or Causal Relations*, contains an analytical list of the ways in which one thing may depend upon another from the perspective of our mental life. One of the theories discussed is that of *arammana*. This is essentially an object relations theory that states that the mind is conditioned by the objects, real or imagined, which surround it. The mind hones in on an object, cognises it and is hence determined or conditioned by it. The most important object around which the mind turns is the idea of self, and techniques such as the meditational experience of all encompassing compassion, and that of deconstructive meditation on death and dissolution favoured by earlier Buddhists, help to overcome it. Such techniques focus on a reorientation of the mind towards objects which will, in the long term, act as ways of transcending the very idea of self.

The Abhidharma categories of *upanisssaya*, *pacchajata* and *asevanna* are an attempt to analyse the phenomena of inducement and habit. We become conditioned to act in certain ways following inducements, dependence is increased through ongoing reliance and support, and finally the conditioning crystallises into habit. In the beginnings of conditioning, therefore, consciousness has a larger role as we will only act in a certain way if induced to do so by the belief that it will have certain advantages for us. Our continued action relies on being supported by external phenomena, such as the continued presence of the stimulus and our continued positive mental reaction to it. As time goes on, however, the conscious element in the process falls away and the pattern of behaviour becomes nonconscious: a disposition. At this point, the external and internal support mechanism are not necessary to bolster the continued behaviour pattern.

Finally, for our purposes, there is the category of *ahara paccaya* that suggests that we maintain our conditioning through feeding it. This idea is broken down into the elements of contact, will and consciousness. The theory states that we tend to stay in contact with that which reinforces the mental condition in question, often not realising that we have been put into such situations by the nonconscious action of the dispositions, and that this in turn will affect conscious thought patterns by the hardening of attitudes.

Several useful propositions lie behind these excerpts from Buddhist psychology that can be mobilised for our purposes. The first is that the self can be used as a tool to change the mental substrates that lie beneath it. This is an idea we have already encountered in earlier chapters, but the differences in the Buddhist conception are that the self can be seen as nothing more than a tool to facilitate such a task, not as an end in itself. Buddhism also offers, through its meditation techniques, ways in which the nonconscious can operate on itself. Such therapeutics are underpinned by the idea that nowhere in our mental or physical life is there any entity that is unified or permanent enough to act as a point of mental stability. That which is desired and that which desires are both forever movable feasts and it is this that lies at the core of our deeper existential worries.

This dynamic view of mental process, with its diminution of consciousness, can be linked to Deleuze and Guattari's project in *Anti-Oedipus*. One of the useful concepts in that work is the co-original nature of mental processes and social, political and economic structures. Rather than linking the contents of the unconsciousness, or the dispositions, to the economy, as in Marx, or early familial relations and childhood experiences, as in Freud, one of the central propositions in *Anti-Oedipus* is that desire and the drives form part of the external infrastructure itself. They 'create within economic forms their own repression, as well as the means for breaking this repression'.[19] The Buddhist notions above help analyse the question in *Anti-Oedipus* of why we fight as hard to maintain the systems of our psychological repression as to free ourselves from them. Our dispositions are formed by the social structures that surround us, as well as our relationships with others. The will to fight our oppression is, therefore, conditioned by that from which it would seek to be free, rendering its effectiveness somewhat blunted. For Deleuze and Guattari, schizophrenia is as much a condition of surrounding society as it is of internal mental content. We live in the age of partial objects and fragments with massive flows of energy (in economic, political and cultural terms) that are not subject to any central control and which all jostle and impact on each other to constantly create friction and new formations.

Thus, we arrive at a point wherein consciousness is not a major player in our mental lives. It constitutes a mental outgrowth of the fact that we have evolved as social animals. It is shaped, for the most part, by external phenomena and responds to the currents that move underneath it, which are themselves the result of external conditioning as well as automated, routinised action. A change in any of these three points (conscious, nonconscious, external structure) can serve to bring about changes in the other, although how a change in the nonconscious can bring about a change in the external world is a little more opaque than the other links in the triad. One answer is found in the actions of Deleuze and Guattari's schizophrenic who, as we have seen in the last chapter, mirrors the external world he or she finds themselves in and who, through harnessing an excess of desire, provides the mental dynamism to create new patterns of thought and behaviour, which will bring about a change in the sociality by forcing it to respond to them.

Another answer, which has a lot in common with the previous, is the Buddhist method of bringing about a change in mental life through analytic techniques which deconstruct the idea of self to the point wherein one may move beyond it, coupled with meditative work on gradually directly changing the underlying nonconscious or dispositions. The practical ways for effecting the latter are very much akin to the ways of changing the instincts identified by Nietzsche.

Freud, in his conception, essentially vilifies the unconscious. Following Schopenhauer, it is seen as the repository of opaque and antisocial forces that, although they provide the dynamism that drives much of our mental life, must be thwarted, diverted and controlled. The way to do this is to strengthen the position and functioning of the ego as a controlling mechanism. This is, therefore, a theory of control, not change, as regards the unconscious. Nietzsche is a lot more useful in that he provides a series of techniques for achieving changes at mental levels below consciousness. He also has a more positive view of these levels as something that should not be feared, loathed and sacrificed to rationality.

As we have seen in Chapter 2, Nietzsche's view is of a natural unconscious, one that internalises its form and function in opposition to earlier supernatural visions that sought to externalize it. With the folding of the unconscious into the core of human functioning and especially in linking it so closely to the body, Nietzsche is in a powerful position to affect change within it. The neurological material of Chapter 1, the social nature of affect in Chapter 3 and the

Buddhist material in the present chapter all point to a more mechanical conception of the unconscious, however, akin to that of Leibniz, Carpenter and Huxley. Herein the nonconscious is a series of subroutines. It is the machinery that ticks along in the background doing all the actual work of mental life, with its activities forming the deep currents for the surface flows of conscious thought. This idea of the mechanic is picked up by Deleuze and Guattari. Deleuze, however, in *Difference and Repetition*, adds a supernatural, or idealist, element to the mechanic functioning of the nonconscious with the concept of the virtual. Nevertheless, the mechanic conception has the advantage over previous notions that a machine is inherently neutral and can be reprogrammed. As such, it lends itself to remoulding the totality of mental life.

A useful way of assessing the thoroughness of any thought that arises from such a process is by referring to Iain Mackenzie's characterisation of partial, total and pure critique. Mackenzie's project is also an exercise in the possibility of thinking differently. He aims to establish an idea of pure critique in opposition to partial or total critique. Partial critique merely serves to tinker with the operational end of a system, such as democracy or capitalism, whereas total critique still shares a second order relationship with that which it engages through a set of shared background assumptions with the criticised that are used as a justificatory framework. Pure critique, on the other hand, sets nothing beyond the bounds of the critical endeavour; even the ideas of 'critique' and 'critic' must be interrogated.[20] This is achieved through a mobilisation of Deleuze and Guattari's vision of philosophy as the creation of concepts.[21] Pure critique must consist of pure concepts that, at the level of their creation, in effect owe nothing to the psychosocial thinker through whom, rather than by whom, they are filtered. As such, the goal of absolute purity will always be aspirational.

My concern in the present work has been with the machine through which the concept is thought. As such, it has been an exploration of the necessary impurity of the critical concept as filtered through the thinker. From the point of view discussed throughout this work, critique will always be total at best, in that the thoughts that a human brain may generate will always contain some investment with the external world and that which is critiqued. As Mackenzie rightly points out, the actors of the anti-capitalist movement, when they accept this tag, automatically engage in a total critique, as it will be articulated with reference to the capitalist system. It will therefore share points of reference with the system it critiques. It will say capitalism creates injustice, for example, thereby appealing to a notion of 'justice' the components or expression of which will then be fought over by both sides. We may now add to this the effects of emotion, the nonconscious, the limited and conditioned role of consciousness. All of these reterritorialise the idea of the 'impure thought' from something to be mumbled in the confessional to an inescapable part of mental life. This is not to say that such thoughts should be critiqued as best we can however.

Notes

1. Freud, 'Civilisation and its discontents', in *Civilisation, Society and Religion*, p. 286.
2. Frosh, *Politics of Psychoanalysis*, p. 40.
3. Freud, 'Civilisation and its discontents', p. 313.
4. Ibid. p. 286.
5. *The Century of the Self, episode 1: Happiness Machines*, television programme, Curtis.
6. Ibid.
7. Beetham, *A Magazine of Her Own?*, p. 142.
8. Ibid. p. 146.
9. Bowlby, *Just Looking*, pp. 1–6.
10. Ibid. p. 18.
11. Benjamin, *The Arcades Project*, p. 7.
12. *The Century of the Self, episode 2: The Engineering of Consent*, television programme, Curtis,
13. The next step in the progress of desire marketing is illustrated by an article by Robert Winnet in *The Sunday Times*, 17 August 2003, entitled 'Admen seek "buy button" in our brains'. This article discusses attempts by lottery firm, Camelot, and Ford to use neuropsychologists to pin-point areas of the brain triggered by advertising.
14. *The Century of the Self, episode 3: 'There is a Policeman Inside all our Heads'*,television programme, Curtis,
15. Freud, 'On the universal tendency to debasement in the sphere of love' in *On Sexuality*, p. 258.
16. Nietzsche, 'Twilight of the idols', p. 479.
17. Lilly quoted in Norretranders, *User Illusion*, p. 266.
18. One can also point to Jung's depth psychology that, in its conception of the collective unconscious, comes very close to the later Buddhist notions of the storehouse consciousness and Buddha-nature.
19. Deleuze and Guattari, *Anti-Oedipus*, p. 63.
20. Mackenzie, *The Idea of Pure Critique*, pp. 26–7.
21. Deleuze and Guattari, *What is Philosophy?*, p. 5.

Conclusion: Skilful Means

Buddhism likens its psychological techniques to a raft that is used to cross a river, the river being *dukkha*. The raft is merely a tool to be used to gain the further shore and then to be abandoned, its task fulfilled. Likewise, the conceptual apparatus used by Buddhism to effect change should not be clung to after their task is fulfilled. (One may ask whether the task of positive mental transformation is ever at an end and schools such as Zen do posit an ongoing process). These techniques are dubbed 'skilful means' and are the conceptual toolkit of Buddhist philosophy and psychology. The means by which change is brought about differs from person to person, society to society and time to time giving rise to the variety of practices one finds in Buddhism. At a deeper level, however, the very mental apparatus that is both utilised and worked upon is likewise to be seen as a means and not an end in itself.

This idea is reflected in the lines of argument pursued through the present work. In Chapter 1, neurological material on the nonconscious was introduced in contrast to previous conceptions of the unconscious, which had focused on the element of our mental life which lies below consciousness as either an external phenomena or as an essentially alien and unknowable part of mental functioning. By contrast, the conceptualisation of the nonconscious is of a machine, a series of subroutines, essentially neutral and mechanical in nature. This was linked in Chapter 2 to a functionalist philosophy of mind as being one that embraced the complexities of the relationship between mental functioning and culture and language, as well as avoiding the pitfalls of dualism. Though an essentially materialist conception, functionalism allows for a more nuanced interaction between the internal and external worlds as well as a hierarchical vision of mental processes. Both of these advantages can be strengthened through linking functionalism to material on embodied cognition. In contrast with dualism, materialist functionalism can begin to show how interaction may be achieved along the two connected axes of mind/body and consciousness/nonconsciousness.

In Chapter 3, a deeper conception of the role of social environment was deployed through an investigation of affect. This also had served to problematise the role of consciousness in our mental lives as it showed how deeply programmed, culturally specific emotions functioned neurobiologically to shortcut conscious processing. As LeDoux explains, the thalamus is able to respond to an event by sending signals to both the cortex, in which higher level processing takes place, and the amygdala, which triggers the physical response. The connections between the thalamus and the amygdala are much stronger than those between the latter and the cortex and, by the time consciousness kicks in, the amydala has already responded with some low level physical response such as adrenaline. The flooding of the body with such a chemical will then trigger a flight response and we may find ourselves fleeing even while beginning to consciously engage with the threat.

What is important about the role of affect, however, is its capacity to be socially conditioned. Herein a neurochemical affectual response becomes a socially inscribed emotional response. The physical affectual response is tears and the emotional response the socially appropriate feeling that accompanies them. This works in much the same way as the explanatory function of the left brain interpreter in the P. S. study. Our body does something and either consciousness seeks to explain it or, at a deeper level, an emotional response accompanies it. Herein, again, the functionalist conception lets us conceive of such operations in terms of levels or hierarchies. Chapter 3 then went on to examine one major element of social conditioning that takes place in contemporary Western society, consumer capitalism. In our present climate, the emphasis could just as easily have been on the climate of fear that helps to bolster and maintain the various current 'wars on terror'. Other societies will have their own structural emotional regimes that serve to condition affectual and emotional responses.

On the next rung of the hierarchy towards consciousness, different societies will also provide different narrative frameworks to facilitate social explanation in Nietzschean fashion, and it was this to which the investigation turned in Chapter 4. The conscious self was explored in terms of a socially conditioned set of explanations. As Gazzaniga and LeDoux state, 'it is as if the verbal self looks out and sees what the person is doing, and from that knowledge interprets reality'.[1] The two key components in such an idea are that the conscious self is essentially a verbal self and that its function is that of interpretation. As such, the role of the narrative self in consciousness was explored. This was closely linked with the idea of time as a mean of conceptualising the link between memory, conditioning and the capacity for change. The loops of narrative identity, as they are played and replayed in different settings across the span of a life, were analysed at the end of the chapter using Deleuze's conception of passive synthesis and repetition. Therein, Deleuze unfolded a way in which the repetitions of habit and memory could still give rise to originality and new creative thought by means of small differences in each repetition. As the layers of mental sediment build up over time and experience, the platform from which repetition is deployed differs slightly each time. For Deleuze, a large part of the capacity for originality comes from the intersection between the planes of the virtual and the actual. It is argued though that a purely mechanistic or materialist conception of mind can adopt the metaphors of difference and repetition without recourse to the metaphysical plane of the virtual. The virtual could, however, be seen as the external conditioning factors of our surrounding environment. The combination of the passive syntheses of habit and memory with affectually conditioned responses and socially conditioned narratives form sheets of past that are the foundations for response in each situation.

As well as presenting a mechanics of mental functioning, these chapters also used Bauman's *unsicherheit* to try to conceptualise one of the elements of our current emotional regime. Using the material so far outlined, *unsicherheit* was conceived of on a number of levels. On the cultural level, it resulted from the mismatch between the demands of a consumer society, the existential imperative of self-creation along individual lines, and the methodology for so doing extolled by consumerism that functions only to constantly manufacture desire. It was also conceived as the disruption of coherent whole-life narratives by the segmentation and fragmentation of time that contemporary society inspires, leading to a frustration of the explanatory function of consciousness so well exhibited by the P. S. study. It was stated that our present mode of social life might, therefore, have created an emotional and structural regime which produces *unsicherheit* as an affective mental response. Consumerism functions to create desire in order to sell its products. The way in which this desire is put forward is under the rubric of individual self-creation and the promise that one can create oneself anew with the aid of the market's products and services. Because our sense of self is created with reference to the background meanings in our culture, we latch onto the market as the dominant meaning creator in our Western society at present. We therefore try to create ourselves on its terms to facilitate social interaction with those in the same society. What we find, however, when we attempt this is not a unified existential sense of self but a fragmented and disjointed set of personae based on concatenations of consumer products, which is always nagged by a sense of near completion because of the functioning of consumer desire. The world this creates is one of individuals who come together in social groups that never get past the instrumental individuality of their composite members. They are single-issue socialites, which we select and deselect along consumer lines. The effect of these processes is *unsicherheit*: insecurity, uncertainty and unsafety, essentially existential anxiety.

A collective remedy to this situation is precluded by the aforementioned effects it has on people's relations to social networks. Therein lies another possibility for critique, however, in the utilisation of the psychological and social state imparted to us by consumer capitalism as found in the concepts of post-structuralist thinkers and exhibited by the functioning of the anti-capitalist movements.

Chapters 5 and 6 then go on to investigate the possibilities for mental change occasioned by both the foregoing conceptualisations of mental functioning and the current forms of its external patterning. In Chapter 5, the conscious potential for radical changes in thought is examined within the parameters of our current social environment of consumer capitalism. Baudrillard had been pessimistic about the possibilities thus afforded, but a more positive engagement was highlighted in the thought of Foucault, Deleuze and Guattari. Deleuze and Guattari suggest pushing the conditioning of capitalism to its limits. They point to a schizophrenic system that produces schizophrenic subjects only to repress the tendencies therein. This is similar to consumer capitalism producing *unsicherheit* as a result of the mismatch between the existential imperative of individual self-creation and the realities of mental functioning on one hand and the tools which it provides for such a project on the other. Such a process ties in with the ideas of *Anti Oedipus* through what they see as the liberating potential of desire (or the creative potential of power in Foucault). Consumerism serves to create and exacerbate desire that can never be fulfilled; indeed, if we are to believe Freud, there is something in the instincts that can never fully discharge. The schizophrenic process, when rendered revolutionary, seeks to harness the dynamic potential of such desire and use the deterritorialising effects of capitalism to force thought along new lines of flight. If we look back at the effects of consumerism on self-identity, as outlined in Chapter 3 we may see how such conditions can be created. First is the fragmentation of core sites of communal and traditional identity through the prevalence of commodity culture and the effects that the commodity form has. Second is the substitution of these sites with the market and the various products it holds out, Bauman's habitat. This entails the inculcation of a new form of identity construction with reference to products framed with meaning in a brand structure in such a way that the actual product falls by the wayside and its symbolism takes over as the primary exchange value. The mining and selling back of cultural meaning by brands has the effect of further fragmenting cultural identities and transplanting them to the arena of consumerism. The presentation of these branded identities leads to their equivalence in the catalogue of consumable possibilities and has the effect of endowing us with multiple partial identities or *personae*.

In this conception, capitalism, through its ever-changing nature and indeed through the effects of the commodity form outlined by Goldman of atomisation and reification, actually helps to create a machinic subject. Whereas from a consumer standpoint, the decentred vision of self can be seen as a lack to be filled with products, the idea of a self as a dispersed cognitive engine taking place at the fringes of mental functioning and essentially externalised into the social environment certainly provides opportunities for the type of schizophrenic lines of flight highlighted by Deleuze and Guattari. To quote their revolutionary prescription again:

> The schizophrenic escape itself does not merely consist in withdrawing from the social, in living on the fringe: it causes the social to take flight through the multiplicity of holes that eat away at it and penetrate it, always coupled directly to it, everywhere setting the molecular charges that will explode what must explode, make fall what must fall, make escape what must escape, at each point ensuring the conversion of schizophrenia as a process into an effectively revolutionary force.[2]

The anti-globalisation movement is one myriad set of practices and opportunities that may be seen as doing this.

The question was asked in Chapter 5, however, of whether the immanence to that which it resists in such a conception can really engender a thorough-going critique. One may turn to the nonconscious to seek a deeper potential for mental change. In Chapter 6, the Freudian and Nietzschean conceptions of the unconscious were examined as a springboard for discussing ways in which the nonconscious could be rendered political. Freud, however, seeks not to change those mental elements that lie below consciousness, but rathe sees them as something to be controlled. Herein we see Plato's cor scious charioteer, in the form of the ego, winding its way between th demands of the superego and the id. Nietzsche was more positiv about what he referred to as the instincts, mostly because he wa inherently distrustful of an over concentration on rational consciou ness as being the pathway to decadence. It is with Nietzsche that w see the consciousness being used as a tool to effect change at the lowe mental levels. Both Freud and Nietzsche's conceptions can of cours be traced back to Schopenhauer, whom both admired. As in Freud Schopenhauer seeks to avoid slavery to the Will and, as in Nietzsch consciousness, which is merely an epiphenomenon, can be turne about as an instrument to combat the Will. Though the Will could nc be forced to change at a deep level, it could be denied through th force of the intellect. Nietzsche, however, supplied tools for effectin such a change at a deep level.

These tools can be expanded upon through a brief examination c some of the tenets and techniques of Buddhist psychology, which ha served to influence both Schopenhauer and Nietzsche. Therein or finds the systematic application of tools to create multiple effects a both the surface level of consciousness and at the deeper level c what are termed the dispositions. In terms of linking in with th neurological material already presented, it is interesting to note tha Buddhist psychology also proceeds from a position of regarding th self as something that should not be reified into an essential elemer in mental life, as well as emphasising the connected nature of th body, the external world, dispositions and consciousness. The way i which such processes are seen to operate in terms of karmic accre tion can be linked back to the Bergsonian idea of pure duration an memory utilised by Deleuze in his concept of repetition at the end c Chapter 4.

The Buddhist conception helps us to tie together the threads an possibilities of the foregoing discussion into the skilful means nece sary to facilitate psychological change. In summary one may, throug introspection, consciously analyse the components of mental life t gain insight into the changing and nonessential nature of both o self-conception and the world around us. The former of these is aide in our case, by reference to the neurological material presented i Chapter 1 and the affectual material of Chapter 3. Such material ca help us see cognition and selfhood in a different way. In Buddhism, is not enough simply to understand a principle, however. In order fc it to actually effect change, it has to be planted deeper down in the mental structures through meditative absorption combined, in Zen at least, with absorption in physical tasks through which the body also can be used as an engine to go beyond consciousness. Thus can consciousness and the body be used to actually alter the dispositions. Given that, from a neurological perspective, we have seen that most processing occurs at these deeper levels, it makes sense to assume that this is where change must take place. This in turn will lead to different patterns of behaviour and affect, as well as changes in conscious selfhood.

When connected to politics, it is from these changes that original thought may spring. An aid to such changes is also to immerse oneself in different socialities to disrupt engrained thought patterns and make new neural connections. This has the effect of both jolting old patterns of thought and helping to appreciate the plasticity of mental life. This is why the alternative social experiments and ways of living of the anti-capitalist and environmental movements are important. It is also what Foucault is getting at in claiming that, for the gay community, the issue should not be a question of trying to integrate itself into a heterosexual framework of definition. Given that his genealogical analysis, as well as the foregoing material, shows that there is no natural 'truth' underlying things such as sexuality, the need for one to conform to a 'natural norm' diminishes. One may, therefore, seek to create space for a multiplicity of relationships; homosexuals may seek to absent themselves from hegemonic conceptions and create a uniquely gay lifestyle. Judith Butler's concept of performativity may serve in this regard as a way of both jolting existing patterns of thought and creating new ones through engaging the world in different ways using the body.

As Althusser claimed, the prevailing ideology in a society is never monolithic. The intersection of different concepts on different levels will serve to create critical possibilities from within a system, as Deleuze and Guattari suggest. There will therefore be material to foster difference in conscious thought even though it may be through the disassembling and reassembling of pre-existing concepts to create new ones through combination. Once the virtual realm in Bergson and Deleuze is taken out of the picture this seems to be all that we are left with. At the nonconscious level, however, our hope may come in disavowing the central principle of our present society, the individual conscious self created in line with the consumer existential imperative. This can be done through utilising threads of thought, such as elements of neuropsychology, Nietzschean philosophy and Buddhism, to begin to inaugurate difference not so much by thinking differently as by feeling, acting, moving and experiencing differently. We come then to a realisation that the satanic question of how does one think differently may be posed in such a way as to fail to take account of the full mental picture and the possibilities afforded therein. It too makes the mistake of privileging conscious thought as the engineer of difference whereas we should be examining what happens at the intersection of conscious thought and self, affectual biochemistry, embodied experience and cultural conditioning and how these bleed together. We must also be careful, however, not to address this task merely with the conscious mind, as to do so would be to miss the point. Rather, there is a time for sitting back, staring into space and casually observing what floats through mind and body on the cognitive and visceral levels. In a society that seems to abhor an experiential vacuum, maybe beginning critique by striving to attain as close to conscious cognitive inaction as possible is one truly adversarial or satanic stance.

Notes

1. Gazzaniga and LeDoux, *The Integrated Mind*, p. 150.
2. Deleuze and Guattari, *Anti-Oedipus*, p. 341.

Bibliography

Printed sources

Assoun, P. L. (2000), *Freud and Nietzsche*, London: Continuum.

Augustine [AD 397–400] (1991), *Confessions*, Oxford and New York, NY: Oxford University Press.

Barthes, R. [1957] (2000), *Mythologies*, London: Vintage.

Bartley, III, W. W. (1978), *Werner Erhard: The Transforming of a Man: The Founding of est*, New York, NY: Clarkson N. Potter Inc. Publishers.

Baudrillard, J. (1968), *Le Système des Objets*, Paris: Gallimard.

Baudrillard, J. (1975), *The Mirror of Production*, St Louis, MO: Telos Press.

Baudrillard, J. (1983a), *Les Strategies Fatales*, Paris: Bernard Grasset.

Baudrillard, J. (1983b), *Simulacra and Simulations*, New York, NY: Semiotext(e).

Baudrillard, J. (1988), *Selected Writings*, ed. M. Poster, Cambridge: Polity Press.

Baum, W. H. (1994), *Understanding Behaviourism: Science, Behaviour, Culture*, New York, NY: HarperCollins College Publishers.

Bauman, Z. (1992), *Intimations of Postmodernity*, London and New York, NY: Routledge.

Bauman, Z. (1998), *Work, Consumerism and the New Poor*, Buckingham and Philadelphia, PA: Open University Press.

Bauman, Z. (1999), *In Search of Politics*, Cambridge: Polity Press.

Bauman, Z. (2000), *Liquid Modernity*, Cambridge: Polity Press.

Bauman, Z. (2001a), *Community: Seeking Safety in an Insecure World*, Cambridge: Polity Press.

Bauman, Z. (2001b), *The Individualized Society*, Cambridge: Polity Press.

Beckett, S. [1970] (2000), *First Love and Other Novellas*, London: Penguin.

Beetham, M. (1996), *A Magazine of Her Own? Domesticity and Desire in the Woman's Magazine 1800–1914*, London and New York, NY: Routledge.

Benjamin, W. (1999), *The Arcades Project*, Cambridge, MA and London: Belknap Press of Harvard University Press.

Bennett, M. R. and Hacker, P. M. S. (2003), *Philosophical Foundations of Neuroscience*, Oxford: Blackwell.

Bergson, H. [1896] (1991), *Matter and Memory*, New York, NY: Zone Books.

Bergson, H. [1913] (2001), *Time and Free Will: An Essay on the Immediate Data of Consciousness*, Mineola, NY: Dover Publications.

Bircham, E. and Charlton, J. (eds) (2001), *Anti-Capitalism: A Guide to the Movement*, London: Bookmarks Publications.

Boadella, D. (1973), *Wilhelm Reich: The Evolution of his Work*, London: Vision Press.

Bowie, M. (1991), *Lacan*, Cambridge, MA: Harvard University Press.

Bowlby, R. (1985), *Just Looking: Consumer Culture in Dreiser, Gissing and Zola*, New York, NY and London: Methuen.

Broadbent, D. E. (1961), *Behaviour*, London: University Paperbacks.

Brown, N. and Szeman, I. (2002), 'The global Coliseum: on *Empire*', *Cultural Studies* 16(2).

Butler, J. (1990), *Gender Trouble: Feminism and the Subversion of Identity*, London: Routledge.

Butler, J. (1993) *Bodies that Matter: On the Discursive Limits of Sex*, London: Routledge.

Cacioppo, J. T. and Berntson, G. G. (2004) *Essays in Social Neuroscience*, Cambridge, MA and London: MIT Press.

Cattier, M. (1971), *The Life and Work of Wilhelm Reich*, New York, NY: Discus Books.

Chalmers, D. (1996), *The Conscious Mind: In Search of a Fundamental Theory*, Oxford: Oxford University Press.

Churchland, P. M. (1979), *Scientific Realism and the Plasticity of Mind*, Cambridge: Cambridge University Press.

Churchland, P. S. (1986), *Neurophilosophy: Toward a Unified Science of the Mind/Brain*, Cambridge, MA: MIT Press.

Churchland, P. S. (2002), *Brain-Wise: Studies in Neurophilosophy*, Cambridge, MA: MIT Press.

Clark, A. (1997), *Being There: Putting Brain, Body and World Back Together Again*, Cambridge, MA and London: Bradford Books, MIT Press.

Connolly, W. (2002), *Neuropolitics: Thinking, Culture, Speed*, Minneapolis, MN: University of Minnesota Press.

Crick, F. (1994), *The Astonishing Hypothesis*, New York, NY: Scribners.

Damasio, A. (1994), *Descartes' Error: Emotion, Reason and the Human Brain*, New York, NY and London: Papermac.

Damasio, A. (2000), *The Feeling of What Happens: Body, Emotion and the Making of Consciousness*, London: Vintage.

Darwin, C. [1872] (1965), *The Expression of the Emotions in Man and Animals*, Chicago, IL: University of Chicago Press.

DeFilippis, J. (2001), 'Our resistance must be as local as capitalism: place, scale and the anti-globalization protest movement', *City*, 5(3).

Deleuze, G. [1968] (1994), *Difference and Repetition*, London and New York, NY: Continuum.

Deleuze, G. [1989] (2005), *Cinema 2: The Time Image*, London and New York, NY: Continuum.

Deleuze, G. and Guattari, F. [1972] (2000), *Anti-Oedipus: Capitalism and Schizophrenia*, London: Athlone Press.

Deleuze, G. and Guattari, F. (1987), *A Thousand Plateaus: Capitalism and Schizophrenia*, London: Athlone Press.

Deleuze, G. and Guattari, F. (1994), *What is Philosophy?*, London and New York, NY: Verso.

Deleuze, G. and Parnet, C. (1987), *Dialogues*, London: Athlone Press.

Dennett, D. [1992] (1993), *Consciousness Explained*, London: Penguin.

Dixon, T. (2003), *From Passions to Emotions: The Creation of a Secular Psychological Category*, Cambridge: Cambridge University Press.

Dreyfus, H. [1979] (1992), *What Computers Still Can't Do*, Cambridge, MA and London: MIT Press.

Dreyfus, H. L. and Rabinow, P. (1983), *Michel Foucault: Beyond Structuralism and Hermeneutics*, Chicago, IL: University of Chicago Press.

Du Gay, P. et al. (eds) (2000), *Identity: A Reader*, London: Sage Publications (in association with Open University Press).

Elias, N. [1939] (1994), *The Civilising Process*, Oxford: Blackwell.

Elster, J. (1994), 'The nature and scope of rational choice explanation', in M. Martin and L. C. McIntyre, *Readings in the Philosophy of Social Science*, Cambridge, MA: MIT Press.

Featherstone, M. (1991), *Consumer Culture and Postmodernism*, London: Sage Publications.

Foucault, M. (1977a), *Language, Counter-Memory, Practice: Selected Essays and Interviews*, Ithaca, NY: Cornell University Press.

Foucault, M. (1977b), *Discipline and Punish: The Birth of the Prison*, London: Penguin.

Foucault, M. (1978), *History of Sexuality, vol. 1: The Will to Knowledge*, London: Penguin.

Foucault, M. (1997), *Essential Works of Foucault 1954–1984: vol. 1: Ethics*, ed. P. Rabinow, London: Penguin.

Foucault, M. (2000), *Essential Works of Foucault 1954–1984: vol. 3: Power*, ed. J. D. Faubion, London: Penguin.

Frederick, C. (1974), *est: Playing the Game the New Way*, New York, NY: Delta Publishing.

Freeman, M. (1993), *Rewriting the Self: History, Memory, Narrative*, London and New York, NY: Routledge.

Freud, S. (1894), 'The neuropsychosis of defence', in J. Strachey (ed. and trans.) *Standard Edition of the Complete Psychological Works of Sigmund Freud* , vol. 3. London: Hogarth Press.

Freud, S. [1900] (1991), *The Interpretation of Dreams*, London and New York, NY: Penguin.

Freud, S. [1901] (1991), *The Psychopathology of Everyday Life*, London: Penguin.
Freud, S. [1912] (1977), *On Sexuality*, Harmondsworth: Penguin.
Freud, S. [1929] (1991), 'Civilisation and its discontents', in *Civilisation, Society and Religion*, Harmondsworth: Penguin.
Freud, S. [1933] (1991), *New Introductory Lectures on Psychoanalysis*, London and New York, NY: Penguin.
Freud, S. (1991a), *On Metapsychology*, London and New York, NY: Penguin.
Freud, S. (1991b), *Psychoanalysis: Its History and Development*, London and New York, NY: Penguin.
Freud, S. and Breuer, J. [1895] (1991), *Studies on Hysteria*, London and New York, NY: Penguin.
Frosh, S. (1987), *The Politics of Psychoanalysis: An Introduction to Freudian and Post-Freudian Theory*, London: Macmillan.
Gazzaniga, M. (1998), *The Mind's Past*, Berkeley, CA: University of California Press.
Gazzaniga, M. and LeDoux, J. E. (1978), *The Integrated Mind*, New York, NY: Plenum Press.
Geertz, C. (1973), *The Interpretation of Culture*, New York, NY: Basic Books
Geoghegan, V. (1981), *Reason and Eros: The Social Theory of Herbert Marcuse*, London: Pluto Press.
Giddens, A. (1991), *Modernity and Self: Self and Society in the Late Modern Age*, Cambridge: Polity Press.
Goffman, E. [1959] (1990), *The Presentation of Self in Everyday Life* London: Penguin.
Goldie, P. (2000), *The Emotions: A Philosophical Exploration*, Oxford Clarendon Press.
Goldman, R. (1992), *Reading Ads Socially*, London: Routledge.
Goodchild, P. (1996), *Deleuze and Guattari: An Introduction to the Politics of Desire*, London: Sage Publications.
Greenfield, S. (1997), *The Human Brain: A Guided Tour*, London: Phoenix Paperbacks.
Haber, H. F. (1994), *Beyond Postmodern Politics: Lyotard, Rorty, Foucault* New York, NY and London: Routledge.
Hahn, L. E. (ed.) (1995), *The Philosophy of Paul Ricoeur*, Chicago and La Salle, IL: Open Court.
Hampshire, S. (1994), 'Introduction', in B. Spinoza [1667], *The Ethics* Oxford: Penguin.
Hardt, M. and Negri, A. (2000), *Empire*, Cambridge, MA: Harvard University Press.
Harris, D. (2001), *Cute, Quaint, Hungry and Romantic: The Aesthetics of Consumerism*, Cambridge, MA: Da Capo Press.
Heidegger, M. [1962] (2000), *Being and Time*, Oxford: Blackwell.

Hollis, M. (1994), *The Philosophy of Social Science: An Introduction*, Cambridge: Cambridge University Press.

Hölscher, L. (1986), *The Reality of the Mind: Augustine's Arguments for the Human Soul as a Spiritual Substance*, London and New York, NY: Routledge and Kegan Paul.

Horsman, M. and Marshall, A. (1994), *After the Nation-State: Citizens, Tribalism and the New World Disorder*, London: HarperCollins.

Jackson, F. (1982), 'Epiphenomenal Qualia', *Philosophical Quarterly*, 32: 127–36.

James, W. (1884), 'What is an emotion?', *Mind*, 9: 188–205

James, W. [1890] (1950), *The Principles of Psychology* (2 vols), New York, NY: Dover Publications.

Jaynes, J. (1976), *The Origin of Consciousness in the Breakdown of the Bicameral Mind*, Harmondsworth and New York, NY: Penguin.

Kaufmann, W. [1980] (1993), *Nietzsche, Heidegger and Buber: Discovering the Mind vol. 2*, New Brunswick, NJ: Transaction Publishers.

Kenny, A. (1993), *Aquinas on Mind*, London and New York, NY: Routledge.

Kerslake, C. (2007), *Deleuze and the Unconscious*, London and New York, NY: Continuum.

Kitayama, S. and Markus, H. R. (1994), *Emotion and Culture: Empirical Studies of Mutual Influence*, Washington, DC: American Psychological Association.

Klein, N. (2002), *Fences and Windows: Despatches from the Front Lines of the Globalization Debate*, London: Flamingo.

Kripke, S. A. (1980), *Naming and Necessity*, Cambridge, MA: Harvard University Press.

Lacan, J. [1966] (1993), *Écrits: A Selection*, London: Routledge.

Lasch, C. (1979), *Culture of Narcissism: American Life in an Age of Diminishing Expectations*, New York, NY: Warner Books.

Laver, M. (1997), *Private Desires, Political Action: An Invitation to the Politics of Rational Choice*, London: Sage Publications.

LeDoux, J. (1998), *The Emotional Brain*, London: Phoenix.

Leibniz, G. W. [1695] (1998), *Monadology*, in L. P. Pojman, *Classics of Philosophy*, Oxford: Oxford University Press.

Leibniz, G. W. [1704] (1981), *New Essays on Human Understanding*, Cambridge: Cambridge University Press.

Libet, B. (2004), *Mind Time: The Temporal Factor in Consciousness*, Cambridge, MA: Harvard University Press.

Lupton, D. (1998), *The Emotional Self: A Sociocultural Exploration*, London: Sage Publications.

Lutz, C. (1988), *Unnatural Emotion: Everyday Sentiments on a Micronesian Atoll and Their Challenge to Western Theory*, Chicago, IL: University of Chicago Press.

Mackenzie, I. (2004), *The Idea of Pure Critique*, New York, NY and London: Continuum.
Maffesoli, M. (1996), *The Time of the Tribes*, London: Sage Publications.
Marcuse, H. [1955] (1987), *Eros and Civilisation: A Philosophical Inquiry into Freud*, London: Ark Publications.
Marshall, S. and Turnbull, J. (eds) (1996), *Cognitive Behaviour Therapy: An Introduction to Theory and Practice*, London: Baillière Tindall.
Massumi, B. (1992), *A Users Guide to Capitalism and Schizophrenia: Deviations from Deleuze and Guattari*, Cambridge, MA and London: MIT Press.
Massumi, B. (2002), *Parables for the Virtual: Movement, Affect, Sensation*, Durham, NC and London: Duke University Press.
Miles, S. (2000), *Consumerism as a Way of Life*, London and Thousand Oaks, CA: Sage Publications.
Moran, D. (2000), *Introduction to Phenomenology*, London and New York, NY: Routledge.
Morris, B. (1991), *Western Conceptions of the Individual*, New York, NY and Oxford: Berg.
Nietzsche, F. [1886] (2000), 'Beyond good and evil', in W. Kaufmann (ed.), *Basic Writings of Nietzsche*, New York, NY: The Modern Library Classics, Random House.
Nietzsche, F. [1887] (1974), *The Gay Science*, New York, NY: Vintage Books.
Nietzsche, F. [1888] (1976), 'Twilight of the idols or, how one philosophizes with a hammer', in W. Kaufmann (ed.), *The Portable Nietzsche*, New York, NY: Penguin.
Nietzsche, F. [1892] (1976), 'Thus spoke Zarathustra: a book for all and none', in W. Kaufmann (ed.), *The Portable Nietzsche*, New York, NY: Penguin.
Nietzsche, F. [1908] (2000), 'Ecce Homo', in W. Kaufmann (ed.), *Basic Writings of Nietzsche*, New York, NY: The Modern Library Classics, Random House.
Norretranders, T. [1991] (1998), *The User Illusion: Cutting Consciousness Down to Size*, London: Penguin.
Nye, R. D. (1992), *The Legacy of B. F. Skinner: Concepts and Perspectives, Controversies and Misunderstandings*, Pacific Grove, CA: Brooks/Cole Publishing Company.
Petit, J., Varela, F., Pachoud, B. and Roy, J. (eds) (1999), *Naturalising Phenomenology: Issues in Contemporary Phenomenology and Cognitive Science*, Stanford, CA: Stanford University Press.
Pinker, S. (1997), *How the Mind Works*, Harmondsworth: Penguin.
Plato (1987), *The Republic*, London: Penguin.
Ramachandran, V. S. (1998), *Phantoms in the Brain: Human Nature and the Architecture of the Mind*, London: Fourth Estate.

Reddy, W. M. (2001), *The Navigation of Feeling: A Framework for the History of the Emotions*, Cambridge: Cambridge University Press.

Reed, E. S. [1994] (2002), 'The separation of psychology from philosophy', in C. L. Ten (ed.), *The Nineteenth Century: The Routledge History of Philosophy vol. 7*, London and New York, NY: Routledge.

Rhinehart, L. (1976), *The Book of est*, New York, NY: Holt, Rinehart and Winston.

Ricoeur, P. (1988), *Time and Narrative vol. 3*, Chicago, IL and London: University of Chicago Press.

Rorty, R. (1991), *Essays on Heidegger and Others*, Cambridge: Cambridge University Press.

Rosen, M. (1991), 'Must we return to moral realism', *Inquiry*, 34

Sahakian, W. S. (1968), *History of Psychology: A Source Book in Systematic Psychology*, Itasca, IL: F. E. Peacock Publishers.

Sartre, J. P. [1943] (2000), *Being and Nothingness*, London: Routledge.

Schopenhauer, A. [1819] (1995), *The World as Will and Idea*, London: Everyman, Dent.

Shields, R. (ed.) (1994), *Lifestyle Shopping: The Subject of Consumption*, London and New York, NY: Routledge.

Smith, N. H. (1997), *Strong Hermeneutics: Contingency and Moral Identity*, London: Routledge.

Spiegelberg, H. (1960), *The Phenomenological Movement: A Historical Introduction*, The Hague: Martinus Nijhoff.

Spinoza, B. [1667] (1994), *The Ethics*, Oxford: Penguin.

Sulkunen, P. (1992), *The European New Middle Class: Individuality and Tribalism in Mass Society*, Aldershot: Avebury.

Tallis, F. (2002), *Hidden Minds: A History of the Unconscious*, London: Profile Books.

Taylor, C. (1985a), *Human Agency and Language: Philosophical Papers 1*, Cambridge: Cambridge University Press.

Taylor, C. (1985b), *Philosophy and the Human Sciences: Philosophical Papers 2*, Cambridge: Cambridge University Press.

Taylor, C. (1989), *Sources of the Self: The Making of the Modern Identity*, Cambridge, MA: Harvard University Press.

Toffler, A. (1970), *Future Shock*, London: Bodley Head.

Varela, F., et al. (1991), *The Embodied Mind: Cognitive Science and Human Experience*, Cambridge, MA and London: MIT Press.

Vázquez-Arroyo, A. Y. (2004), 'Agonized liberalism: the liberal theory of William E. Connolly', *Radical Philosophy*, 127, September–October.

von Hartmann, E. [1884] (2000), *The Philosophy of the Unconscious: Speculative Results According to the Inductive Method of Physical Science*, London and New York, NY: Routledge.

Wegner, D. M. (2002), *The Illusion of Conscious Will*, Cambridge, MA and London: Bradford Books, MIT Press.

Williamson, J. (1978), *Decoding Advertisements: Ideology and Meaning in Advertising*, London and New York, NY: Marion Boyars.
Wilson, T. D. (2002), *Strangers to Ourselves: Discovering the Adaptive Unconscious*, Cambridge, MA and London: Belknap Press of Harvard University Press.
Winnet, R. (2003), 'Admen seek "buy button" in our brains', *The Sunday Times*, 17 August.

Television programmes

The Century of the Self, episode 1, Happiness Machines, television programme, written and produced by Adam Curtis, London: BBC television, 13 March 2002.
The Century of the Self, episode 2, The Engineering of Consent, television programme, written and produced by Adam Curtis, London: BBC television, 24 March 2002.
The Century of the Self, episode 3, 'There is a Policeman Inside all our Heads. He Must be Destroyed', television programme, written and produced by Adam Curtis, London: BBC television, 31 March 2002.

Websites

http://www.camping-07.de/content/view/11/138/lang,en/
www.wombles.org.uk/lessons.htm

Index